And Then Life Happens

And Then Life Happens

A Memoir

Auma Obama

Translated by Ross Benjamin

ST. MARTIN'S PRESS NEW YORK

 Printed in the United States of America. For information address St. Martin's Press, 175 Fifth Avenue, New York, N.Y. 10011.

www.stmartins.com

Design by Steven Seighman

ISBN 978-1-250-01005-6 (hardcover)
ISBN 978-1-250-01059-9 (e-book)

First published in Germany by Lübbe

First U.S. Edition: May 2012

10 9 8 7 6 5 4 3 2 1

In loving memory of my father, Barack Hussein Obama,
I dedicate this book to my family

Out of respect for their privacy, the names of some people who appear in this book have been changed. The dialogue in this book has been reconstructed to the best of my recollection.

—Auma Obama

Contents

Author's Note

This book was originally written in German. Some may wonder why, when English is actually a language I grew up with. But the fact that I studied and worked in Germany made it seem natural to tell my story in the language in which I had spent my formative adult years. The writing came more easily to me, and in many ways my main audience was a German one. They, I knew, would be able to relate immediately to many of my experiences.

I was, of course, thrilled to receive an offer for an English version of my German book. Finally, all my friends and family who had been asking when they, too, would get to read my memoir would have the opportunity to do so. But I underestimated the challenge of "reproducing" the narrative. I realized that the way I think and express myself in German differs from the way I think and express myself in English. Moving between the two cultures, I had always transitioned smoothly from one to the other, and so I had never noticed this difference until I dealt with telling the same story in both languages. It became necessary to work in close collaboration with my editor, Daniela Rapp, and a German-English translator, Ross Benjamin, to render a version that best captured my voice in English. I believe this process has been a success.

KENYA

1.

"Oh, my God! Oh, my God! I can't believe it!"

For the second time, Lucy, my assistant, read the letter she was holding in her hand. Flustered by its unexpected arrival, I had desperately needed to show it to someone.

I stood next to Lucy's desk and could tell clearly by the look on her face that she was itching to read the letter once again—this time aloud. Immediately, I emphatically gestured to her not to do so. The last thing I wanted was for the whole office to find out what was in the letter—or even worse, who had sent it. For some time now, I had been getting an enormous amount of attention—because my brother Barack had, against all odds, become the first African-American president of the United States. Almost overnight, I—as a member of his family in Africa—found myself in the spotlight. And now it seemed that even levelheaded Lucy was getting caught up in all the excitement.

"You absolutely have to frame the letter! Absolutely!" she cried. Laughing, I took the letter from her. "Really, Auma!" she added in earnest. "Imagine how much it will be worth in a few years." Now I really had to laugh.

"You Kikuyu," I teased, feigning reproach.

The Kikuyu, the largest ethnic group in Kenya, have a reputation for good business sense. Lucy grinned. She is actually Kamba, a different ethnic group, but is married to a Kikuyu man.

"Must have rubbed off on me," she replied with a shrug and a mischievous smile.

I noticed our coworkers looking at us with growing curiosity.

"Don't you think it would make more sense to answer the letter instead of keeping it as a museum piece?" I went on, lowering my voice and trying to bring not only Lucy but also myself back down to earth. All the while, another question was whirling around in my mind: How on earth was I to go about answering a letter from Hillary Rodham Clinton?

Only a few minutes earlier, the letter had been brought to me personally by a U.S. embassy staff member. It was preceded by a call to my office at the international humanitarian organization CARE to confirm that I would be available to take delivery of the letter. Before I knew what this was all about, my immediate reaction was to go on the defensive. I thought it was just another of the numerous interview requests I had been receiving. Overwhelmed by the volume of calls, I had started to feel like a cornered animal trying to take cover from the journalists. The fact that those inquiries always reached me exclusively on my cell phone and that only a few people knew my office number had at that moment completely slipped my mind.

At the height of the election in 2008, I had intentionally given out my cell number, so that anyone with questions about the Obama family could contact me. I had believed that I could easily deal with the media. After all, I thought, I had worked as a journalist myself when I lived in Germany. By providing my number, I had mainly wished to protect my grandmother, whom everyone called Mama Sarah, from all the media fuss. But I had not been prepared for such a flood of calls.

Because Mama Sarah was also Barack's grandmother, everyone wanted to speak to her. They wanted her to tell them about his family, to bring to light the missing pieces of the puzzle that Barack Obama was for them. Who exactly was this black man and son of an African who had dared to aspire to the office of president of the most powerful nation in the world? Where were his roots? Who was his family?

In search of answers to these questions, scores of reporters from across the globe boarded planes and traveled to Nairobi, the capital of Kenya. From there they continued on to rural western Kenya, to Alego Nyangoma Kogelo, an unassuming little village not far from the shores of Lake Victoria that was our ancestral home. There, on the Obama family homestead, lie the mortal remains of Barack Hussein Obama Sr. (1936–1982) and Onyango Hussein Obama (1879–1975), the father and grandfather, respectively, of the forty-fourth American president. And to this day, it is the home of our grandmother, Mama Sarah.

On many occasions I was at my grandmother's side when she was interviewed, and I never ceased to be amazed and delighted at how well she, eighty-seven years old at the time, was able to grasp the intricacies and dynamics of the American electoral process. She answered all the questions with intelligence and humor, sticking to the point and not digressing. That being said, I was also always conscious of not wanting to overtax her at her age and tried to keep the media interest from getting out of hand.

I carried Hillary Clinton's letter around with me for days. I felt that any response had to be well thought through. Not only was I in a state of mixed emotions—overjoyed at my brother's success, while at the same time not fully prepared for the unrelenting attention I now received as a member of the Obama family—but the letter from the U.S. Secretary of State also brought back some painful memories. During the primaries, she had run against my brother for their party's nomination. Both were Democrats, but they had also been the fiercest opponents. Recollections of negative attacks on my brother from the Hillary camp were still fresh in my mind. And because I was not accustomed to the rules of political campaigning, at the time everything had seemed to me to be playing out on a very personal level. I had feared that his rival's team wanted not only to win the election, but also to ruin my brother's political career. And now here was a letter from Hillary Clinton thanking me for the wonderful moments we shared in Washington and wishing me all the best. I could hardly believe it.

On the occasion of the inaugural luncheon, I had been seated with Hillary and Bill Clinton and other dignitaries of American politics. As we ate, the conversation revolved around Barack's swearing-in, global politics, development aid, Kenya, and my work with CARE. I even received a number of tips to pass on to my brother and his wife, Michelle, wise advice on how to lead a somewhat "normal" life in the White House.

Even though I was not sitting next to Hillary, the opportunity arose for a brief one-on-one chat. To my pleasant surprise, the former senator from New York was a charming, amusing, and engaged conversation partner. I really enjoyed talking to her and would have gladly spoken longer with this energetic, intelligent woman. I could see why so many people had so passionately supported her during the campaign. From up close, I also realized why female voters in particular had wanted to help Hillary become the first female president of the United States. She simply exuded enormous "woman power."

The dialogue with Hillary—during which I crouched down next to her—was interrupted when it was time for dessert. Feeling the strain in my thigh muscles, I returned to my seat next to her husband, the forty-second president of the United States.

Almost a month went by before I finally found the right words to reply to Hillary. It was not an easy task. On the one hand, I wanted to keep open the possibility of getting to know her better—a response along the lines of "Thank you for your letter" seemed insufficient. On the other hand, I was aware that this letter was most likely just a polite gesture, a matter of political etiquette without further implications. I was not sure how to take it. This was all very new to me. With my brother taking center stage in global politics, I could not help questioning all the interest in me as "Barack Obama's sister."

2.

GROWING UP, I NEVER UNDERSTOOD why there were so many things I was not allowed to do merely because I was a girl, while my brother Abongo—who was just two years older than I was—not only had more freedom than I did but also felt entitled to boss me around.

I fiercely resisted this situation. Being the only, somewhat headstrong girl in a patriarchal African family—my siblings were all boys—I had no choice but to fight to hold my own. On many occasions, I sought refuge in books, where I could lose myself in the lives of others.

Stories about compassion, suffering overcome, and powerful emotions were my favorites. Not only did they suit my temperament, but their gripping content also enabled me to block out my own reality. In high school in Nairobi, I discovered German postwar literature and immediately took to it. I was sixteen at the time, and like most teenagers, I was intense and soul-searching, struggling to establish an identity.

First I read the books in English, and later on in German. I devoured Bertolt Brecht, Heinrich Böll, Günter Grass, and Wolfgang Borchert, and I admired Christa Wolf. These authors' protagonists felt things deeply, and I felt with them. For hours, I buried myself in their books. Sometimes I even read two books at a time, one before falling asleep at night and the other during the day.

It was only by chance that I came into contact with German literature and the German language. Kenya was once a British colony, and not until 1963 did it gain its independence. As a result, the official European language of the country is English, next to Kiswahili, a regional East African language. In those days, German was an unlikely language for a Kenyan to encounter, but in 1976, German classes were offered at my high school. The subject was new, and none of us students really knew what you could do with it. Up to that point, the only foreign language offering had been French. And since most of us were busy enough with that, only a few students registered for the German class. I was one of them. That was my first step toward my later decision to go to Germany and study in the land of my literary heroes.

But long before my escape into German literature, I questioned many things and searched for a way to free myself from the constraints of our traditions. My family belongs to the Luo people, in which the man occupies the undisputed role of patriarch.

The Luo are one of more than forty ethnic groups living in Kenya. They are among the Western Nilotic peoples, who migrated centuries ago from Sudan, from the banks of the White Nile, to Uganda and onward to Kenya, settling on Lake Victoria. Today the region of the Luo-speaking peoples extends across southern Sudan, Ethiopia (Anuak), northern Uganda, and eastern Congo (Democratic Republic of Congo, DRC), as well as across western Kenya into northern Tanzania. In Kenya, the Luo are the third largest ethnic group after the Kikuyu and the

Luhya; in total, over four million people are said to speak their language.

I was the only girl in our nuclear family. While our city life had modern features, in the countryside with my grandparents, where things were particularly traditional, I experienced how the boys were always treated differently than the girls. Women and girls were constantly occupied with various activities in house and home—at least that was how it seemed to me—while the male family members did next to nothing in the household and only rarely made themselves useful on the homestead.

I remember that my grandfather Onyango, in accordance with Luo custom, always ate with the boys and men of the house, never with the girls and women, who dined separately in the kitchen. We women—among us were also cousins and aunts—cooked, served the meals, cleaned up, and did the dishes, while the men and boys had everything brought to them. It especially rankled me that my older brother visibly enjoyed this allocation of duties. But it bothered me even more that most of the women and girls seemed not to mind waiting hand and foot on the male family members. I resisted fiercely what I experienced as gender inequality and tried not to subordinate myself—though without great success. I had to fall into line.

Years later, when I delved deeper into Luo traditions, I learned that the gender roles in our ethnic group had originally been distinct but rather balanced. The main tasks of the male family members were raising livestock (usually they herded cattle), hard physical farming work, fishing, building huts, and producing a variety of objects. For example, they made musical instruments, did metalwork and carpentry, wove baskets, and tied fishing nets. Their jobs also included herbalism and the protection of the community in times of war. Girls and women were responsible for the household. They fetched water in gourds, plastered the house walls, made pottery, and, like the men, wove baskets. It was their duty to sow the fields, to bring in the harvest, and to store the grain. Among the animals, they were responsible for the goats, sheep, and calves; in case the men went to war, they learned how to herd the cattle as well. And, of course, they took care of the children and their upbringing.

By learning these tasks, girls and boys prepared for their future lives as husbands and wives. Taught obedience, a sense of responsibility, and deference from an early age, they largely accepted these traditions. Only by passing them on could the Luo ensure the economic and social survival of their people.

But then the time-honored structures, as they had existed for centuries, fell victim to the colonization of Kenya. The colonial rulers introduced the so-called hut tax: Overnight the native Africans had to pay taxes on their huts in the form of money. As a result, they were forced to work on the farms of the white people, because not paying the taxes was a punishable offense—at the worst, with imprisonment. Because the men could only earn money from white people, they had to leave their own land and seek wage work in the areas of Kenya settled by white people.

While the men now worked for the colonists, the women and girls who had stayed behind had to take over their duties. When the men returned home, it was usually only for a few vacation days. During those stays, they did not have the necessary time to participate in a meaningful way in the farming activities. As a result, they did not take on larger tasks; most of the time, they just let their wives and daughters serve them, until it was once again time to return to the cities or to the white peoples' farms.

In this way, all the farming work became the women's responsibility. In marriage, great value was attached to the bride's ability to work in the fields and perform all the necessary tasks on the homestead. This did not, however, alter her position in the hierarchy of the family.

As an eight-year-old girl, I did not grasp this development. Though the traditional societies had changed under external pressure, which also affected how boys and girls were brought up for adult life and the customary division of their roles, the Luo families preserved their child-rearing principles. They did not question all too much how and whether these were compatible with the altered circumstances. And I, too, was expected to submit unquestioningly to the old values.

Unfortunately, no one took the time to explain contexts and backgrounds to me, the inquisitive girl. My grandmother Sarah was only amused by my constant questions, or shook her head when I was too persistent. Occasionally, she jokingly threatened to marry me off to an old neighbor, who was already over fifty, if I would not stop questioning everything. She would certainly get a few fine cows from him in exchange, she always added with a laugh.

I couldn't for the life of me wrap my head around this custom either: How was it possible that a man could simply take a woman as his wife without her consent—with only the agreement of the parents, or the father? This prospect unsettled me so much that I had a recurring dream in which a very old man—even older than my grandmother's neighbor—forced me to marry him. In the dream, he hid in the bushes and suddenly seized me when I was about to return to the homestead after fetching water from the river. No one heard me crying for help as the man tried to drag me home with him. Eventually, I managed to break free from him and run away. But when I finally got back to my parents, I found out that he had already given my family several cows as a bride price. So I was already married, and no one had thought it necessary to ask me or even inform me. For nights on end, I was haunted by this nightmare, and whenever I woke up from it, I would lie sleepless and sweating in my bed for hours.

In general, marriage among the Luo was actually far from being as dramatic as it was in my nightly fantasies. Although the Luo regard it (along with death) as one of the most important events in a person's life—that goes for men as much as for women—a marriage in those days amounted to little more than a contract between two families.

In this, the woman often had no choice—that is, she had no say at all in the marriage negotiations. In most cases, however, the fears and anxieties of both partners abated quickly. It was simply not expected that getting married necessarily had anything to do with love.

Thus my grandmother married my grandfather when she herself was only nineteen and he was already around fifty. When I asked her how she felt about having a husband who was so much older than she was, she answered with the simple declaration that it didn't bother her at all. My grandfather was a reputable, well-off man, and for my grandmother it was important that her family viewed him as "a good match." With that, it was settled for her that he was the right man, and that was enough for her.

"But he was so old!" I replied, indignant at her explanation. "Did you even love him?" I could not just accept the reasons she had given for her consent. At the age of eight, I already found the idea of not being able to choose my future husband for myself unbearable.

"You really are a true Baker granddaughter," my grandmother often rebuked me. "That's why you don't understand our customs and traditions." Baker was the maiden name of my North American stepmother, whom my father had married when I was four years old. As an American, she abided by Luo customs only to a minor degree, if at all. And although my grandmother never criticized her in my presence, I knew that she did not always approve of this.

Even though I adored and respected Granny Sarah, I decided that I would definitely not follow her example. I would never permit a man to rule over me just because I was a woman, and I would certainly never let anyone else decide whom I had to marry. I was convinced that life (and marriage) meant more for a woman than submitting to a man. And although I had no idea how I would do it, I was already pretty certain back then that I would one day leave Kenya to find this "more." Not forever, because I loved my country, but for a certain period of time.

In fact, the older I got, the more intensely I longed for a place where I could simply be myself, without having to subordinate myself to the cultural constraints and expectations of my family and my fellow Kenyans. In short: a place where no one demanded that, just because I was a girl, I behave any differently than my headstrong and independent nature inclined me to.

Like the books in which I buried myself for hours on end, my journey to Germany was ultimately an escape. I wanted to avoid at all costs a fate as a submissive wife.

My path to Germany actually began when I was in high school. In Nairobi, where I lived from the age of four onward, I attended Kenya High School, an all-girls boarding school still renowned today. The original name of the school, European Girls School, was also reflected in its architecture, for it had been built during the colonial period in the style of a British private school exclusively for the daughters of the European colonists; in those days, admission was denied to native Africans.

At the time of British rule, separate schools were established for the children of the Africans, usually by missionaries. These schools had substantially fewer resources than the European ones. In his day, my father had attended such a school, the Maseno Boys Secondary School, founded in 1906.

But when I went on to high school after the seven years of primary school customary in Kenya, that era was past. Now my boarding school was no longer called European Girls High School, and although there were some white students—along with a few Indian ones—the Africans clearly outnumbered them. But, despite the fact that the student body of Kenya High School was now predominantly African, the rules in force there were far from being tailored to Africans. On the contrary: It was *we* who had to conform to regulations dating from the colonial period. For example, we were not allowed to braid our hard-to-control curly hair, even though braiding gave us a neater appearance and spared us the painful morning combing. Nor were we permitted to speak our respective native tongues at school. We were also prohibited from stepping on the meticulously tended lawn of the school grounds, and running around anywhere was strictly forbidden. Sometimes I had the feeling that they were trying to educate us to be little British girls.

On the whole, though, these rules didn't bother me much. In my primary school, Kilimani Primary School—which, just like Kenya High School, had formerly been a school for white children—I had already been prepared for this to some extent. There, too, we had been obliged to follow countless rules similar to those at the all-girls boarding school later on. As a consequence, many Kenyan men and women of my generation did not master their native tongue and destroyed their skin and hair with chemicals, just to adapt their appearance to the British norm.

Before I entered Kilimani Primary School, I had attended another primary school—also modeled on the British system—for over a year: Mary Hill Primary School. Run by Catholic nuns, the boarding school was a short distance outside Nairobi, in Thika, and was regarded at the time as one of the best all-girls schools in the country. I was sent there at the age of six, and there was a reason for that: My father had the same high standards as the other members of the small group of "chosen ones" who were the first generation of Kenyans to have completed their studies in the United States or Europe. In a sense, they represented the hope of the nation. And it was important to all of them that their children receive the best possible education.

The daughters of many prominent Kenyans went to Mary Hill Primary School, including the daughter of the politician Tom Mboya, who played a significant role in Kenya's history. Mboya was a leading Luo politician and, in 1960, one of the founders of the Kenya African National Union (KANU), the party that led Kenya to independence. Later, he was the first Minister for Economic Planning and Development. Our families were close friends at the time. At the beginning of each school trimester, the Mboyas drove me to school or we took their daughter with us. A few other girls carpooled with us as well, allowing our parents to take turns with the long drive to and from the school.

I can still see a bunch of us girls packed into one of those cars. One car in particular I remember clearly, a Citroën, at the time a state-of-the-art, posh model with a long, wide front. The car was unusually low, and in the back, where we children sat, the vehicle seemed practically to touch the ground. On the wide backseat, I always had the feeling that I was almost sitting on the road. I could barely look out the window; it was like being in one of those large spinning cups on a carnival carousel. At the same time, the Citroën reminded me of the huge tubs in which the bigger girls washed us younger students every day in the large washroom of the school.

Mary Hill Primary School was run by the Missionary Sisters of Our Lady of Africa, an order that had settled in Kenya in 1907. First and foremost, this educational institution admitted children from culturally mixed families. In those days, each individual cultural community in Kenya—European, Asian, African—had its own school, but at Mary Hill the unique attempt was made to integrate the groups.

In this nuns' school, religious education was central, of course. They were determined to make us into good, devout Catholic girls, as required by their missionary duty. We had to go to church regularly, and not a day went by without some religious activity. But to this day, one question remains for me: What affiliation did my father, who was never religious to my knowledge, indicate when he enrolled me in this school? If he didn't specify one, how was it possible that I was admitted there as a child who belonged to no denomination?

We non-Catholic girls were not expected to go to confession, but I remember well that participation in the Sunday Mass was obligatory. After church we walked around the cemetery with the priest, gathering nuts that had fallen from large trees. Although I have fond memories of those walks, I still shudder today at the thought that on those cemetery paths we might have consumed bodily remains that had turned into nuts.

Entirely in the British tradition, we wore school uniforms. Even on the weekend, standard attire was obligatory: There was a Saturday uniform and another for going to church on Sunday. Like all first-graders, I was assigned an older student as a "big sister." She had to look out for me and help me with everyday things like the above-mentioned washing or getting dressed.

In retrospect, I have the impression that everything at Mary Hill Primary School was organized according to strict rules. We were under permanent supervision and were constantly kept occupied with something. And it seems to me that we were not given a minute simply to do what we wanted.

Since the introduction of the British educational system, it has been common in Kenya—unlike in many Western countries—to attend boarding school, particularly for high school students. The best Kenyan schools were and still are boarding schools. At six years old, however, I did not appreciate the fact that I had gotten one of the most highly coveted places at such a school. I would have much rather stayed at home.

I burst into tears when my parents brought me to the boarding school and said good-bye to me. For a long time after their departure, I could not settle down, and, especially during the early days, I suffered from horrible homesickness—much to my father's disappointment. Many nights I cried myself to sleep. At that time I shed so many tears that my father had to come to the school several times to bring me a new pillow. But during those brief visits, I was rarely allowed to see him, even though I had longed so terribly for him and my family. I can still see myself standing at the window of the dormitory, watching him drive away, once again in tears.

The cause of my difficulties adjusting was probably not only that I was still so young. The fact that my little brother Okoth was born at that time must have been very much on my mind. With the arrival of a younger brother, I, the littlest, suddenly lost my position as the baby of the family. On top of that, by moving to boarding school, I had lost the safe space of my home. I must have felt cast out. And although I do not remember clearly the separation from my biological mother, Kezia, two years earlier—when I was only four years old—I would imagine that must have also left its marks. So I most likely experienced my stay at Mary Hill Primary School as a double banishment from a familiar environment: I had to part from my biological mother and from my second mother, my father's American wife.

The strictly regimented life of the boarding school was frightening for me. In class, it was the nuns who scared me. I seem to recall that they threatened to lock us in a "dungeon" if we weren't good. None of us children knew for sure whether this dungeon really existed, but our fear of it was so great that we preferred not to find out. Out of sheer terror, I often did not dare to ask whether I could go to the bathroom during class. Once I waited so long that, to my despair, a warm stream suddenly ran down my leg to the floor.

Things did not go much better for us in the living quarters. There, too, we were surrounded by nuns, who watched us like hawks. On both ends of the dormitory, a crucifix hung on the wall, and there was constant praying, to which I was unaccustomed. My father, as mentioned, was not religious, and my stepmother Ruth was Jewish, though she didn't practice her faith.

Each evening before going to bed and each morning immediately after getting up, we had to kneel down in front of our beds facing the crucified savior. At bedtime, the nuns painstakingly made sure that our hands lay virtuously on the blanket. Why that was so important to them was a mystery to me at the time. At home, I was used to covering myself up to my neck. With my arms lying "out in the open," I had trouble falling asleep.

One night the nun on duty caught me with my hands under the blanket. I was startled out of sleep in confusion as someone yanked the blanket from my body. Completely bewildered, I saw the Sister standing in front of me and heard her scolding me, without understanding what I—while fast asleep!—had done that was so bad. Only years later did I realize that the nuns wanted to prevent us from sinning under the blanket by playing with certain body parts—even though we were only six, at most seven! Eventually, my father had to give in to my obvious unhappiness and take me out of Mary Hill Primary School.

My older brother Abongo didn't fare much better. He, too, attended a top boarding school, the Nairobi School, which was in the middle of the capital. And he, too, was apparently unhappy there and loathed life in that educational institution. But he expressed his aversion in a different way. Instead of shedding tears, he made other children cry, by getting into fights with them. My father was summoned to his school so often that he eventually realized there was no point in leaving Abongo there any longer. So both of us returned home—I was in second grade, my brother in third—and spent the rest of our primary school years happily as day pupils at Kilimani Primary School. At that time, my stepmother Ruth gave birth to my brother Opiyo, her second son.

The harmonious family life did not last long. While I was still waiting for the results of my final primary school exams, my father and Ruth got a divorce. When I was accepted into Kenya High School, with my thirteenth birthday approaching, my stepmother had already moved out and had taken my two younger brothers, Okoth and Opiyo, with her.

My father and stepmother's divorce was hard on me. A large void opened up. Fortunately, I could escape it to some extent with the entrance into boarding school life. The new school would turn out to be a blessing for me.

When I arrived at Kenya High School, people seemed to have heard of me already. The word was that I was the girl with the strange way of expressing herself (at the time, influenced by my stepmother, I used many American terms). And because I behaved rather self-confidently, people at first found me arrogant. Even some older girls looked in on our class to get a glimpse of the new student. Of course, the message behind that was: "Watch out, we're keeping an eye on you!" I was not to think that I could act as if I were something special; instead, I was to conform immediately to the strict hierarchy that prevailed in the boarding school subculture.

But I was not intimidated by the behavior of the older students. My stepmother's modern parenting—she had always tried to explain things to me in detail and allowed me to express myself—had made me into a rather self-assured young girl, who was not impressed by the big girls. And so I quickly settled in and found my place at Kenya High School.

3.

MY STEPMOTHER HAD LEFT US—and I fell into a deep hole. The house was suddenly quiet and empty without her, Okoth, and Opiyo, and even though Ruth had reassured us in parting that she had only separated from our father and not from us, I knew that wasn't true. She had also separated from my older brother and me.

A sad time began. Because my relatives had always mocked me for my supposed closeness with the Baker family, my stepmother's family, I was firmly resolved not to show my pain. But no one could fail to see that I was suffering.

I had lived with Ruth since I was four years old. She was the only woman I had consciously experienced as a mother. My father had insisted from the beginning that we call her "Mummy," and in the next nine years she really had become a mother to me.

My memory of my biological mother, Kezia, had largely faded. I no longer recalled how I had felt when I had to say goodbye to her. Very soon after we moved in with my father and his new wife, Ruth, he had his younger sister Zeituni come and look after us. Getting used to a new mother was hard for us, so they assumed that the adjustment would go faster with our familiar aunt.

I can still remember well Aunt Zeituni being there. She was tall and beautiful, and she became a very strong presence in our lives. She washed us, combed and braided my hair, and spent a lot of time with us. On many occasions she settled disputes and protected me, because Abongo was quick to fly into a rage when I did something he didn't like.

At first, my biological mother, Kezia, came regularly to see us at home, but I can scarcely remember those occasions. Only the sweets she brought us stuck in my memory. Her visits never lasted long because, supposedly, we often got upset and burst into tears. My father eventually refused further meetings. I was five or six years old at the time, and I wouldn't see my mother again until I was thirteen.

Except one time—at a brief encounter in her new home—I didn't see my stepmother again, either, until many years after her departure. By then I was already an adult.

At the age of thirteen, after having to cope for the second time with being abandoned by a mother, I began to brood and seriously question who I was.

Until that point, apart from regular visits with Granny Sarah in the countryside, I had been under the dominant influence of my stepmother. In my early childhood years, I had not really been aware that she was not my real mother, but as I got older, it became clearer to me. Besides the obvious fact that Ruth was white and I was black, she also spoke quite openly with me about the fact that she was not my biological mother, which also explained why she sometimes treated her own children differently than she treated Abongo and me. When her separation from my father was imminent, she tried several times to make me understand why this step was necessary for her. And she told me once again that we were not her children and therefore could not go with her.

It is possible that I repressed everything that had to do with my biological mother in order to preserve my familiar world. I knew only my stepmother and our small family, and I desperately wanted it to remain the way it was. As long as my real mother stayed away, I thought back then, nothing would change. No wonder my brother, who could still remember her well, often got annoyed with me. Abongo probably viewed me as a horrible traitor.

And it was also he who, soon after our stepmother's departure, began to talk about the return of our biological mother.

My brother's efforts are best understood against the background of Luo traditions. In our ethnic group, polygamy is customary, and a man is permitted to have several wives. He may, without having to get divorced, get married a second, third, or even fourth time. Thus my father and my mother, because they had had a traditional marriage, were, in the eyes of Kenyans, especially the Luo, not divorced—particularly in light of the fact that, for the Luo, after the delivery of the bride price (usually a certain number of cattle) and the birth of children, an official divorce is, as a rule, no longer possible. Even in the case of a separation, the couple continues to be regarded as married. If they remain childless, however, the wife is frequently blamed. In that case, if the man does not simply take another wife, a divorce is possible.

As a consequence of the payment of the bride price, if there is a separation, all the children born from the marriage belong to the husband. They become his property, so to speak. And his wife is permitted to go back to her own family only after a return of the bride price. If she leaves her husband's compound, for whatever reason, the children living with the father can demand her return. Usually, this is the responsibility of the oldest son.

In the life of a Luo woman, another change occurs with marriage. As a result of the strict customs, she now loses her place in her original family. One ritual makes this particularly clear: Among the Luo it is customary to bury a deceased family member within the homestead. A married woman is traditionally buried on her husband's compound. A divorced woman, however, even if she lives on her former family's compound, is permitted to be buried only outside the homestead—because, despite returning home, she does not belong to her parents' family, but still belongs to that of her husband. Both families are acquainted with this tradition and adhere to it.

When my brother began, at the age of fifteen, to make an intense effort to get our biological mother back, he was familiar with all this. He turned to her family to get in touch with her.

One day a schoolmate of mine approached me and explained that she was related to me; our mothers were cousins. Over the years, I had been introduced to so many close and distant relatives that I didn't think much of it. Now and then we visited each other, until one day this schoolmate came running over excitedly and urged me to accompany her home. I asked what was going on, but she answered only that I had to come with her immediately. It all sounded extremely mysterious.

Since we did not live far away from each other, we were at her house in a few minutes. She led me into the living room, in which many people were sitting. I remained standing at the door nervously, because I didn't know anyone except my aunt. But my cousin pushed me into the room from behind, and her mother called to me:

"Come in, child. We have a surprise for you!"

Shyly, I entered the room. I still hadn't grasped what this was actually about.

"Don't you recognize her?" my aunt asked excitedly.

I looked around without a word.

"Don't you recognize your mother?"

Confused, I looked around the room once again. My mother? No, I didn't recognize anyone.

One woman in the group was looking at me particularly intently. Embarrassed, I began to smile. Then the woman beamed at me, stood up, and came toward me with open arms.

"My child, don't you know anymore who I am?"

"Hello," I replied uncertainly, walking toward her. What else should I have said?

I was aware of the fact that I had a biological mother, even if she had not participated in our lives over all these years. Sometimes, when I was particularly unhappy or was troubled by a burdensome problem, I imagined her as a good fairy, who at any moment would conjure me away and free me from all my difficulties. But, ultimately, I did not view her as part of our family. At an early age, I had accepted things as they were. For me, my mother had therefore always stood outside our life. I had never seriously thought about what would happen if she ever returned.

Now this stranger was standing in front of me, and I couldn't bring myself to say a word. And even though I sensed that everyone was waiting for a reaction from me—excitement, joy, some expression of emotion—I remained silent.

"Let her be," my aunt exclaimed. "Don't you all see that she's shy?"

My mother took me by the hand and led me to the chair next to her own. After that, the room filled with conversation again. Tea and juice were served with light snacks.

I continued to sit silently next to my mother, grateful that she hadn't made a dramatic scene out of her return into my life. I eyed her furtively from the side and listened to her chatting and laughing casually and self-confidently with her relatives. And I wondered whether, now that she was back in my life, everything would finally get better.

The next encounter with my mother took place at our home. She had brought along a relative I didn't know—another one. I assumed she might have been afraid of confronting my father without support. But as it happened, only my brother and I were in the house at that time.

After we had greeted each other, my mother took a large silver can out of her handbag, which looked as if it had gone straight from the factory onto the store shelf before anyone had time to stick a label on it.

"For you," she said, handing me the container. I accepted the mysterious gift and looked at her questioningly.

"For your skin," she explained.

I went into the kitchen and got a knife to pry open the tightly closed lid, which resembled that of a paint can.

"Thank you," I said after a while, when I was back in the living room with my mother. The can contained Vaseline. Suddenly I had a wonderful sense of security. After my stepmother's departure, I had barely taken care of my appearance. I had retreated into a sort of apathy as a way to stop time, so to speak—if I couldn't turn it back. And at the same time, I had persuaded myself that the less I took care of myself, the less I would miss my stepmother. There was no one who asked whether I had bathed, put on lotion, or brushed my teeth. My brother and I barely talked to each other, and my father withdrew into his work and usually came home late in the evening, when I was already in bed.

At our first meeting, my mother must have noticed my neglected appearance and my dry, lusterless skin. While I at first saw only a stranger, she was looking at me from the beginning through maternal, caring eyes. From then on, she brought me a can of Vaseline on each visit.

Full of conviction and commitment, my older brother waged the campaign to get my mother back. I don't know whether he spoke openly with my father about it at the time, but he often met with relatives, and some of them supported him energetically and encouraged him not to let up.

I myself hung back and didn't say much about his efforts because, even though I had finally gotten to know my biological mother, I still longed to have our recently broken-up family back. I missed my little brothers terribly, especially Opiyo. But the more Abongo campaigned for the return of our mother, the less probable the chances seemed that my stepmother and my little brothers would one day come back to live with us.

4.

THERE WERE EVENTS that occurred several months before I was born that had an enormous impact on my life. When my mother found out that she was pregnant for a second time, it was already planned that my father would go to study in the United States.

At that time, Kenyan students were being sent to the United States to be educated at universities there. Most of them received support from a scholarship program initiated by Tom Mboya. The program was funded by private sponsors—later by John F. Kennedy, among others. This exodus of students to the United States, which took place between 1959 and 1962, has been dubbed the "airlift."

Tom Mboya was not only a politician, but also a union leader. He advocated tirelessly for Kenya's independence. His vision of an Africa free of colonial rule could only be realized, in his view, with the help of a sufficient number of well-educated Africans. In his eyes, there was a need for qualified Kenyans who would take over the leadership of the country after the end of colonialism—which he never doubted was coming. But to attain those qualifications, the journey abroad was necessary. As senior officials, diplomats, and representatives of the educational system, the young academics would lead the nation to independence and ensure its self-government.

Unfortunately, Mboya didn't live long enough to see his vision become a reality. In 1969, six years after Kenya's independence, he was shot. He was thirty-eight, and the forces behind the assassination were never fully determined. But it was speculated that the government had something to do with it. My father, who was hit hard by the murder of Mboya, was himself firmly convinced that it was a politically motivated act.

Though my father was not an airlift student, he traveled to the United States at the same time with private American support. Once he was there, he to some extent joined the "airlift family." Thus the program's records reflect that he received financial aid for the purchase of books and that he was supported a few times with tuition payments. But the main funding was actually organized by two American women, whom my grandmother curiously remembers today only as "Monica and Mary." She means Elizabeth (Mooney) and Helen (Roberts). The two of them had come to Kenya with the organization World Wide Lit to teach the people there reading and writing. My father participated in this program as a teacher. Both women were impressed by my father's intelligence and wanted to help him get into a university in the United States. They requested applications from several universities, and members of Elizabeth's family mailed books so that he could prepare for the entrance exams. After he had passed those, he was accepted by the University of Hawaii in Honolulu to study mathematics and economics.

By my grandmother's account, my father met the two American women at a time when he was employed by East African Railways, the railroad company founded in 1948 that served the three East African countries of Kenya, Uganda, and Tanzania. He and my mother really liked to dance, and Helen and Elizabeth must have, too, because they supposedly picked up my parents often to go out with them.

My grandfather at first reacted with concern when my father came to Alego to give the family the good news that he had the opportunity to attend a university in the United States. It was not exactly cheap to study in the States, and my father, who was only in his early twenties, already had a wife and son to provide for. A second child (I) was on the way. But by mentioning the support from the two American women, he managed to reassure his parents. All he asked of them was to take care of his wife and children in the meantime.

Incidentally, my father maintained contact with his two sponsors even after his return from America.

Some of the young students who went to the United States at that time took their families with them. But my father wanted to leave us behind so that he could complete his studies more quickly and thereby return home sooner. However, when he finally did come back to Kenya, things turned out differently from what our family had imagined.

Before his departure, my father visited a photo studio with his wife and son, accompanied by my grandfather, to have a farewell picture taken of the family. To this day, that portrait hangs on the wall of my grandmother's living room, and whenever I look at it, the thought crosses my mind that, although I am not visible in the picture, I, too, was present, comfortably nestled in my mother's womb.

After my father's departure, my pregnant mother and little Abongo moved in with her parents-in-law in Alego, the small village in Siaya District near Lake Victoria and not far from the border of Uganda. There she awaited the birth of her second child. She was seventeen years old at the time.

With my grandparents, my mother and Abongo—and, shortly thereafter, I, too—led a glorious life. The family property consisted of numerous fields, pastures as well as untilled land, and in the middle was the compound with its thatched clay houses. A tall hedge of dense trees and bushes protected it, and my grandfather's house, in which he lived with my grandmother, formed its center. In front of this house was, on one side, a small hut that served as a kitchen, and a short distance away my mother's house, which was in the place traditionally designated for the first wife of the oldest son. Further places were reserved for my grandfather's other sons, though they were not yet married at the time.

My grandfather owned many cows and goats, which were kept in a pen. My grandmother Sarah took care of the poultry, which were driven back every evening into their coop in the rear of the cooking hut.

Numerous fruit trees grew on the homestead, all of which had been planted and carefully cultivated by my grandfather: mango, papaya, guava, orange, and avocado trees. He could even show off an apple tree, of which he was especially proud. Here, in western Kenya, apple trees have a very hard time thriving. He had managed to raise such a tree and from time to time even to harvest an apple—always only one, because, despite loving care, only one fruit ripened at a time on the somewhat puny plant. We children always eyed that apple full of curiosity and with intense longing. We were strictly forbidden to pick it, and to break that rule would have definitely meant a beating. My grandfather was a very strict man, who suffered no disobedience. Thus we did not dare even to touch this forbidden fruit.

I no longer recall who ultimately got to eat each of those single apples. But I seem to remember that I, too, at one point enjoyed the coveted fruit. In any case, its sweet and sour taste has stuck in my memory.

About one and a half years after my father's departure, a letter from the United States was delivered to my grandfather. Many years later, my grandmother told me in detail about the excitement that its arrival provoked.

Apart from the letters my mother received at wide intervals from overseas, no one in the family got mail from distant America. So it was understandable that my grandfather immediately feared the worst. Why should anyone write to him from the United States, if not to inform him that something terrible had happened to his oldest son? After the message that he had arrived in Hawaii, Barack had not sent his father another line.

My grandfather hesitated to open the envelope. The family had gathered around him, and everyone was looking with anxious concern at the letter in his hand, as if it were a bomb that would explode when opened. My mother, holding me in her arms, fearfully held her breath.

Finally, her father-in-law opened the envelope. The handwriting was that of his son Barack. With relief, my grandfather read the lines—and breathed in sharply. No one dared to ask a question; everyone waited silently for an explanation.

"What is he thinking?" he suddenly cried. "And what will become of his studies now?" he went on with irritation.

My grandmother could no longer contain herself and asked the question that was burning in everyone's mind. "What happened?"

"Your son wants to get married again!"

I believe my mother had expected the worst. Now she took a deep breath; she was relieved that her husband was still alive, but at that same moment, something died inside her.

Occasionally, I have imagined how she must have inwardly screamed at my grandfather's words—and how she nonetheless remained silent, because she did not dare to show her true feelings in front of her parents-in-law. For the news that the letter contained was nothing out of the ordinary. Since a Luo man was permitted to have several wives, it would not have done my mother any good to protest against it. She knew that. But the fact that she should lose so quickly everything that connected her and my father struck her like a terrible blow.

For my grandfather, the message posed a different problem: The new bride was not Luo, not even Kenyan. She was American, and so came from an unknown country with foreign customs and traditions. And she was a white woman. Having grown up under colonialism, and after many years in the service of the colonial regime, he could simply not imagine how such a marriage could turn out well.

"And she's pregnant, too," he added after a while.

My mother had to sit down.

"Her father is insisting that the two of them get married," my grandfather explained.

"So Barack is being forced to marry her?" my mother ventured to ask, hopefully.

"No. He writes that he intends to marry her anyhow. He only needs my blessing. So I am supposed to give my consent—but I don't really have a choice."

"Oh," my disappointed mother let out.

"And he wants to know from you whether you have anything against it." With this remark, he turned to his daughter-in-law.

My mother gave no reply. What did it matter if she had something against it or not? In the end, all that counted was what my grandfather decided. On top of that, a child was on the way. Thus her husband and the new woman were practically already married.

"Is this girl going to come with Barack when he returns to Kenya?" my grandfather asked his wife. The concern in his voice was unmistakable.

He didn't doubt for a second that his son would come home immediately after his studies. But what would become of his second marriage, what of the child, in the event that the mother did not want to follow Barack to Kenya?

My mother must have felt horrible in light of the news. The letter meant the end of the dreams she had associated with her marriage. Despite the fact that polygamy was customary among the Luo, she later told me she had not expected to be affected by it herself one day. After all, she herself had defied tradition and gotten married against her father's will. Barely sixteen years old, she had met Barack at a dance when he was staying in Kendu

Bay on Lake Victoria, where he was visiting family. At the time, he was working in Nairobi. For both of them, it was love at first sight. Without thinking twice about it, my mother followed her heart, dropped out of school, and ran off with my father. After a seemingly endless back and forth between the two families, the new lovers were finally permitted to get married.

For them, ballroom dancing was more than just a hobby. Soon they participated in contests held in the various African social halls around Nairobi. And often the two of them were the winners. Abongo was born, and they went on dancing. If no babysitter was available, they wrapped the little one in a warm blanket and took him along in a Moses basket. While his parents enjoyed themselves on the dance floor, Abongo slept peacefully, looked after by the many friends who loved to watch his parents.

My mother had agreed to the temporary separation from my father only because she had firmly believed that there was something special between her and the man she loved. She had been willing to wait for him, and she had assumed my father would feel the same way.

But now he would no longer belong to her alone. On that fateful day, she had to swallow her despair. Because there had also been several previous wives in my grandfather's household, in which Sarah now lived, she knew that her tears would not be met with understanding. And even my grandmother would have been able to console her only far from my grandfather's eyes—in the cooking hut, for example, where the two of them could talk to each other undisturbed. For the cooking hut was exclusively the domain of women, and men were traditionally not allowed to enter.

Without long hesitation, my grandfather made his decision: He would give his son permission for a second marriage. In matter-of-fact terms, he informed my mother of this, too. She was not asked, although her husband had requested her consent in his letter. But even if she had been asked, she would not have been able to oppose my grandfather's decision. His word was final. As much as it hurt, she had to accept the inevitable.

A short time later, after my grandfather had answered his son, my father married eighteen-year-old Ann Dunham, who, like him, studied at the University of Hawaii. She was an anthropology student.

On my grandparents' compound, life took its usual course. My father continued to write to my mother, and he still sent clothing and gifts for us children. If no one had known that the weighty letter was in one of my grandfather's trunks, they could have assumed that it had never existed.

When my father earned his bachelor's degree in Honolulu, he was offered the opportunity to pursue a doctorate at Harvard University. There was a new decision to make. Ann decided not to follow him to Harvard. She stayed behind in Hawaii with Barack Jr. and resumed her anthropology studies.

Years later, when I met Ann, I asked her why she had stayed in Hawaii at that time. She explained to me that, although my father had asked her to come with him, she had not wanted to go. She had loved him, but she had feared having to give up too much of herself. She had married my father when she was very young and naïve, without realizing how hard it would be to bridge the great differences between them.

Ann was an independent spirit and a dreamer, who wanted to contribute by her own efforts to making the world a better place. She was also the type of woman who felt most at ease in comfortable sandals and casual clothing. Rather than devoting hours to her appearance, she preferred to discuss political events with like-minded people. My father appreciated her sharp intellect, but he himself placed great value on external appearance, not only for the sake of following social conventions, but also because he loved to dress particularly well. When we met, Ann told me that my father often bought her "useless" things, such as makeup, high-heeled shoes, and dresses that were not her style. She wore them reluctantly and only because he liked to see her in them. I had to smile at her words. From his journeys abroad, my father always brought me back the most beautiful dresses, which made my friends envious.

At that point, Ann must have known that she would never be able to be the wife my father desired. If she had gone with him to Harvard, sooner or later she would have had to change for him and give up her individuality to be that woman—at least, that is what she feared. Would her fears actually have come true? Would she actually have had to give up so much of her own identity? Would she have begun to hate my father and thus destroyed the wonderful memories she now shared with me?

As we spoke to each other, I sensed how important it was to her to make clear to me that my father, regardless of his fondness for high-heeled shoes, lipstick, and a fine wardrobe, had been a caring and highly intelligent man. Clearly, however, the two of them had come up against unbridgeable differences, which went beyond the question of clothing and had to do with their very distinct cultures. I could easily put myself in Ann's shoes. At that time, I was living and studying in Germany, and every day I was confronted by the difference between how the Germans perceived me and how I viewed myself. They often saw in me only the exotic creature from Africa, from whom they expected a very particular way of behaving, instead of recognizing me as an individual. The experience of living in Germany had made preserving my own identity into a very real and personal matter for me, too.

The conversation with Ann took place in Maryland in 1990. We had come together there to celebrate the wedding of Abongo, who had in the meantime become a Muslim and taken the name Malik. Our father had died almost ten years earlier, in 1982.

The circle of wedding guests was not very large; most of us, sitting together in Abongo's home, were close family members. His bride, Sheree, had a daughter, Hanifa, who was among the guests. Barack and his girlfriend, Michelle, as well as Barack's sister Maya, Ann's daughter from her second marriage to an Indonesian man, had also come. I myself had brought my then-boyfriend, Karl, from Germany. My mother, Kezia, had been living with Abongo for a month to help him and Sheree with the preparations.

The wedding ceremony took place at Abongo's house and was performed by a Muslim cleric.

It was, incidentally, not the last time we were to meet in this family grouping. With the exception of my mother, Sheree, Hanifa, and Karl, we saw each other again a couple of years later in Chicago, at Barack and Michelle's wedding. Toot, Barack's maternal grandmother, who had not been at Abongo's wedding, was also there that time.

Because Abongo's wedding brought together almost exclusively close family members, it was easy for us to speak openly with each other. Many stories of the past were told, and everyone shared memories of my father, who connected all of us.

With the exception of Abongo and me, the other siblings had spent most of their lives apart from each other. And yet we all felt very close. At that moment, it didn't matter that we had different mothers or fathers. For me, Maya was the little sister I'd never had and Ann the "little mother" (as the Luo call the father's second wife) we had wanted to meet for years.

To my surprise, our mothers immediately had a similarly intimate connection. Although they had never seen or spoken to each other before Abongo's wedding, they did not give the impression that this was their first encounter. Even before the day was over, they were sitting close together, holding each other's hands, reliving the wonderful times they had spent with our father and assuring each other what a great man he had been.

With fascination, we children watched our mothers—one from Africa, the other from America, one black, the other white—and listened to their conversation. Soon we contributed our own experiences with our father to their exchange. We fondly called our father "the old man." Still, we children were harder on him than our mothers were. With the anecdotes that we shared, old feelings of loss, disappointment, anger, and pain welled up. Many tears flowed, tears for neglected opportunities and for the fragmented family we children symbolized.

I will never forget one image from that evening: my mother and Ann, the two of them almost the same age, crying in each other's arms. And since that day I often wonder what an extraordinary man my father must have been that two women who came from completely different worlds clearly still loved him even after so many years, although much in their respective relationships had gone so differently from what they had expected. In light of these memories, I cannot help thinking how large the hearts of these two women were that after all that had happened they were able to embrace each other without ill feeling.

Little Barack was two when Barack Sr. left Hawaii. He would not see his father again until he was ten years old, at a time when Barack Sr. was living in Kenya again and was married to his third wife, Ruth.

Ruth Baker was the daughter of a Boston family. My father met her during his time at Harvard. In contrast to Ann, Ruth was willing to leave everything behind to follow him to another country. I cannot say whether my father planned at the time to live with her in Kenya. I was told that he had actually returned from the United States alone with the intention of living once again with my mother, brother, and me. But then Ruth unexpectedly came back into his life.

Besides love, what induced her to follow my father might have been the feeling that her fate was now to be by his side. It was the early 1960s. As a young white American woman from an upper-middle-class family, she had alienated herself from them by crossing the "color line" and beginning a relationship with a black man. Did she have any choice but to take this step and go to Africa?

Having arrived in Nairobi, she supposedly began searching for my father, whose name was all she knew. It helped that the group of students who had returned home from the United States was quite small. They all seemed to know each other. On top of that, the name Obama was not common. We were practically the only family in Kenya with that name.

Ruth found my father. She traveled as far as Kisumu, a city

on the shores of Lake Victoria, and from there a messenger was sent to Alego to fetch Barack, who was visiting his family—at least that is how Ruth's reappearance was later recounted to me.

But what I have never learned is whether she knew at the time that my father already had a wife and two children in Kenya. My attempts to talk to her about that have failed. After their painful divorce and the hard work of building a new life for herself and her sons, she must have decided never to look back at the time she spent with my father—in stark contrast to Kezia and Ann.

Ruth's appearance in our lives back then presented my father with the choice of either staying with my mother or leaving with Ruth. He did not make that difficult decision on his own. As before, while my mother had little say in the matter, he asked his father for advice. My grandfather reminded him how he had once had to fight for the hand of my mother. It further complicated things that both my father's father and my mother's father were Luo elders, so they knew and respected each other.

Barack, my father, thus had to think carefully about what he would do now. He knew that Ruth had taken the long journey from America to Kenya and would definitely not give up her love so easily. My grandfather ultimately suggested marrying Ruth and living with her in Nairobi, almost four hundred miles from Alego. There, because of his education, my father had already gotten a good job. His first wife, my mother, would live with my brother and me on the homestead. This suggestion was absolutely in keeping with our tradition. Ruth would become the second wife, and everyone could go on living "happily" with this solution. That was how my grandfather imagined it. That was all right with my mother. She had previously accepted Ann as her husband's second wife; to avoid at all costs the breakup of her small family, she was now prepared to accept Ruth, too. But in contrast to my mother, Ruth was by no means willing to share her husband with another woman.

After days of discussions came the decision. My father decided to go to Nairobi with Ruth. But with her he opted for a Western marriage, which did not allow him to have more than one wife. The ensuing separation from his first wife, my mother, was akin, in a way, to a divorce. And that meant that she had to leave our compound and return to her family in Gendia, in Kendu Bay.

With his departure from a traditional Luo marriage, the tug-of-war between two cultures began for my father on a personal level. It would accompany him for the rest of his life.

For my mother, this decision was life-shattering. She had assumed that she would certainly be favored as the first wife. In her eyes, my father had to respect tradition and allow her to remain with his parents in the countryside. But not even that option remained for her.

It is not inconceivable that there was already a deep rift between my father and my mother at that time, after his years of absence and due to his relationship with Ann. Perhaps he thought he would be happier with Ruth.

So it happened that my father left us for a second time. Ruth and he set off to begin a new life in the Kenyan capital, while we children and our mother moved in with her family in Gendia. At the time, she was twenty-two years old, my brother Abongo six, and I four.

After my mother had to leave Alego, she went through an incredibly difficult time. As a young girl, her prince charming had appeared before her and enchanted her out of a mundane life. Now, only a few years later, she returned to her own family, cast out and without prospects for the future, dependent on her relatives and their support.

Years later, my mother told me how inconsolable she was after the separation.

"I almost went mad," she said, describing to me her state back then. "I was devastated and ran naked through the house, panic-stricken and confused."

The woman who, in order to please her husband, had always dressed well and carefully maintained her appearance, not only to go dancing but also in everyday life, now neglected herself, stopped washing herself and refused to do her hair or change her clothes. She was embittered. For years she had waited for her husband, only to be cast out by him now, on his return. Where would she go from here? Her situation did not allow her to pay for her two children's sustenance and schooling. But in the sixties, a good education was the highest goal to which parents aspired for their children. Up to that point, her husband and his family had provided for their financial needs.

I do not know the exact arrangement between my parents, but one thing is certain: Financially, my father was doing substantially better than my mother. Attractive professional opportunities really did await an academic educated abroad. He quickly got a job with the oil company Shell and a lavish salary, which enabled him to lead a very comfortable life—much to my mother's chagrin. She must have asked herself why she should be the only one to suffer. If she hadn't dropped out of school to follow my father, she would now at least have had the possibility of finding a job to provide for herself and her children and to obtain a good education for them. In light of this dilemma, my mother decided with a heavy heart to bring Abongo and me to our father. With him we were guaranteed a proper education. And so my brother and I moved in with our father and Ruth in Nairobi.

I no longer recall the journey to the city any more than I do the parting from my mother and the first real encounter with my father. Today, all I know is that for us children a completely new stage began in our lives.

Some time ago, my grandmother gave me a picture that she was given by Sally Humphrey, an old acquaintance of my father's from that period. It shows a young man with a little girl and a boy. Sitting behind the children on a wall and smiling confidently at the camera, the man has his arms protectively around the two children, who are standing between his spread legs. Shyly and a bit anxiously, the girl is holding on to the man's leg. Her face is slightly averted. The boy, on the other hand, is looking fearlessly into the camera. One of the man's hands is on his shoulder. The picture radiates a sense of unity between the three people; for the children, the man seems to be a place of security. On the back of this photo of my father, Abongo, and me, the year it was taken is noted: 1964. That is also the year in which our new life in Nairobi began.

5.

WHEN MY BROTHER ABONGO and I moved in with my father, he was living with my stepmother in Roselyn, an affluent neighborhood in Nairobi. A highly modern bungalow built on a slight hill became our new home. The building had two levels: On the upper level were the kitchen, bathrooms, and bedrooms; on the lower level was the living area. One of the living room walls was almost completely made of glass. Large sliding doors led outside into a huge garden, at the end of which was a small wooded area with tall trees. A plantation of coffee shrubs planted neatly in rows abutted the garden on the side. We children loved the ripe coffee berries that hung on the branches, deep red and enticing. Despite all warnings, we often ate the delicious fruits, which regularly gave us bellyaches.

The large garden was on the whole a glorious place for us children. In a number of ways, it reminded me of our grandfather's homestead. There, too, we had a lot of space to play and numerous trees, and there, too, tilled fields abutted the compound. But the property itself was surrounded by a hedge of tall trees and bushes as protection from uninvited visitors. In Nairobi, on the other hand, the property was open on all sides.

Without difficulty, anyone could intrude, either from the woods or from the coffee plantation. That marred the wonderful feeling of living in open nature. And there were, in fact, several break-ins; among other things, our television and record player were taken. It was easy for the thieves to escape unhindered through the plantation.

For that reason, my father one day—to our great joy—brought home a dog to guard our property. We would have loved to have him as a playmate, but we were only rarely allowed to run around outside with him. The night watchman, who made his rounds with the dog on the property after dark, frowned on our having contact with the animal. So that the watchdog did not become too playful and did not get too accustomed to us, he was ultimately locked in a doghouse during the day and only let out into the garden at night. From that point on, we saw him so rarely that he didn't even recognize us when we came home from boarding school. I remember that he always had to be restrained when we got out of the car so that he wouldn't attack us. It was much easier for us after all that he had to stay in his doghouse.

Unfortunately, the time in the glorious house in Roselyn did not last long. Perhaps my stepmother no longer felt comfortable in the secluded bungalow after the break-ins. In any case, we moved to Hurlingham, a somewhat more densely developed neighborhood in Nairobi. There, a hedge of thorny Kei apple trees surrounded our property.

I only faintly recall our life in Hurlingham, because I was in boarding school most of the time we lived there. But there is one image I can still see clearly in my mind's eye: I am sitting in our car, frightened and perfectly still, as one of our household workers runs alongside it, pulling at the collar of our fiercely barking dog up on his hind legs.

Kilimani Primary School, which I began attending as a day pupil after my unhappy time at Mary Hill Primary School, was only a few houses down from the Hurlingham house. But by the time I entered the new school, we had once again moved, this time to Woodley, another Nairobi neighborhood, not far from Hurlingham. Woodley had at one time been reserved for mid-level colonial officials, but in the aftermath of independence, the white families, with a few exceptions, had left the area. When we moved to Woodley, our neighborhood consisted mainly of Africans and a few Indian families. My best friend Barbara's parents came from Poland and England. They lived only a few houses down from us, at the end of the street. And my second closest friend, Sharon, and her family, who lived next door, were Kenyan, though originally from Goa, an Indian state. Barbara, Sharon, and their brothers attended Kilimani Primary School, too.

In Woodley, there were almost only young families with children our age, so that we never lacked playmates. Sometimes up to fifteen children met in front of the houses to do things together. For, although all our bungalows were surrounded by gardens, we almost always played in the street, which barely had any traffic during the day and offered us a lot of space. There we could be as loud as we pleased, because the properties had large front gardens and the buildings were situated at some distance from the street.

We could play outside to our hearts' content only on weekends and school breaks. During the week we had to do our homework after school, which left us barely any time for anything else. We made up for that on weekends and vacations, rushing outside right after breakfast. At lunch we all disappeared to our respective homes, because we did not eat in each other's houses without our parents' permission. Since both parents typically worked on weekdays, each family had domestic help, who were available at least six days a week and cooked for the children. After lunch, we would then meet again to continue the interrupted play.

Generally, girls and boys played together without reservations. Only my brother Abongo never wanted me to join in with his friends. He would have been happier if I spent my time only with girls or preferred dolls to soccer. But dolls bored me. I found the athletic activities and competitions we organized with the boys much more exciting. Most of the girls in our neighborhood felt the same way, with the exception of a few who only wanted to watch.

It bothered Abongo not only that I didn't stay away from his friends, but also, on a quite general level, that I participated fearlessly in everything they did. He would make that particularly clear to me whenever there were scuffles for some reason. If, for example, I got into a fight with a girl who had provoked me, he kept out of it as much as possible. While the other girls usually received support from their older or even younger brothers, Abongo only watched aloofly as we went at each other. Even when I was really in a tight spot or was getting clobbered by several children at once, he did not abandon his observation post. Often one of the other children would get our cook, Obanda, for help. Or Obanda would find out about the fights when I returned home with my clothing stained from a nosebleed. Then he would always get angry with Abongo.

"Why don't you help your sister?" he would ask him furiously.

"It's her own fault," Abongo would grumble. "She's the one who's always asking for trouble."

"What did you say?" Obanda would ask in a threatening voice.

"She can never keep her mouth shut. I'm not responsible for her!"

At that point, Obanda would raise his voice.

"Are you crazy?" he would scold. "You are responsible for her! You're her older brother, aren't you? Who else is going to look out for her?"

Abongo would shrug and look down at the floor. Both of us were afraid of Obanda. He had worked in our house for a long time and, besides the cooking, dealt with many other matters of importance to my father. As a result, the two men were very close. We children always feared that Obanda would tell our father—who was a great, awe-inspiring mystery to us—about our misbehavior, and then we would get in a lot of trouble. On top of that, Obanda would not have shied away from raising his hand against us, if need be. For that, he had our father's blessing. In our culture, it is not only the parents who bring up the children; in their absence, it is completely natural for someone like Obanda to slip into their role. Although the cook was very strict and we were quite afraid of him, he nonetheless mercifully overlooked a lot and thus ultimately spared us from our parents' reprimands many times.

I relished it when my brother was scolded. Now Abongo would get what was coming to him, I thought, that idiot, who never stood up for me. While I felt in all my bones the painful effects of the skirmishes with the other children, I waited intently for my brother to get his justly deserved beating. That was the only way he would finally realize that it was his job to defend me. Especially since I myself always jumped into the fray when he got into fights with other children, and often walked away with bruises. More often than not, however, Abongo got off with only a scolding.

At the time, I didn't understand why my brother never helped me and why he was so often standoffish or angry with me. Only years later, when we were grown up and I began to grasp the intricacies of our complicated family life, could I divine what was going on with him in those days. At the age of six, he was separated from his biological mother and transplanted from his familiar rural surroundings into the city and, on top of that, into a strange family. The head of that family, his own father, was a stranger to him, and the woman he was now supposed to call "mother" even more so: She was a white woman. Up to that point, we children had scarcely had any contact with white people, at least never consciously. And like many children from the countryside, we were probably at first afraid of the woman with the pale complexion.

Abongo, who was two years older than I was and already grasped to some extent what was happening to him, must have really struggled with this new situation. He must have missed our mother terribly, and at the same time he had to watch as I, a clueless four-year-old, adapted quickly to the new circumstances. No wonder that my "betrayal" seemed to provoke great anger in him. And because I later sometimes received preferential treatment from our parents, for I remained the only girl, that anger intensified. Thus, for better or worse, I had to learn not to rely on my brother or anyone else to help me out of a jam.

We children from Woodley loved to model our games on current sporting events, such as the Safari Rally (better known as the East African Safari Rally), which started every year around Easter in Nairobi and was then continued in other parts of the country. Parallel to that exciting event, we organized with great seriousness our own mini Safari Rally in our neighborhood. On the basis of the rally schedule that could be consulted in the newspaper, we prepared for our own race with colorfully painted Dinky racecars (the competitor to Matchbox cars). We carefully planned the course of the racetrack and marked it on the ground. Then we tied a long string to the front of each little car and checked the condition of the wheels to make sure that they turned properly and evenly. And off we went.

As soon as the starting whistle sounded, each racing pilot pulled his racecar by the string over the bumpy ground, through puddles and small hollows. Now *we* were Joginder Singh, Shekhar Mehta, Hannu Mikkola, or Bert Shankland, the famous drivers who raced their cars through the land. And like those professionals, we too, their doubles, raced toward the finish line. As chance would have it, the racetrack of the true heroes ran along Ngong Road, of all places, which was only a few hundred yards from our house. Of course, we excitedly stopped our mini-rally to see them hurtle past. We then returned to our parallel event with heightened enthusiasm.

Our other games, too, usually revolved around who did something fastest, best, or most skillfully. I will never forget the day when I tried to prove to myself that I could climb higher than anyone else—and almost broke my neck in the process. At the time, there was a fir tree in our garden, which was over thirty feet tall and which I had already climbed many times. That day, I swiftly and easily climbed the tree and didn't stop at the usual spot, but instead kept going higher. Having almost reached the top, I didn't even notice how the thin branches were bending. Suddenly, a branch broke under my foot, depriving me of support. I began to slip and tried in vain to cling to the branches. They broke off in my hands, and I fell farther and farther down.

Luckily for me, the lower and thicker branches broke my fall. Frozen in shock, I stayed where I was, half-lying, half-sitting. Everything had happened incredibly fast. After a few minutes, I pulled myself together, looked down, and realized with alarm that it was only a few yards to the ground. If I had fallen farther, I definitely would have broken my neck.

After that plunge, it hurt everywhere on my body where the branches had jabbed and scratched me. I felt like crying. But I clenched my teeth and swallowed my tears. I had undertaken that adventure on my own initiative, and no one would find out about my fall, which fortunately had ended well. It was a long time before I climbed that tree again.

I always took part when we organized the garbage can race, which, in retrospect, was not entirely without risk either. In those days, the streets of Nairobi were in very good condition, which is hard to imagine for anyone who knows their present state. In any case, the well-maintained asphalt surface was excellently suited for our garbage can race. For that game, we utilized the sturdy, bucket-shaped garbage cans, just over three feet high, which stood on every property. We took off the lids, which sat loosely on the containers, and laid the cans on their sides on the ground. At most, four garbage cans fit side by side on the street. Every can pilot now stepped onto his vehicle and balanced on it until the starting whistle sounded. As fast as possible—without falling down, of course—the metal container now had to be rolled with the feet to the finish line at the end of the street. That worked best if you took many tiny steps. But until you had really mastered this special technique, you fell repeatedly onto the hard asphalt and got scrapes and bruises. This was especially true if you were so courageous—as I was—that you organized the race on a slope instead of on a flat stretch. Although I was an enthusiastic fan of this game and got more and more skilled at it over time, some of the scars I got back then remain visible today.

Although I often played with the boys, I spent just as much time with my friend Barbara. We met practically every day, when we were not busy with schoolwork, usually at my house. At her place, I always had the feeling that her mother was not thrilled about my presence. She never said anything to that effect, but I sensed from her manner that she didn't like me, just from the way that she would look at me and from the fact that she would very rarely talk to me or allow me into the house. I think that she was not comfortable with the fact that her daughter's best friend was a black girl. In the early sixties, shortly after the end of the colonial era, she had to accept that many Africans moved into her neighborhood, in which only white people used to live. The fact that my stepmother was white probably mitigated my blackness in her eyes a bit—and I suspect that was the only reason she tolerated my friendship with her daughter—but Ruth's marriage to an African must at the same time have been a considerable demerit.

My friendship with Barbara lasted only until the end of primary school. Afterward, our ways parted because I went to a different school than she did. Shortly thereafter, Barbara's family became one of the last white families to move away from Woodley. Little by little, all the white people had left the neighborhood, and besides the African families, only a few Indian families now stayed behind. I never saw Barbara again. Thus ended an almost six-year friendship, without either of us ever inquiring about the other again.

Shortly before Barbara's departure, my friend Sharon's family had also moved away. They left the country when it became known that the Ugandan head of state Idi Amin was expelling the Indian population en masse from his country. He claimed that they would exploit the country and deprive the indigenous people of the chance to participate in Uganda's economic success. Fearing that the same fate could befall them in Kenya, Sharon's parents ultimately decided to immigrate to Canada.

Suddenly, due to events beyond my control, my world changed radically once again. From the familiar primary school, I entered high school, my two best friends moved out of the neighborhood, and—what hit me hardest—my stepmother then divorced my father and left us forever, taking my two younger brothers with her.

This time, I was actually glad to go to boarding school, because an oppressive emptiness had permeated our home. Not only because my stepmother was gone, but also because she took many household objects with her, which made the rooms look bare and dismal, as if no one was living in them anymore. The house turned into a quiet, depressing place. On top of that, Ruth was awarded our father's only real estate—it was in Lavington, an elegant neighborhood of Nairobi—after the divorce. He thereby lost the bulk of his wealth.

One might have thought that Abongo and I would have grown closer in our shared fate. But the opposite was the case. My brother showed barely any interest in me, took pleasure in teasing me, and acted as if it meant nothing at all to him that three important people vanished from our lives. Only years later did he confess to me that he, too, had cried himself to sleep at night in his room out of sheer grief.

6.

As a thirteen-year-old girl, I experienced the new boarding school as a true salvation. Without the security of Kenya High School, I might not have recovered my shaken balance so easily—for the six years I spent there were among the most difficult in my life. Far from the ruins of my former family, this all-girls high school became a second, more stable home. The school's orderly world with clear rules and structures provided me with an urgently needed foothold.

The large offering of academic and extracurricular activities proved to be an additional source of help in that. We were advised to make full use of them, and with this wide palette of possibilities we were instilled with the sense that the world was at our fingertips. There were no limitations at all, and the school subjects generally reserved for boys were regarded at Kenya High School as fully appropriate for us girls. As long as our grades permitted it, we could learn anything we pleased in addition to the required curriculum. Apart from our own laziness, nothing and no one could stop us from becoming whatever we had set our mind to. And that really was the case. To this day, over thirty years later, I run into alumnae of "Boma"—as we fondly called our school (*boma* means "cattle pen" in the Maasai language)—who have since become scientists, engineers, lawyers, judges, professors, or politicians. Most former students go through life with a confidence that can certainly be traced back to their Boma education.

While during the week a packed academic and extracurricular schedule provided me with the necessary distraction from the pain smoldering inside me, on some weekends the emotions kept in check in the midst of the school routine rose powerfully to the surface. This happened most often when we girls dealt with typically female questions, which a mother would have been best equipped to answer. Such topics usually came up on Saturday evenings after dinner—because we were free to do what we wanted with those evenings. In the common rooms of the several residence halls, we could play records and dance and visit each other in our respective living quarters.

In a group of friends, we moved from one residence hall to another, usually boisterous and laughing loudly. We stayed longest where songs were played that we knew by heart and could sing along to at the top of our voices. In that joyful atmosphere, I was sometimes seized unexpectedly by a profound sadness. My friends struck me as so happy and carefree; their only concern seemed to be the choice of a common room with the best dance music. But I sank deeper and deeper into a feeling of loneliness, which threatened to nearly suffocate me. On such evenings, I withdrew from the group of friends unnoticed, in order to be alone. I crept over to the "Five Acre," an elevated semicircular stretch of land that separated the residence halls, each of which housed about a hundred students, from the academic buildings. There I sat in the dark for hours on a bench, from which I watched all the girls walking back and forth between the various residence halls. The bench was under a large tree directly in front of the residence hall in which I was living.

I spent many Saturday evenings in that familiar place. Sometimes I only wept softly, but often my emotions rumbled fiercely in me, and I stared angrily into space. I felt betrayed by my father, blaming him for not holding the family together, and abandoned by my stepmother. If the separation only applied to my father, then where was she now? I asked myself, furiously hurling the words into the darkness. My father had promised me that everything would turn out all right, after I had asked him for the hundredth time what was going to happen now that they had left. But everything was not all right! Why else was I so unhappy? And why hadn't my stepmother been in touch with me at all?

One evening, I almost cried my heart out on my favorite bench. I had been sitting with a few friends, and our chat had turned to the problem of eyebrow plucking. Should we or shouldn't we? Was plucking your eyebrows part of becoming a woman? Suggestions, considerations, and arguments went back and forth, but we did not reach a clear conclusion. Actually, none of us really knew at that point what it meant to be a woman. Even though I was looking forward to it, I was at the same time afraid of it, as many other girls must have been as well. One of my schoolmates finally suggested that we ask our mothers what they had to say on the topic. Everyone nodded enthusiastically, and I nodded, too—knowing all the while that there was no mother I could ask. I barely held back the tears. Shortly thereafter, I stole away and visited my spot under the tree. And there I longed desperately for the mother who would have been able to advise me on the difficult question of eyebrow plucking, among other things.

Even more difficult for me than those Saturday evenings were the weekends when the students went home. Every other weekend we were allowed to visit our families. On Saturday morning, we were picked up at an appointed time by our parents or a relative and had to be back at the boarding school punctually the next evening. All the girls seemed to look forward to it, and it was considered the worst punishment to lose the privilege of going home. For me, however, it was not a punishment; I was happy to be able to stay at school.

To be in our empty house, without my stepmother and little brothers, was much worse. If I spent a weekend there, I was mostly alone. My father worked a lot, putting in long hours, and did not come home immediately afterward, but instead spent the evenings with his friends. That was nothing out of the ordinary in those days. Kenyan fathers rarely dealt with the children; that was a woman's job. Only there was no woman in our home anymore. Abongo, who attended his school as a day student, came home every day, but after a brief greeting spent most of his time elsewhere. Both of them, my father and my brother, seemed to flee the silence of our house as often as possible. Frequently, I was already asleep when they got back. And from time to time, it would happen that my returning father would wake me up to talk with me.

While I sat on the sofa in the living room, rubbing my eyes sleepily and pretending to be listening to him attentively, he talked to me late into the night about all the great things he was planning for us. He spoke about his love for us children, about the fact that he was doing everything in his power to provide for us.

On those nights, my father would also talk about my brother Barack and his mother, Ann. Over the years, I had heard a lot about this brother in the United States whom I had never met.

But I was never particularly curious about him. Despite the fact that my father spoke regularly about Barry, as he called him, to us children and our extended family, ensuring that he was definitely part of the Obama family, he was too far removed from my everyday life for me to show real interest. Even now I only listened with half an ear as my father repeated the stories from letters and showed me photos sent to him by Ann updating him on Barack's progress. He was very proud of Barack and also seemed to still care a lot for Ann.

Longing for a return to a tight-knit family circle, I would prick up my ears only when my father talked about Barack and his mother coming to live with us in Kenya. I detected in his voice a desperate need to believe that with the two of them he could re-create a home that was not tarnished by a sense of failure and discord. I did not question how likely this reunion was. When talking about it, my father's voice was tinged with sorrow and loneliness, and deep down I probably knew it would never become a reality.

Sometimes he simply played a piece of classical music and told me this and that about the composer. I thus became acquainted on those nights with Bach, Schubert, Brahms, and other great figures of European classical music.

I often have vivid recollections of those nighttime scenes. I can see us sitting together on the couch, my father talking, me nodding. I rarely respond to what he is saying and am distant toward him. I did not understand his deep sadness, and his loneliness did not arouse my sympathy. At that time, I firmly believed that he himself was to blame for the situation into which he had brought all of us, which had resulted in a broken family.

Ultimately, my father's attempt to get closer to me during those late-night conversations was doomed to fail. My pain was simply too great to allow any intimacy. I remained distant and mistrustful and felt as if I were sitting opposite a man I didn't know at all. I resented the fact that he made me sit through his suffering when I felt that he did not acknowledge mine, when in my eyes he was, in fact, responsible for it. Not only did I sense that he did not grasp how great my loss was, behaving as if everything would soon be back to normal, but he had also been too much of an absent father for me to share my feelings with him. Previously, he had only rarely done anything with us of his own accord. When my stepmother was still living with us, she always planned a family outing on the weekends, and my father always submitted to her wishes. Or if nothing was planned with the family, he met up with friends after he had read the newspaper and solved the crossword puzzle. At the time, it was basically quite all right with us children that we didn't have all too much to do with him. We were in great awe of him and were glad when he didn't meddle in our affairs. We also had my stepmother and each other.

But there were also times when I asked my father for help, such as one day when Abongo was playing soccer with his friends and he refused to let me join them despite my persistent pleading and begging. I fetched my father, who put his foot down. My brother reluctantly gave in and made me goalie. Unfortunately, I did not last very long. After a short time, a ball hit me with full force in the belly, knocked the wind out of me, and brought tears to my eyes. That ended the game for me for the time being. I ran to my father, who immediately rushed out of the house and reprimanded my brother.

"You have to do a better job of looking out for your sister," he shouted at Abongo, comforting me.

"That's why she shouldn't play with us," my brother replied angrily, trying very hard not to sound impertinent, for fear of getting in trouble.

"If she wants to play, she can play," my father said decisively.

Although I sometimes took advantage of my father's authority to prevail against my brother, and Abongo himself constantly threatened to tell my father about my misdeeds, we usually tried to resolve our quarrels between ourselves and preferred not to get him involved.

To sit with my father relaxing and listening to music on a weekend at home seemed completely absurd to me. It was not only that I was afraid of him as a figure of respect, but also that the anger over our lost family and the longing for my vanished mother were rumbling in me rather powerfully. If only my father had taken an interest in us earlier, we might have had a different relationship, I thought repeatedly as the poignant music filled the room. Now that he had to deal with us on his own, without my stepmother, he knew how to relate to us only as an authority figure whose word was law—or, on nights like this, as a broken man.

Agitated and full of conflicting emotions, I listened to the flutes and violins of Schubert's *Fifth Symphony* and could not shake the thought: Why can't everything go back to the way it used to be?

At that time, I fully comprehended that my father needed the music and the conversation to drown out the emptiness that had permeated his life, but I did not grant him that escape. What about me? Didn't he see that I was going through the same things he was? Had he ever seriously thought about my feelings at all? I suspected that my father didn't ask me any questions about my emotional state because he was afraid of the answers.

Nor did I demand an explanation from him. I avoided an honest conversation, because as a well-bred child I was not allowed to rebel against my parents' decisions. I was strictly forbidden to talk back to an adult. So I remained silent and merely listened in frustration to the music.

With the distance of years, I grasp better what was going on in my father's life in the sixties and seventies and what political struggles dominated his everyday professional life. He had returned highly motivated from his studies in the United States and believed that he could make a significant contribution to building up his native country. He moved from the private sector into government service, taking a post in the Ministry of Finance, where he was convinced he could be of real service. But the first thing he discovered was that he would have to align his visions of the country's development with the prevailing political climate. The powers that be seemed to have no real interest in fostering Kenya's progress. They seemed much more concerned with consolidating their own positions. My father's honest efforts to support the government in word and deed were met with inaction and even hostility.

What ultimately became my father's undoing was the fact that, with his academic background in economics, he was frequently more competent than his superiors and did not shy away from making that clear to them. On top of that, he was Luo, which did not make things easy for him in the political landscape at that time, since the government posts were occupied mainly by the Kikuyu. In the conflict resulting from the mistrust that had developed between the various ethnic groups under colonial rule, and through ethnically motivated cronyism, the Kikuyu had gained the most advantages for themselves. My father refused to play along with the game of corruption and nepotism. He criticized vocally those two elements of political praxis—and was thus systematically chastised as a "know-it-all" Luo and marginalized to the point that he ultimately lost his position. His efforts to find a new job were blocked nationwide. He even had to surrender his passport so that he could not go abroad.

His growing professional discontent also put ever-greater strains on his relationship with my stepmother, Ruth, until it finally fell apart. Thus, on top of his lost job, he no longer had familial support either. In this situation, he tried in vain to be there for my brother and me. Today, I can understand why he didn't succeed in that. Without employment and without money, and politically ostracized to boot, he couldn't get back on his feet no matter how hard he tried.

I've often wondered how things would have gone for us if my father had held his tongue and bowed to the pressure of the power relations at that time. Would he have managed to move his country forward, stay true to himself, and hold his family together at the same time? Would things have gone better for us? But there's no answer to this question. My father simply could not hold his tongue.

Under the prevailing circumstances, school break was always particularly trying for me. The boarding school shut its gates, and all the students had to go home, whether they wanted to or not. Now came hard weeks—for in our motherless household there was always something new to contend with. One day stuck in my mind with particular clarity, when my father appeared at home with friends and asked me to prepare lunch for all of them. Obanda was gone by then. I was told that my stepmother had fired him shortly before her separation from my father because he had shown up drunk for work. And she had taken our domestic help, Juliana, with her.

For us, a warm meal typically consists of vegetables, meat with sauce, and the traditional *ugali,* a cooked maize flour paste. The vegetables and meat sauce needed only to be warmed up, but I was supposed to prepare the *ugali.* My father was not aware that I didn't know how to do it. And I didn't dare to confess this to him.

First, I put water on the stove, as I had observed Obanda and the various maids do. Then I waited for it to heat up. But that seemed to take forever—and my father was inquiring about the food from the next room. Nervously and uncertainly, I stared at the slowly heating water. Once again I heard him call. On the spur of the moment, I reached for the packet of maize flour, which was only a third full, and poured the whole contents into the steaming water. It bubbled up, flour spraying out of the pot onto the stove. I quickly began to stir the mixture with a large, flat wooden spoon. I pushed the spoon forcefully back and forth in the thickening paste, in the way I imagined Obanda would have done it.

After a while, I noticed that my *ugali* was not getting firm, though there was no longer any bubbling and spraying. But I had already been stirring for some time. I turned up the temperature, to no avail. The soft sludge simply refused to harden. I knew that *ugali* had to be firm, even though it wasn't clear to me how to get it that way.

"Where's the food?" I heard my father calling once again in a joking tone. "We're gradually starving."

I was in anything but a laughing mood. My face was sweating from agitation and heat. I sampled a little of my *ugali* to check whether it was cooked now, but it still tasted raw. I wondered whether I should add more maize flour—but the packet was empty anyway.

Fifteen minutes had passed, and I was still moving the spoon back and forth. Usually it took at most ten to fifteen minutes to cook *ugali*.

"Where's the food, Auma?" a voice suddenly said directly behind me. I was startled and turned around. My father was standing in the doorway.

"I cooked it, but it just won't harden," I answered, almost crying, as I pointed at the pot.

"Why?" My father stepped closer to me. "Let me have a look."

He took the spoon from my hand and briefly stirred the soggy *ugali*.

"When did you put in the maize flour?"

"After the water had been on the stove for a while."

"Was it boiling?"

"I think so. I'm not sure," I answered timidly.

"Why aren't you sure?" my father asked perplexedly. "You must know what you did."

I didn't say anything.

My father hated it when people did things thoughtlessly. His own actions were only rarely the result of chance. In my eyes, he was someone who always knew what he was doing and why he was doing it. And he himself seemed barely capable of comprehending that other people sometimes did rash things—things they could not necessarily explain.

"Was the water boiling when you poured in the maize flour?" He repeated his question somewhat more gently.

I still didn't say anything and looked at the floor. I felt terrible. What if he now told his friends how out of my depth I was in the kitchen?

"Is there any maize flour left?"

"No," I answered sheepishly.

"Then nothing will come of this *ugali*."

And before I grasped what was happening, he turned off the stove, took the pot, and poured the whole contents in the garbage bin.

"But, but . . ." I stammered, aghast.

At that time, my father had considerable financial problems—I knew that it was sometimes a struggle for him even to put food on the table for us. Under those circumstances, how could he simply throw away a meal? I was surprised that he had brought friends home with him in the first place. What would we serve them now?

"When you prepare *ugali,* the water has to boil before you pour in the maize flour," he explained to me with a sigh. "It probably wasn't boiling at all. You could have gone on for hours like that, and it never would have turned into *ugali*. Here," he added, pressing some money into my hand. "Run quickly to the kiosk and buy a packet of maize flour. Then I'll show you how to cook *ugali*."

"And your guests?" I asked uncertainly.

"They can wait."

As fast as I could, I ran to the kiosk. On the way, I thought that my father wasn't so bad after all. He actually wanted to teach me how to make *ugali*. I didn't have to be afraid of him. This superman was, in fact, just a completely normal person.

His absence in my life, due to his work and his traditional paternal role, along with the image of him as a strict authority figure that Obanda in particular had painted for us in order to be able to discipline us with it—along the lines of "Do what I say, or you'll get in trouble with your father!"— had stirred up a fear of him inside me that was hard to overcome.

The *ugali* episode ultimately ended with a crash course in cooking, during which my father explained every single step as he himself prepared the *ugali,* while I stood next to him and watched. Under his supervision, I then got to warm up the meat sauce and vegetables. When I finally served the meal to the patiently waiting guests, he praised me and didn't say a word about the fact that I was not the one who had cooked the food.

Our financial situation deteriorated drastically when my father was taken to the hospital after a serious car accident. Among other injuries, he had broken both legs and had to spend several months in the hospital. The accident occurred shortly after he had finally gotten a new job, but because he was out on sick leave for so long, he lost it and was now once again unemployed. In Kenya, he could receive no unemployment benefits, no child benefits, and no other financial support at all.

We sometimes didn't know how we would get through the next day. For us children, that was a very frightening feeling. Only a few relatives still provided me with a sense of closeness and intimacy. During school break, Aunt Zeituni, my father's younger sister, regularly brought us something to eat. Aunty Jane also did what she could to help us. She worked in the city center, and during the weeks when I was not in boarding school, I sometimes stopped by and picked up some pocket money. She was my mother's sister, a full-figured, upbeat, and fun woman.

In those difficult times, it happened repeatedly that I was sent home from school due to unpaid school fees. A week after the beginning of each trimester, a list of names would be called in the morning when we had lined up in the hallway outside our dorm rooms to go to breakfast. Those whose names were called were instructed to report to the school bursar after breakfast. Whenever my name rang out, it was clear to me that it was about the school fees. With a slip of paper in his hand on which my name and the outstanding amount were written, the bursar informed me with a serious expression that he unfortunately had to send me home again. I could not come back until my father had paid the noted sum. I would then return to my residence hall, take off my school uniform, and head home. Other girls who had been summoned did the same. The school did not, however, feel obligated to inform our parents that we were released. So we set off without their knowledge; in my case, that meant about a two-mile walk.

When I showed up unannounced on such days—in the hospital or, after his release, at home—my father always gave me a reproving look, as if I were skipping school. Each time, he tried to send me back immediately. He called a few friends, who promised to help him with the payment of the school fees. Then he made out a check and sent me off again.

I dreaded those checks—for I knew, as my father did, that they weren't covered. There was simply no money on hand. It was extremely rare that my father's friends kept their promise to support him. And so I was sent home more than once within a few days and had to ask my father for the school fees again. This was particularly bad during the time that he was in the hospital, because I knew beforehand that I wouldn't get anything from him. With each visit I had to grow a thicker skin in order to cope with the terrible situation. The skin thickened and thickened until I had distanced myself completely from my father and all the pain I read in his face.

7.

THE DOMESTIC DIFFICULTIES left their mark; I became quiet and reserved with my family. Although I had a reputation at school for being extroverted and self-confident, someone who always had a joke on her lips and was up for any mischief, at home I withdrew into myself and became very taciturn. I felt misunderstood—because in comparison to what many other family members had to suffer, my problems were not considered too bad. My sensitivity was called "European"—and I was teased about that. Yes, my stepmother was gone, but I still had my father, it was said. Even though he was in financial straits, he nonetheless managed somehow to pay for my excellent education at the expensive Kenya High School. At least I still had that. On top of that, no one doubted anymore that my biological mother would soon return. It was the time when Abongo was making an intense effort to get her back.

How that was supposed to happen, however, I could not imagine. We weren't living in a traditional, polygamous Luo household, in which each wife had her own lodgings and the man his *simba*, as the man's house was called in the Luo language. On such a homestead, even spouses who preferred to avoid each other could live together relatively free of strife. We lived in the city, in a single-family house. How would the married and family life work, if my mother came back only for our sake? What would happen if our parents did not get along?

My brother apparently did not ask himself all these questions. All he cared about was having our mother back with us. But when he finally achieved this goal, she stayed only one week. I was fifteen years old at the time. The same number of years had passed since the time when my mother had lived with my father, and it was eleven years since we children had been separated from our biological mother. Too much had happened in the meantime. However much Abongo wished it, our parents did not reconcile. And that did not surprise me. My father felt trapped and my mother neglected.

The single week the family experiment lasted was, in a word, a disaster. My father kept away from the house and my mother was restless and irritable. It was obvious that they both felt forced into a situation dictated purely by Luo tradition. I still remember that I was getting ready for a school trip at the time, an adventure expedition into the wilderness that included the climbing of Mount Kenya. Before the journey began, I spoke to my mother. I sat down with her, looked her directly in the eyes, and told her that I did not want her to stay with my father for my sake. If she was there only on our account, she should know that she should not force herself to live with us for me. With my fifteen years, I was now old enough and no longer needed mothering. It was too late to make up for the lost years.

When I returned from the expedition, my mother was gone. Not until years later, with the death of my father, did she become part of our family again. As his first wife, she buried him in accordance with our traditions and took her rightful place again as the first wife of the first son on the family homestead in Alego.

Whenever I was back at boarding school after break, I felt as if a huge burden had been lifted from my shoulders. The girl who at home didn't speak much and was most content hiding behind a book vanished, and in her place appeared the rambunctious child of my primary school years. Like most of my classmates, I was loud and playful. At school, I successfully suppressed the family problems that weighed on me at home. When there was laughter, I laughed loudest. When antics were hatched, I was game from the very beginning. I did not want anyone to notice the anguish that was gnawing at me.

Then Peggy Flint arrived, a young American teacher who had been sent to our school by the Peace Corps to teach music. What she found there did not at all meet her expectations. As she later told me, she was already wide-eyed on her arrival. From the window of her taxi, she glimpsed the imposing entrance gate to the school grounds, on the wrought-iron bars of which the impressive motto of the school was displayed: *Servire est regnare* ("To serve is to rule"). And above these three words was a roaring lion. When the taxi drove through the stately gate, Peggy Flint found herself on a campus reminiscent of the atmosphere of a British private school. Her eyes wandered over a well-tended lawn, along green hedges and flower beds. In the distance, she made out an open-air theater half hidden by tall trees. A sign showed the taxi driver the way to the school garden and the sanatorium. Then he turned and stopped in front of a massive, three-story building, one of several that served as dormitories for the students. Just within sight, she glimpsed the pretty chapel.

During her later tour, Peggy Flint discovered excellently maintained tennis courts and hockey fields, a gymnasium, and a large swimming pool. The well-equipped classrooms appeared no less remarkable to her; there were no ramshackle desks anywhere. On top of that, Kenya High School was located on several acres of lush land. No huts or windowless flat buildings with corrugated iron roofs could be seen far and wide. No barefoot African children who had to walk for miles to their school with their books on their heads struggled there to acquire knowledge in a language they could scarcely understand, let alone read or write. At Kenya High School, it was easy to forget that you were in Kenya—if it weren't for the many black faces.

Peggy Flint had come to this country with completely different visions. From my conversations with her, I gathered that she had assumed that her job would consist of helping needy African children, only to be disappointed. Most of the students she would henceforth be teaching by no means suffered from a lack of money. There was not a trace of poverty about them—at least not visibly. For most of them came from well-off families, who did not in the least correspond to the image of poor, underdeveloped Africans. Therefore, as I later learned, after a short time Peggy Flint made an intense effort to be transferred to a rural, more "indigenous" school.

But apart from her disappointment in the face of the "Europeanized" students, Miss Flint, as we called her, got along very well with us girls. I gravitated toward her from the first moment on. She was a genuinely cheerful spirit, and unlike me, she showed her feelings openly and wore her heart on her sleeve. She entertained us with exciting and amazing stories from her life in the United States. There she had taught in a poor neighborhood at a high school attended predominantly by black children, where she made it her mission to help them out of their misery. Now she wanted to do the same thing here in Africa.

Miss Flint lived on the school grounds, and because she at first knew barely anyone, she spent a lot of time with us students. Often I talked with her for hours about everything under the sun. Because I liked to read, she recommended books to me; in return, I explained Kenyan customs and traditions to her. She was particularly interested in why we "Bomanians" were so "British," so different from what she had expected. I watched with amusement how she tried to arouse our enthusiasm for African culture and music. But her efforts had to compete with our passion for Michael Jackson, Marvin Gaye, and Luther Vandross, and in that contest, the American R&B singers always emerged as the clear winners. In our eyes, those musical preferences were by no means in conflict with our "African identity." We took that identity for granted, as something we had grown up with. We did not question it and did not try to prove it. The "Britishness" that Peggy Flint saw in us—which, as our musical taste demonstrated, was infused with a great deal of "Americanness"—we either scarcely noticed or experienced as a mere addition to what we were anyhow. Thus this teacher who promoted everything "indigenous" only confused us with her zeal, instead of freeing us from the "yoke of imperialism" as she intended.

Despite her passionate fascination with everything "African," she was a great help to me in difficult times. I trusted her and felt like I could tell her anything, without her judging or rejecting me.

I also received support from some other teachers in those years, such as Miss Wyatt, who was from England, and Miss Ismail, a Kenyan of Asian descent. Miss Wyatt taught home economics, but encouraged me to get more involved in my sport of choice, swimming. Miss Ismail, our physical education teacher, also promoted my athletic skills. Plus, if a teacher complained about me at faculty meetings, she always put in a good word for me. It was also Miss Ismail who provided me the opportunity to give swimming lessons at our school at an early age.

Although other teachers helped me, these three in particular created the necessary space for me to express myself, make progress, and develop my potential. Later on, my German teacher, Mrs. Kanaiya, who was from East Germany and was married to a Kenyan, would also play a part in that.

Our German class was made up of only four students, all of whom were highly motivated. Mrs. Kanaiya taught us with great enthusiasm and worked with us not only on a technical level, but also interacted with us personally. From her we learned a lot about the German language, German culture, and German history. We had extensive discussions about human rights, the position of women in society, and numerous other topics that we never would have been able to cover in such depth in a larger class. She gave us *Stern, Der Spiegel,* and other German magazines and newspapers to read. It was Mrs. Kanaiya who shaped my early image of Germany and laid the groundwork for my later entrance into German society.

In the meantime, the problems with the troublesome school fees had fortunately been overcome because I had received a scholarship from Kenya High for the last two years before graduation. It had been donated by a group of women in England who met regularly and raised money for various humanitarian purposes. I was chosen by the school administration as the beneficiary of this support.

Now I could focus, free from worries, on life and learning at school. My achievements as a swimmer and swim teacher soon made me popular with the younger girls. We also laughed a lot and thought up pranks together. I thereby incurred the disapproval of the house matron Miss Ndegwa. She did not especially like me anyhow and did not take kindly to my self-confident and assertive nature, so that over time a sort of ongoing battle developed between us. I made sure to avoid her as much as possible. If it hadn't been for my good relationships with some teachers, Miss Ndegwa would probably have managed to get me expelled from school. In a moment of anger, she had assured me that she was working on that.

Unfortunately, I was not entirely free of blame for her antipathy toward me. Like many other girls, I got a kick out of making fun of the matron for her strong local accent and her somewhat ill-proportioned figure. And instead of trying to win her over, I showed her only too clearly that I didn't care whether she liked me or not.

On top of that, Miss Ndegwa was somewhat fearful of my father. Whether that was due to his imposing baritone voice or something more, I never found out. In any case, she did not threaten, as she often did with other girls, to tell him to punish me for my misdeeds. Instead, the mere mention of my father reduced her to silence or made her resort to the feeble threat that she would get the school administration to expel me.

Miss Ndegwa did not understand why an African girl did not simply do as she was told, but constantly questioned everything and even spoke her own mind. When I learned to my great surprise that I had been appointed deputy head girl, I was convinced that this happened partly because with this new function I had to move to another residence hall and Miss Ndegwa was finally rid of me.

As deputy head girl, I was responsible for ensuring order. That meant that I had to attend to the disciplined behavior, manners, and well-groomed appearance of the students. In addition, together with the head girl, I had to represent the students before the administration and the teachers. One reason for this "promotion" was most likely that I was very popular with the younger girls, and the administration as well as the teachers wanted to take advantage of this. While I had previously, as a "mere mortal," worn the regular school uniform—gray skirt, short-sleeved white shirt, red and black tie, and gray sweater—I now became a prefect and got to wear a blue sweater. From that point on, I was one of the powerful "Blue Rags." At our side stood the "Red Rags" (also prefects, they wore wine-red sweaters and ties), who were chosen from the upper grades, but had far from as much responsibility as we did.

Years later, when I taught at the University of Nairobi after my studies in Germany, I lived not far from Kenya High School. One day, as I was heading for a telephone booth, Miss Ndegwa, of all people, stepped out of it. I was startled and felt as if I'd been transported back in time. Instinctively, I wanted to turn around and get out of there. But because I was standing directly in front of her, that was not possible. She, too, looked at me uncertainly and seemed to want nothing more than to vanish into thin air. But then she composed herself, put on a friendly face, and greeted me with a cold smile. I had no choice but to greet her back. She asked me a few superficial questions, behind which there was no discernible genuine interest.

"How are you doing? What do you do now? Are you married? Children?"

Inwardly, I told myself that she would definitely not expect a success story in my case, but would be more inclined to assume—as she had always predicted—that I had "amounted to nothing." I answered her questions succinctly and said goodbye, without making my phone call. Although many years had passed, my antipathy toward the house matron had not abated. As I walked away, I smiled to myself, filled with satisfaction. I had told her with relish that I had come from Germany some time ago, was currently teaching German at the University of Nairobi, and would soon return to Germany to pursue my doctorate there. Not bad, I praised myself, and thought: Her prophecies did not come true.

Despite my differences with Miss Ndegwa, I enjoyed the years at Kenya High. But eventually the school days neared their end, and the closer that end came and the more space the preparations for the final exams took up, the more tense I became. I had not yet thought about what would come next. Though I had applied to the two public universities in Nairobi and looked for an international scholarship, I did not know how things would go on at home in my family. I simply could not imagine returning to the domestic void.

My pent-up fears vented themselves in roundabout ways. Such was the case on a school trip with the Blue Rags. We were on our way back from an evening at the New Stanley Hotel, where we had seen Cilla Black in concert. About thirty girls had seen a worldwide star and were exuberant and exhilarated. Everyone was talking at once. Each of us wanted to give her commentary on what we had seen, and the noise level in the bus rose tremendously. As always, I sat all the way in the back and took part enthusiastically. The two teachers who were accompanying us, Miss Oluoch and Miss Doyle, had a great deal of trouble keeping our volume in check. Just as we were entering the school grounds, one of us made a dumb joke, and we again burst into irrepressible laughter. It was loudest in the back of the bus.

Suddenly, Miss Doyle, a British woman, stood up and came marching to the back.

"That's enough! I've had it up to here with you!" I realized with surprise that I alone was the target of her anger. "Who do you think you are?" she shouted at me. "I will not tolerate this behavior. Do you understand me?" Her face was completely red with rage.

"What did I do?" I asked in shock. I had been behaving no differently than all the other girls.

"You must think I'm stupid. But I'm not! I know for a fact that you started this noise."

For a moment, I was speechless. Why me? Weren't all of us laughing?

"We—" Again I tried to defend myself.

"I don't want to hear another word from you!" she broke in. "You will be quiet immediately!"

It had gone dead silent on the bus. All the girls were staring at Miss Doyle. We had never seen a teacher so angry, and none of us comprehended what had made her so furious.

"But it wasn't me!"

"Don't say it wasn't you. I know it was you. You think you can do whatever you want. But not with me!"

She did not let up. I was the instigator, I should admit it and stop lying, she shouted.

Then something inside me suddenly cracked. Completely unexpectedly, I burst into tears. I doubled over. Like a limp rag doll, I sat there and wept uncontrollably. A floodgate had opened, and the flow of tears could simply no longer be stemmed. Everyone was shocked, especially Miss Doyle, who now tried every means to calm me down. But it was futile. However hard I tried, I could not stop crying.

And suddenly, to the utmost surprise of my schoolmates and the other teacher chaperone, Miss Doyle began to weep as well. No one knew what to do. In tears, the British woman said that she had always known that I hated her. That was why I was constantly making fun of her, just to provoke her. Sobbing, she apologized for her angry outburst and for not handling the situation differently.

I didn't understand what she was talking about. My crying fit shook me and would not stop. When she tried at one point to draw me consolingly toward her, I recoiled. Then she started weeping again. None of the stunned girls left the bus. There was a pervasive sense of helplessness. We had long since arrived at one of the boarding school houses. It would not be long before the lights went on inside and the sleepy faces of curious girls appeared at the windows.

Suddenly, one of the Blue Rags suggested fetching Peggy Flint, because it was known that I got along well with her. Shortly thereafter, my favorite teacher came on the bus. Thirty pairs of eyes watched her intently. When she saw me sitting in the back weeping, she immediately came over to me, bent down, and asked what was going on. I tried to answer, but instead of words there came only sobs and tears.

"You need something to calm you down," Peggy Flint finally said, and asked the driver, who was still sitting patiently, though somewhat uncertainly, at the wheel, to drive us to the school sanatorium. The other girls reluctantly got off the bus, and I was brought to the sanatorium. There I was given a tranquilizer, and it was decided to keep me there overnight. Miss Flint stayed with me until I had fallen asleep.

I never found out what my favorite teacher told the school administration about my crying fit. In any case, I was kept in the sanatorium for five days. And I seemed to really need that time, for I still remember waking up completely exhausted that first morning and doing nothing but sleeping in the days that followed. I was told that my breakdown had been a delayed burnout reaction to the difficult situation at home. Miss Flint wanted to send for my father, but I was opposed to that because I shied away from speaking to him about my problems.

Miss Flint visited me every day. I found out that Mrs. Wanjohi, our headmistress, had reacted to the incident with shock and astonishment. No wonder, for she knew me only as a cheerful, lively, extroverted student, who shrank from nothing and was always in the thick of things. When I finally returned to classes, everyone helped me find my feet again. Only Miss Doyle avoided me as much as she could. I actually felt sorry for her. How could I explain to her that I had not cried so hard because of her, but because of everything that had happened in my life over the past several years? Among those things were my experiences at the home of my Uncle Odima, where I had had to seek shelter during one school break.

8.

RENEWED ACUTE FINANCIAL DIFFICULTIES had forced my father to give up our rented house in Woodley, where we had lived for almost eight years. Now we had nowhere to stay and were dependent on relatives and friends to put us up. There was no space anywhere for our things. Many things got lost at that time: the classical music records my father loved so much, as well as books, paintings, clothing, and kitchenware. We children watched our home disintegrate—and could do nothing to stop it.

When the next break began, my father brought me directly from school to Ngara, the neighborhood where my Uncle Odima lived with his family. I was to spend the next several weeks with him.

Uncle Odima, whom I later called "Soda Uncle," because he worked at a beverage company for years, had come to Nairobi as a teenager. At that time, my father had found a school for him and taken on the payment of his school fees. My father let him live with us until he had graduated from high school. Years later, my father and I now stood at his door. No sooner had we entered the house than I sensed that something was wrong. There was tension in the air. The atmosphere in the small living room was oppressive. Uncle Odima's wife, Catherine, whom I knew from previous years, did not smile when she—with obvious reluctance—gave me her hand. She was quite clearly not pleased about my presence. I felt like an intruder.

My aunt's behavior toward my father and me was unambiguous. Outwardly, my father didn't let it bother him, instead behaving as if he were at home. In retrospect, I assumed that he did that for me. He knew quite well that Catherine did not want us in her home. But he needed a safe place for me to stay.

Uncle Odima was not yet home when we arrived. As soon as he returned from work, all would be well, I thought. Surely he would set his wife straight and demand that she treat us, his closest relatives, with the necessary respect. After all, he had lived with us for years. He would remember that my father had paid all his expenses back then and gotten him his current job. Interestingly, my uncle had even adopted my father's name, because he knew that it would open doors for him. As Bonifus Odima Obama, he enjoyed all the advantages that were initially associated with the name Obama.

But when he returned home to Ngara that evening and stood in the doorway of his small living room, he seemed to have forgotten all that. At the sight of us, he acted just as irritated as his wife had. He didn't smile, greeted us only tersely, and disappeared into one of the rooms, from which he did not emerge until dinner was served. I was completely confused. Was this man really my favorite uncle, who had taken me on his best friend's motorcycle in Woodley and had so often brought us sweets? This man here was a stranger to me. I felt the sense of loneliness that had so often accompanied me since the breakup of our family well up in me again. Besides my father and my brother, this uncle was all that remained of our former family—indeed, of a whole era. He had lived with us; he had to understand what I was going through. But his behavior expressed in no uncertain terms that he wanted nothing to do with us, that we represented too heavy a financial burden for him.

Uncle Odima's apartment was very small; besides the living room, there were two small bedrooms and a tiny kitchen. One of the bedrooms was allotted to my father, while my uncle and his wife shared the other one with their two-year-old son, Daniel. And where was I supposed to sleep? I looked around in confusion. And where did the maid, who was rattling the dishes in the kitchen, spend the night?

Shortly after dinner, everyone went to bed. My father had gone out, which I didn't even hold against him. Because how was someone supposed to remain in an apartment with such an unwelcoming atmosphere? Our whole situation was probably even more oppressive for him than it was for me.

Catherine turned out the light in the kitchen and told me as she walked by that I could sleep on the floor in the living room with the maid. She did not show me where the bed linens were, however. So I asked the maid. She pointed to a thin, rolled-up mattress in a corner and a brown blanket. "You can share my things," she offered. I thanked her and helped her move the furniture against the wall and unroll the mattress in the middle of the room. It was not the first time that I slept on the floor. That often occurred at my grandmother's in Alego. But there it was always an adventure to sleep with other children on a huge papyrus mat. Most of the time we were so tired from playing that we didn't even feel the hard floor and fell asleep immediately. That evening, however, in my former favorite uncle's apartment, I couldn't sleep. The floor was made of cement; I felt its hardness through the thin mattress whenever I moved. On top of that, it was cold with two people sharing the thin blanket. For a long time I lay awake and wondered desperately how I would get through the next four weeks in this house.

The next morning, I had to get up before sunrise with the maid. The living room had to be put back in order because my uncle and his wife ate breakfast there before work. My father, who had not come back until night, was still asleep. I was supposed to help prepare breakfast, which was completely fine with me, because I didn't know what to do with myself. Plus, I already sensed that my aunt would not approve of my sitting around doing nothing in the living room. But at least little Daniel was there. I was looking forward to his company, for it promised distraction. So I would attend to him. Unfortunately, it did not work out the way I'd imagined. With each passing day, my aunt treated me a little bit more like a second maid, and soon Daniel, too, began acting recalcitrant and fresh. Because I did not have to look after him, I ignored him as much as possible from then on.

In Ngara, I didn't know anyone, and the unfamiliar surroundings intimidated me. So I stayed in the house most of the time. Only now and then I was sent to the kiosk or a store. And when I simply couldn't stand it anymore in the cramped apartment, I would visit Aunty Jane in the nearby Kariokor neighborhood. I would stay there until the approaching darkness forced me to return to Ngara. Jane, my mother's younger sister, was always happy to see me and had a smile to spare for me. But apart from the few visits with my father—he had moved into a cheap hotel after he brought me to my uncle—or Aunty Jane, I stayed in the ground-floor apartment, which was dark and cold. It had a tiny balcony, which was in the back, for the building was on a hillside. For hours I would sit there and gaze at the Nairobi River, a brownish polluted sludge that flowed along sluggishly. On our side, the bank consisted mainly of rampant reeds and garbage. On the opposite bank grew corn and *sukuma wiki,* a type of collard greens common in Kenya. But there was filth everywhere there, too. The collard greens were grown by people who resided on the bank in wretched huts made of corrugated cardboard and plastic.

The bleak landscape before my eyes matched my inner landscape only too well. In both, things looked gray and hopeless. Nonetheless, I envied the poor people on the other side of the river their home. I imagined that, despite everything, in the midst of their poverty they had intact families. But at the same time I was aware of what misery that destitution must have involved. I thought of my father, who, although he didn't live in one of those cardboard huts, was now poor. And I sensed that the despair that arose from poverty was not to be underestimated. For that reason, I was anxious, but also sad: Those people were much worse off than I was.

One day, when I was again on the small balcony looking across the river, I was overcome by the horrible feeling that things would never look up again. I could not imagine how my father would ever manage to find a way out of our plight. However hard he tried, he simply could not get a job. (At the time, I had no idea how closely linked this struggle for survival was with political power struggles.) For me, the school exams were approaching, and here with my uncle, in this oppressive apartment, I was incapable of studying. I was constantly freezing—in August it was quite cold in Nairobi without heating, with temperatures around 50 degrees at times—was always hungry, and felt isolated and abandoned. I looked down at the river. The balcony hung over the ground due to the hillside. As I gazed into the depth, I was suddenly seized by the desire to jump, wondering what would happen. Perhaps I would meet my end, I thought naïvely, and then all the suffering would be over. The balcony was probably too close to the ground for the fall to be deadly. But at that moment, I only wanted all the pain to cease.

Just as quickly as the desperate vision had appeared, I recoiled from it. I rushed back into the dark living room, fleeing my own thoughts, and set to work helping the maid prepare dinner.

Despite all my family problems, I passed the final exam and was accepted into Kenyatta University, where I studied fine art and education. (In those days, you could not study German at the university.) I actually didn't want to study in Kenya at all, for I had begun in high school to apply for an international scholarship. And because only four students in our graduation year took German, I was confident about finding financial support. As high school students, we were often invited to German-Kenyan events and cocktail parties. There, I spoke to many people about my desire to study in a German-speaking country in order to improve my knowledge of the language.

At one of these parties, we German students met Munyua Waiyaki, the Minister for Foreign Affairs. He was impressed that we had such concrete plans for the future and promised us to keep an eye out for funding opportunities.

We visited him in his ministry several times. From there he sent us to various people with the request to help us. But even though we met with many influential figures—ambassadors, ministers, businesspeople—our efforts came to nothing.

I had been enrolled at Kenyatta for a year when I finally got a scholarship on my own initiative from the Deutscher Akademischer Austauschdienst (DAAD), the German Academic Exchange Service. My friend Trixi, one of the four girls with whom

I had taken German at Kenya High, had left for Germany a year earlier on a Goethe-Institut scholarship to study the language.

Trixi was from Tanzania and a few years older than I. She was pretty, worldly, and seemed very grown-up. While I lived at boarding school and had to go home to my father during break, she lived with her sister Ade and some others in the Westlands neighborhood of Nairobi. There they ran their own household and could do as they pleased. I was impressed by the fact that they did not have to obey anyone. But Trixi's life was not simple. Besides Ade, she had eight other younger siblings and helped her mother raise them. I had never been saddled with such a responsibility.

Trixi and her flat mates had their own rooms, while the kitchen and bathroom were shared. At the time, I didn't know that I was getting a taste there of what I would later come to know in Germany as a *Wohngemeinschaft*, or *WG*, a communal living situation.

The campus of Kenyatta University, on which I lived, extended over a huge area several miles outside the capital. Because there was nothing but the university buildings far and wide, the place was tailor-made for studying. You also made friends quickly. I enjoyed that time and forged some friendships. But during those days I never lost sight of the desire to go abroad.

More than a year and a half had passed when I received the acceptance letter for the DAAD scholarship. Finally, my dream would come true! I would have the chance to leave the narrow world of my childhood and spread my wings. And although I really enjoyed my art studies, particularly painting and drawing, I told myself that I could pursue that activity any time, even without higher education. The opportunity to study in Germany would definitely not come a second time.

I shared my joy about the scholarship with only a few people—for I was afraid that my father would find out about it and prevent me from accepting it and going to Germany.

Our relationship had remained difficult; the sad events of the past stood between us and prevented us from getting closer. In my eyes, our family situation had improved only minimally, and I still held it against him that he had not fulfilled his fatherly duties—to give us a sense of safety, stability, and financial security.

I was convinced that he would forbid me to study abroad. The mere fact that I had not asked his permission before I applied would surely displease him, the strict father. Not least among the reasons I wanted to get away was the desire to escape the cultural constraints and his authority. But I would not have been able to make that clear to him—especially as I was the only girl in the family and, despite our tensions, he had a special love for me.

The fact that I had the desire to study German, of all things, and not economics, mathematics, law, or medicine—as my father probably would have wished—made everything still more difficult. For my father, the learning of a language was only a means to an end. When he visited me several months after I moved to Germany, he asked me what I wanted to do with my German. The disappointment in his voice was unmistakable. Before I could even answer his question, he added: "Child, it's not enough to be able to speak German. In Germany, every homeless person under the bridge speaks German. It has to lead to something more."

Years later, I had to admit that my father had been right. The German language alone was not enough to practice a "decent" profession in Germany (or elsewhere). The subjects that I chose in addition to my major—pedagogy, sociology, and media studies—formed the actual cornerstones of my later career. But back then, with my nineteen years, when I held the scholarship in my hands, I could think of only one thing, and that was that I would not only be able to "really" learn German, but would also expand my own horizons. That was enough for me.

But there was still one more hurdle, which threatened to destroy all my plans. Because I was not of age, which in Kenya was twenty-one, I could not apply for a passport without my father's signature. According to Kenyan law, my mother, who knew about my travel plans and supported me, could not sign the application on her own. I was beside myself when I found out about this. Why did I need my father's permission, too? Because he was a man? Why didn't my mother's signature suffice? She was a grown woman, after all. My fear of asking my father was based on the fact that he had up to then made virtually all major decisions about what I could and could not do. For me, contradicting him was unheard-of and I did not know whether he would tolerate it. Now I imagined all sorts of scenarios, which all amounted to the same thing: being prohibited from going to Germany. And that must not happen.

I was firmly resolved to accept the scholarship, and because I did not receive support from the Kenyan authorities, I turned to those who had granted it to me. I sought out the German cultural attaché and explained my situation to him, describing to him honestly how things stood between my father and me. Luckily, he had a sympathetic ear and decided to help me. He made some calls and hinted that certain exceptions could be made. He promised to plead with the proper agencies to treat me as a special case.

And, as luck would have it, after some back and forth and a number of sleepless nights, my mother finally received permission to sign the all-important application. I got my passport and the path to Germany was clear. Only once I was there did my father find out that I had left Kenya.

GERMANY

9.

AS THE PLANE DESCENDED and approached Frankfurt Airport, I looked with curiosity out the porthole at the neatly divided landscape below me. The borders between the individual parcels of land looked as if they had been clearly demarcated with a ruler. The city, with its mass of houses, seemed like a compact whole, systematically and precisely sectioned by means of streets, highways, and train tracks.

It was early morning in Germany in October 1980. Was I afraid of what this first day in a foreign land would bring? I no longer recall. In any case, I had gotten through my first long-distance flight. Apart from a scenic flight in a small sport plane, which I had won in a Sunday school competition when I was about ten (I could name the separate books of the Bible by heart), I had never flown before in my life. Back then, I had gotten ill in the shaky plane, and I remember that I was given a pill to settle my nerves and my stomach. But now I was landing in a wide-body aircraft on an unknown continent. I was so curious and excited that there was probably no space left for the fear of being away from home for the first time.

What first impressed me in Frankfurt Airport were its vast

dimensions. Nairobi's airport seemed to me tiny in comparison. Besides the information desks and check-in counters of the countless airlines, there were also stores, cafés, and restaurants here. People walked around, sat on benches and at tables, ate, shopped. Some even lay stretched out and fast asleep on the rows of seats in the waiting areas. The confusing activity all around me reminded me less of a place of arrival and departure than of a shopping mall or a large, indoor market. Only the scattered scenes of farewell that were taking place and the fact that almost all the people had baggage with them confirmed for me that I was in an airport.

The next leg of my journey would be the train ride to Saarbrücken, which was four hours away. Contrary to my expectation that a representative of the DAAD would pick me up in Frankfurt, no one had showed up. But I had also been told that it was no problem to find the way to Saarbrücken: "Just go to the information desk and ask where the train to Saarbrücken departs." That would have posed no great difficulty, if I had found my bearings among the countless signs that confronted me everywhere. But most of them I did not understand, and the symbols were foreign to me. When I realized that the signs were not helping me, I tried asking someone.

"Excuse me?" I said in German to a woman who was coming toward me at a hurried pace. I must have spoken too softly, for she simply rushed past me.

Next, I addressed an older man, who was walking more slowly than his predecessor. When he got close to me, I said, a bit louder this time, "Excuse me! Can you please help me?"

To my relief, the man stopped.

"How can I help you?" he asked with a smile.

He understood me, I rejoiced inwardly. Until now, I had spoken German with another person only during role-playing at school, a relatively stress-free exercise, during which I always knew that I could switch to English if necessary. But this was not role-playing. I really had to get to Saarbrücken. I searched my memory for the German word for "information desk." But it simply would not come to me. The man looked at me patiently.

"How can I help you?" he repeated.

"Um . . . information desk?" I stammered in English. Then, in German, "Please, information. Train?"

Damn it, I thought in frustration. Here was someone who wanted to assist me, and I could not think of the right words. Suddenly, all the German I had learned had vanished into thin air. How often we had practiced such dialogues in class! Actually, I could have recited whole travel scenes, with all the questions and answers.

"Do you want to take a train?" Thank God, the man spoke English—albeit with a strong German accent, but I understood him. All was not yet lost.

"Yes, please!" I answered with relief. "To Saarbrücken. I need the information desk."

The man smiled and said, *"Den Informationsstand."* He took my baggage and said, "Follow me. I will show you where it is."

As we marched to the information desk, the terms came back to me bit by bit: information was *Auskunft,* train station was *Bahnhof,* round trip was *hin und zurück*, one-way to Saarbrücken was *eine einfache Fahrt nach Saarbrücken* . . . I softly said words and phrases to myself as I walked. At the information desk, I wanted to finally show how well I could speak German.

When we arrived there, my companion explained to the man on duty, before I could even open my mouth, that I had to get to Saarbrücken and needed a suitable train connection. The first real chance to demonstrate my German—out the window. But still: I had understood almost everything he had said. When the official spoke to me in German, the helpful older man broke in, "You should explain it to her in English. She can't speak German."

Immediately, I wanted to protest. Just when all the words were coming back to me! Instead, I smiled politely and was silent. The man at the desk explained to me how to get to the train station, which was also in the airport, and how I could buy a ticket and obtain all other travel information there. After I had, to be safe, repeated the instructions to the helpful older man, who was still standing next to me, he pointed to a sign showing a train, the word *Bahnhof*, and an arrow.

"Everything is okay now?" he asked kindly. I nodded and thanked him in German. "I must go now," he said. *"Auf Wiedersehen und viel Glück!"* And with that he turned around and disappeared.

For a few seconds, I stood forlornly next to my duffel bag. In that brief time, I had gotten used to the nice man and had secretly hoped that he would bring me to the train. But then I dispelled the sense of disappointment. He had already done enough for me; I would manage the rest on my own. I took my baggage and followed the sign toward the train station.

All that I remember about the trip to Saarbrücken is that I had several brief conversations with other passengers. At the time, I was happy to provide information and did not shy away from answering unusual questions about myself. I also wanted to use my knowledge of German and test my mastery of the language. If anything from that day has impressed itself deeply in my memory, it is the sense of joy and pride that I could actually make myself understood in German. I still recall that, having arrived in the Saarbrücken train station, I got off the train feeling satisfied with myself and immediately found a taxi that brought me to the university. And once I was there, I made it to student services without any problems.

Outside the office that had been indicated in my documents as the first place to go, several young women and men were waiting. I sat down with them. Finally, I had reached my destination.

With curiosity, I observed the students sitting next to me and passing by, impressed by the fact that they all spoke German, even the foreigners. The African students stood out from the crowd, not only because of their skin color, but also because none of them passed me without looking in my direction and giving me a friendly nod, which I experienced as a greeting of camaraderie.

Finally, it was my turn. I entered a small room, in which there was a huge desk. Behind it sat a man who looked like an Arab and somehow seemed too large for the room. He made a slightly irritated, impatient impression, which I ascribed to the fact that he had had to deal completely on his own with all the students who had been with him before me.

I gave him a warm smile. Something told me that I had to cheer him up. But his eyes showed no sign of friendliness.

"What can I do for you?"

I sensed that I would make headway with him only in German. "Um . . . I'm Rita Auma Obama. I'm from Kenya."

"Na und?"

I didn't understand what he meant by that.

"Excuse me?"

"Na und?" he repeated.

"I don't understand," I said, taken aback. His impolite-sounding answer was not something we had learned in German class. (The expression, I later learned, is akin to "So?")

"What can I do for you?" He sounded more and more impatient.

Now I was the one who was irritated. I had assumed he was informed. After all, I had been accepted into this university as a student.

"I'm here to study."

"Just like all the other students, right?" he replied laconically, and then, at the limits of his patience, asked loudly, "You want to enroll?"

"Yes, please." Finally, he had gotten it. I heaved a sigh of relief.

"What was your name again?"

I repeated it.

The man took a file off the shelf and leafed through it until he found what he was looking for under *O*. Then he gave me a small green book—my *Studienbuch*, which would serve as the official record of my courses—filled out a few forms and closed the file again.

"All right," he said. "You can go."

"And the key?" I asked, again with a smile. He must have forgotten that.

"What key?" Apparently, he considered our conversation finished. He was about to call in the next student. He cast a glance at his watch and stood up.

"I mean the key for my room," I said, remaining seated.

"What room?"

"The dorm room."

The man looked at me as if I were crazy.

"What dorm room? I have no room for you. You have to find yourself a room."

We had spoken German the whole time, and I had not felt as if I had missed anything. But my brain cells refused to understand his last words. In Kenya, you were automatically assigned a room when you began your studies.

"No room?"

"You certainly won't get one from me!"

My German no longer sufficed to continue the conversation. I had to say everything from that point on in English. Was he telling me that I had taken the long journey here from Kenya to find out that there was no room for me?

"I have no room!" I said loudly and clearly in English, emphasizing every single word.

"I don't have a room for you, *either*!" he replied, still speaking German, now visibly annoyed.

"You have to have a room for me. I wrote!"

"Listen, I don't have a room for you. You have to go into the city, buy a newspaper, and find yourself one. Now I have to carry on." With those words he went to the door and opened it. I felt him pushing me out of the room with his eyes. I had no choice but to leave the office.

"I can't find a room. I wrote to you asking for a room, and you never wrote back to say you had no room. Now I'm here, I don't speak enough German, and you have to get me a room!" I said in one breath.

The door now stood wide open and the next student was looking expectantly into the room.

Suddenly, everything was no longer simple at all. I felt the tears coming to my eyes. But I pulled myself together, walked out, and turned around again to the man. "You have to have a room for me."

He gave no reply, and merely indicated to the other student with a nod that he could enter.

In the hallway, I went back to my duffel bag, which was still where I had left it, and sat down. Besides me, there was only one more student waiting. He was constantly looking at his watch and at the door of the room in which I had just experienced that defeat. Only now did it dawn on me that I had not yet even thought about what time it was. I felt as if I had been in transit for an eternity. Kenya was so far away. It was hard to believe that I had still been there the previous evening. For the first time, feelings of loneliness and faint despair welled up in me. Just as I was about to turn to the student next to me, he jumped up, looked at his watch, and hastily strode down the hall.

Now I was sitting there completely alone, disheartened, but firmly resolved not to go anywhere. And where could I go? It was Saarland University that had brought me here, after all. I had been accepted as a student and was informed that everything would be taken care of. And now that man in the gloomy office was telling me there was no dorm room for me. That didn't make sense.

The more I thought about it, the angrier I got. And with the anger the tears ceased. At that moment, the door opened, and the student services employee stepped out of the office with my successor. He seemed to be in a good mood, for he was laughing about something the student had just said. When he saw me, however, his expression froze.

"You're still here?" he asked, clearly perturbed, looking at my duffel bag. As he started to lock his office door, I stood up quickly.

"I need a room," I said again.

I was dead serious with my demand, and my face said: *If necessary, I will spend the night outside your office door.* The man looked at his watch.

"I'm already off work for the day," he replied in frustration. He used the German word for the end of the workday, *Feierabend,* which I didn't know, but I suspected it had something to do with him wanting to go home. *Me, too,* I thought.

The man sighed and reopened the door to his office. I immediately grabbed my duffel bag and followed him.

"I'll see what can be done. But I'm not promising anything!"

I sat down and was silent. There was nothing more to say. All I needed was a room.

The man made various phone calls. I was no longer even listening; I was now really tired. The only thing I wanted was to lie down and sleep.

"You have a room available? In Residence Hall D? Wonderful," the man suddenly exclaimed loudly into the telephone. His relief was unmistakable. I didn't know where Residence Hall D was, but I was delighted to finally have a place to stay.

I no longer recall how I ultimately made it to the residence hall with my heavy baggage. The building was on the campus, not far away from student services. There, a German student helped me find my room, which was on the ground floor of the three-story building. The student's name was Elke. She was a bit taller than I was, very slim, and she had long blond hair that reached down almost to her hips. Elke could speak English very well, and because I was tired, we spoke to each other only in that language. I was glad that the first person I had to deal with in my new home was so nice. At the time, I did not know that this chance encounter would turn into a close friendship, which lasts to this day.

10.

WHEN I ARRIVED in Saarbrücken, my name was Rita Auma Obama. I had never really liked the name Rita, especially as my grandmother often teased me that it was the name of a girlfriend of my father's from his student days in the United States, where he was living at the time of my birth. Supposedly, he had suggested it in a letter to my mother.

In Germany, everyone now thought I had a German first name and asked me why I didn't have an African one. That sounded to me as if they were calling my whole identity into question. As if they wanted to know who I really was, because they could not reconcile me, the African, with that name. In a way, I understood this dissonance. I, too, felt a bit as if the name Rita gave me a false identity.

So I decided pretty soon after my arrival to use my Luo name, Auma, as my first name from that point on. My mother had chosen to name me that after a relative who had appeared to her in a dream shortly after my birth.

Although I no longer called myself Rita, I never completely gave up the name. I regarded it as a gift from my father and retained it in the form of the initial *R*. But that experience enhanced my awareness of myself as an African. There was a growing sense of pride within me that I was Kenyan. Apart from the excessive attention paid to me in public because I looked different, I enjoyed rediscovering, so to speak, my African identity and embracing it consciously. In Kenya, I had never thought about my identity. And why would I have? It had been a given.

It was not only the confrontation with my first name that made me reflective regarding my background, but also people's reactions to my choice of clothing, music, and literature. In a foreign land, I inevitably gained a stronger consciousness of what it meant to be an African.

I had settled into the residence hall well. My room was in Elke's corridor, and I could not have been any luckier, because Elke and I had in the meantime become good friends. We had a lot to share with each other. I told her all about my life in Kenya, about my dearly beloved grandmother, my siblings, and the extended family. Elke, for her part, explained to me much of what seemed confusing in the twelve-month language proficiency course I was required to take in preparation for my studies. She also told me about her family, which, in contrast to mine, was small and basically consisted of only a father, a mother, and two children. She and her younger sister, Gabi, had grown up in a village in Bavaria, where her parents had built themselves a house. For a while, Elke had had a relationship with a Togolese man, whom she had really loved. But for him, it had been settled from the beginning that he would sooner or later return to his native country. She understood and let him go. Once Elke visited him in Togo, but came back to continue her studies. I found the story sad—Elke had liked the man a lot but had nonetheless let him leave. She reminded me a little of Ann Dunham, who had also loved a man from another culture—my father—and had not wanted to hold him back.

I will never forget the day when I first encountered snow (as a young girl I had seen snow from afar only once, when I climbed Mount Kenya on a school excursion).

I woke up in the morning, looked out the window—and caught my breath. Everything was white: the ground, bushes, trees, cars, roofs, everything. I immediately ran over to Elke's room. I knocked hard on her door.

"Open up, Elke. Open up. It's snowing!" I cried.

It was still early, too early for my friend.

"What?" I heard a drowsy voice. "Come back later . . ."

By student standards, it was indeed still very early; in the hallway it was dead silent. But I disregarded that and kept knocking. I was raring to go out in the snow, and I wanted Elke to come with me.

"Five more minutes." Her voice still sounded pretty hazy.

"Not today!" I persisted, my face pressed against the door. "Open up! Please, please, open up!"

I received only a grunt in reply, and I imagined her pulling her pillow over her head.

"Elke, it's snowing! You have to get up," I cried, now somewhat more loudly. Finally, she came shuffling to the door, opened it, turned around, and immediately crawled back into bed.

"You're going to wake everyone up," she murmured. The last part of the sentence was swallowed by the comforter she had burrowed under.

"But you have to come outside with me," I insisted. I can be very stubborn. "It's snowing! Everything is white. I'm seeing real snow for the first time!" We had been speaking German, but in English I exclaimed, "My first snow!" I thought that she would better recognize the seriousness of the matter if I said it in English.

"I heard you the first time," a muffled voice replied from under the comforter. "Another five minutes. The snow will still be on the ground outside tomorrow and the day after."

I sat down at her desk and stared at her—or rather, at the spot where I suspected her head was. And waited. Finally, Elke turned over and looked sleepily out from under the blanket.

"Okay, I surrender." She sat up in bed, her hair tousled, smiling wearily. "I should have known you wouldn't give up."

I laughed.

"By the way, if I were you, I would put on different shoes," she added. "It's going to be pretty wet outside."

I looked down at my feet. In my rush to see the snow from up close, I had not even considered whether winter boots would be more sensible than the slippers I was still wearing.

Finally, we were outside, bundled up warmly and equipped with the proper footwear. We had fetched Manou, a student from the Ivory Coast, to share with him the experience of the phenomenon "snow." Manou had already been awake for a long time. He was a serious, disciplined student, an early riser who always did everything in an organized and conscientious manner. His room was invariably tidy. He liked to cook and was very good at it and occasionally invited us to eat with him. I think he had a bit of a crush on Elke, but did not have the courage to tell her. I teased her about that sometimes, but she always pooh-poohed it. In any case, we really liked Manou. Behind his serious face was a person with a great sense of humor, who could tell wonderful jokes.

Now he had joined us to look at the snow, touch it, taste it, and play with it. It was a wonderful experience. Like children, we frolicked in the white splendor, started snowball fights, did cartwheels and handstands, and even ate the white stuff—and all the while one of us was taking photographs, for I absolutely had to document this event for my family in Kenya. Even though it was cold and wet in the snow, we weren't freezing. The sun was shining, we broke a sweat horsing around, and soon we even took off our winter jackets.

Shortly thereafter came the next impressive experience: my first German Christmas. Elke invited me to spend it with her family. To avoid the expensive train ride to Trunkelsberg, a village in the Unterallgäu district of Bavaria, we arranged a carpool through a ride-sharing agency.

I found the idea of splitting gas costs brilliant, and during the car ride, I wondered whether something like that could work in Kenya. There this form of shared travel would spare many poor people the high costs for public transportation. But then it occurred to me that Kenya lacked several important prerequisites for it—first and foremost, the trustworthiness of drivers and passengers. The danger of being robbed or of something even worse befalling you was great. In Germany, if something was fishy, you could usually find out without too much difficulty from the register of residents where the driver or passengers lived. That fact alone seemed to me a guarantee for a safe journey. In Kenya, there was no comparable registration of the population (nor is there one to this day). And not least importantly, the gulf between poor and rich is simply too wide to inspire you with the necessary confidence in a carpool made up entirely of complete strangers.

Having arrived in Trunkelsberg, I realized excitedly that there was even more snow here than in Saarbrücken. But it was also considerably colder than it had been there.

On the day after our arrival, Elke, her sister Gabi, and I immediately went out and hiked through the snowy landscape to a hill at the edge of the woods, where village children were sledding or hurtling down the slope on black truck inner tubes. At the bottom, they turned around and tramped back up the steep slope to race downhill again.

It was not long before Gabi had found a few schoolmates who were willing to lend us their rubber tube. Clinging to Elke, I hurtled down the slope on the strange vehicle. It was so much fun that we repeated the up and down several times until, tired and soaked with sweat, we gave back the tube.

In Trunkelsberg, I also became acquainted with cross-country skiing, a sport that was actually not difficult, but had unforeseen consequences. As easy as it was to glide on the skis over flat, snow-covered ground with the help of two poles, the aches and pains caused by this mode of locomotion were terrible. The next day I felt muscles that I previously hadn't even known existed. Everything hurt; I could barely move.

"You actually should have done a few weeks of ski gymnastics first," Elke commented sympathetically. "Then you wouldn't be sore now."

Before our arrival, Elke's mother had spent days baking and pre-cooking for the holidays. When I asked in amazement why so much preparation was necessary, it was explained to me that Germans celebrate Christmas over several days, unlike Kenyans, who, like the British and the Americans, observe only December 25, which requires much less effort. *Of course!* I thought at the time, and found my conclusion quite clever. That's why the German word for Christmas, *Weihnachten,* is plural.

The rituals that accompanied my first German Christmas were very foreign to me, but spending the holiday with Elke's family made me appreciate it. The mood in her home was cheerful and relaxed. The fact that this time I was there, an African who was a stranger to everyone except Elke, made the festive gathering into a very special event. To celebrate Christmas Eve, I wore a wide-cut, light-blue West African robe.

The hospitality of this family, who accepted me so quickly and warmly as a third child, restored a little bit the sense of familial security that I had lost in the previous years, and for that I was really grateful. I had been living in Germany for only a few months, and already the country was far from as foreign to me as it had been on my arrival.

11.

As time went by, I learned from certain experiences with which I was repeatedly confronted. Unsuspecting as I was, I at first responded with a polite smile to every stranger who approached me and asked me questions. Some of them, especially men, would then regard this as an invitation.

One day, when I was sitting outside on a bench and enjoying the last warming rays of the sun on a spring afternoon, a man of around forty walked by. He smiled at me, and as usual I smiled back—I was still the "nice little African" who reacted without reservations to encounters with strangers. Visibly interested, the man stopped, came over, and sat down next to me. I thought nothing of it, and so we talked for a while. Finally, he suggested exchanging our addresses and telephone numbers. Because he did not relent, I gave him, naïve as I was, my residence hall address.

That was the beginning of a strange and somewhat unpleasant story, which taught me to be less open toward strangers. For, to my great surprise, the man fell in love with me. He visited me a few times at the residence hall, took me out, and made a lot of fuss over me. I wasn't sure how I should behave. Still rather inexperienced with respect to men, I didn't know how to make it clear to my admirer without offending him that I was not interested in him and didn't want to go out with him. I was too polite for that. He was nice, after all, and behaved like a gentleman.

My new acquaintance, Peter, was a musician and played in an orchestra. One day he took me with him to one of his concerts. Afterward, we went out with his colleagues. But in the group of strangers, I felt like a fish out of water. Peter and his friends were much older than I was; I recall nothing but gray-haired men and women. Although they otherwise acted as if it were completely normal that I was sitting with them, I noticed how they kept glancing over at me. Where had he snagged such a young, exotic thing? their eyes seemed to ask. I smiled courteously, but my whole being screamed silently at them: No! I don't belong to him!

Even though I never encouraged Peter, his invitations became more frequent. At the same time, I felt an increasingly strong need to put an end to the matter. Only I didn't know how. Peter mistakenly believed that our "relationship" was progressing, while I was desperately trying the whole time to figure out how to get rid of him. Finally, I went out with him only when Elke was willing to come along. Up to that point, she had watched Peter's advances with amusement. She knew quite well that I was not attracted to him, but had assumed that I enjoyed going out with him.

When there were thirty red roses outside the door of my room one day, it became too much for me. I knew that I had to draw a line. I dreaded the confrontation, but it was unavoidable.

Shortly thereafter, the unsuspecting man called to ask whether I had received the flowers, and at the same time he invited me to go out once again. Without thinking twice, I interrupted him in the middle of his sentence.

"I'm sorry, Peter, I can't see you anymore."

"We can meet another time, if today doesn't work for you," he said. Apparently, he had not understood.

"No!" I replied, this time with a louder, somewhat shriller voice. I felt hot and cold all over with nervousness. My hands were sweaty. "I mean really, never again. I can't see you anymore."

I felt Peter freeze at the other end of the line. There was a long silence. To create distance, nothing better had occurred to me than to address him with "*Sie*," the formal "you" in German.

"Why?" he asked. His voice suddenly sounded serious.

I was silent.

"You don't want to meet me anymore? Why?"

I still said nothing. There was simply no kind answer to his question. I would have had to explain to him that I had felt nothing for him from the beginning, that the whole relationship had taken place only in his head, and that at our very first encounter I had expected nothing more than a simple "hello" from him.

Instead, I said only, "I just can't see you anymore. I'm sorry. I have to go now. Good-bye."

The clipped sentences had simply come out of me. I didn't even wait for his reply, but hung up the phone and hastily left the telephone booth in the hallway of the residence hall.

Thus the relationship that had never been came to an end. *Nothing crazy like that ever again!* I resolved at the time. But it wasn't long before I was in another jam.

By that time, Elke had gotten her international scholarship and had gone to study in the United States. A large void had opened up in my life in Saarbrücken. I missed her above all as a friend, but also as a daily guide to the German language and culture.

But then I met Nora, who came from Nigeria and also attended the preparatory language proficiency course. When I had complained to her about my unhappiness over Elke's departure and the fact that I had not spoken enough German since then, she said she had the perfect solution for me.

"What is it?" I asked with curiosity.

"You can find a family through the newspaper."

"For what?"

"A German family!" It sounded as if she had discovered the magic formula to win the lottery.

"You place an ad in the newspaper saying 'African student seeks family to improve her German,' or something like that. You wait for the offers and just choose one, and then you visit regularly to practice your German with them! Great, isn't it?" Nora beamed at me and added, "I myself have found a family in this way."

Not a bad idea at all, I thought. With a German family, I would have to speak German the whole time—the ideal language training. The more I thought about it, the better I liked the idea.

"I'll help you," said Nora, after I informed her that I had decided to take her advice. "It's really simple."

Indeed, with her help, I found such a family within a week. They lived near Saarbrücken in the countryside. Where exactly was not so important to me during our first telephone conversation; the fact that it was a young couple with two small children appealed to me more than anything else. They must be nice, responsible people, I assumed, and without thinking twice I accepted their offer to spend the next weekend with them.

On Friday evening, I waited excitedly for my German family, who were picking me up from the university in their car. Today, I can no longer recall any doubts or fears. Nor do I remember whether I told anyone that I would be spending the weekend out in the countryside with complete strangers. The family was there, and I simply went with them.

The young parents and their two children, who were about seven and nine years old, made a nice impression. Most of the forty-five-minute drive took us past tilled fields; only now and then was there a solitary farm or a small village. When we finally reached their house, it was dark. I could only vaguely make out that it was on a sort of farm. Through the long, narrow hallway, we entered a spacious living/dining area. The large table was already set for dinner.

My host parents immediately showed me my room, which their son had had to vacate for me—a typical boy's room with a lot of toys and blue walls. I put my bag next to the freshly made bed and returned to the living/dining area. There the two children were sitting on the floor and playing. Only now did I notice that there were things lying around everywhere and the room looked pretty messy.

Next to the dining table, the door to the kitchen was open, from which I heard noises. For several minutes, I stood around not knowing what to do. Should I stay with the children, or did they expect me to help in the kitchen? The boy and the girl, who had asked inquisitive questions during the drive, seemed in the meantime to have lost interest in me. So I went into the kitchen.

It was large and just as messy as the living room. I was amazed. In our home the kitchen in particular always had to be clean and tidy to avoid attracting vermin. Much of this kitchen looked like an ideal breeding ground for moths, bugs, mice, and other such creatures.

"You don't have to help," the mother said with a cheerful voice. She had just begun preparing dinner. So I retreated into the living room again, sat down quietly on the sofa, and waited. I didn't feel completely comfortable, but I didn't know whether as a guest I was allowed to return to the kitchen uninvited. In Kenya, where even poorer families usually have servants, you would never enter that room without the host's express permission.

When the father entered the living room with a bottle of wine and said, "If you want, you can help put the dinner out on the table," I was saved.

"Yes, thank you!" Relieved, I jumped up and followed him into the kitchen.

"Come on, children. You help, too!" he called to the two little ones. The answer was a moan of "Ooooh." Reluctantly, they stood up and joined us.

I tried to suppress my vermin fantasies and set to work putting the various components of the dinner out on the dining table: several types of bread and rolls, butter, an assortment of sliced cheeses and sausages, and some other things that were unknown to me. To drink there were juices—homemade, as was proudly announced to me; the fruit came from the garden—wine, and mineral water.

Then we all sat around the table. The mood was merry, and I began to relax and lose my shyness. From my visits with Elke's family, I was used to having a cold *Abendbrot* ("evening bread," as Germans call this type of supper) at this time of day instead of a warm meal.

After eating, we remained seated and talked. In the meantime, a brother of the father's who lived nearby had joined the group. The new guest took a small paper bag out of his pocket and poured something out of it onto the table. It looked like dried herbs. He took a portion of it, rolled it in white paper and shaped it into a sort of oversized cigarette. He lit it and took a drag. I watched with astonishment. But I was even more surprised when he handed the huge cigarette to his brother, who then took a drag and passed it to his wife. My eyes grew wider and wider. What were they doing? And now she was holding the thing out to me. Aghast, I stared at her.

"Go ahead and take a drag," the mother said.

"No, thanks," I replied, barely managing to conceal my distaste. "Thanks, I don't smoke."

"Have you never tried a joint before?" asked the brother. "I thought that everyone in Africa smokes pot. Try it."

"No!" I insisted. I suddenly felt miserable.

"Oh, come on. It's not a cigarette. It's a joint." He saw my uncomprehending face and added, "Marijuana."

Marijuana! I'd heard of that; it was called *bangi* in Kenya. Now I grew frightened. *Bangi* was a drug! I had ended up in a house in which the family smoked *bangi,* and I didn't even know where I was! I had no idea where the telephone was and whether they even had one. Suddenly, I realized that I had made a huge mistake. Why had I simply gone off with these people without having the faintest idea who they were? Now I was stuck here. Words like "heroin" and "LSD" were floating around in my head. We had always been warned about drugs, and I had ended up here with drug addicts, of all people. My imagination ran wild; I saw myself lying in a half-stupor in a ditch.

I don't know whether the family noticed any sign of my inner turmoil. In any case, I acted outwardly as if everything were fine. *Just don't show any fear,* I thought. For even though I was telling myself the whole time that everything would be all right, I was afraid of just the opposite.

Apart from the large *bangi,* which continued to go around, the evening actually went quite smoothly and pleasantly. Although I participated in the conversation, my fear did not subside, and I was trying all the while to figure out how I could cut my visit short. There was only one thing I wanted: to get back to my safe room in the student residence hall in Saarbrücken.

The next morning I got up early. The house was quiet; the family was still asleep. I packed my things, made the bed, and went into the living room. There I sat down on the sofa and waited impatiently for the first signs of life.

Eventually, the children showed up in the living room in T-shirts and underpants and began to play with their scattered toys. Shortly thereafter, the father entered the room. He, too, was wearing a T-shirt, but that was all. I froze. I had never seen a naked man before, let alone a naked man who was a stranger and on top of that was in a living room in which small children were playing.

They did not seem to notice anything out of the ordinary. In our home, such a scene would have been completely unthinkable. For Kenyan children, the sight of the naked father was a major taboo. I was experiencing the ultimate culture shock! (Only later did I find out that I had ended up in a typically "alternative" circle of early 1980s Germany.) The effort I had to muster not to sit there with my mouth hanging open made itself painfully felt in my cheek muscles.

If it had been up to me, I would have left immediately with an empty stomach. In the meantime, the horror visions in my head had also expanded: *They could be lunatics, criminals, drug dealers, who could somehow harm me,* I thought anxiously. I worried that my fear could alarm the family, and who knew what they would do to me then? For that reason, I could not leave until after breakfast, lest I attract attention.

Everyone helped set the table. The father had in the meantime put on pants, and the mother had appeared in the kitchen fully dressed, thank God.

At breakfast, I announced that I absolutely had to get back to Saarbrücken because I had forgotten to take care of something urgent. I don't know whether my hosts believed this lie, but to my relief they did not seem particularly irritated. In general, they were quite easygoing about everything.

"No problem," they said. "You'll come again, won't you?"

"Yes," I said, forcing a smile.

"We have to drive to Saarbrücken anyway, so we'll bring you right back."

"Thanks," I replied, sighing furtively.

But I could not breathe calmly again until I was back in my room in Residence Hall D. It was the first and last time I sought out a German host family at random. Fortunately, I learned German grammar anyway, and a year later I passed the entrance exam that qualified me to begin my studies in German literature at Heidelberg University.

12.

After I had been living in Saarbrücken for several months, I received a phone call from my father. He was on the way to what was then the Soviet Union on business and had added a stopover in Germany to see me. Over the past few years, he had found his feet again professionally and was working for the government in the Ministry of Finance.

I was startled when I heard his voice. Fear welled up. Was he planning to send me back home or at least make a big scene because I had left Kenya without his knowledge? My father had always been an authoritarian figure, who made decisions about his children's lives without consideration for how we felt. This was entirely in keeping with family roles in our culture, in which children did not have a voice. I sensed that my father saw me as an extension of himself, not really a separate entity. With my rebellious nature, I had constantly felt the need to fight to maintain my identity and be recognized as an individual. Now that I had gained my autonomy, I feared he might not accept this and might try to reassert his authority over me. In panic at that prospect, I wondered how I could convey to him in a few words that I didn't want to see him.

In the meantime, I had been enjoying the life of an independent adult. During my academic year at Kenyatta University in Nairobi, I had gotten a slight taste of this freedom. But here it meant that I could determine my life completely on my own, without interference from my parents. I had turned twenty, was financially secure through my scholarship, had a place to stay, and didn't have to ask my father for anything. And none of that should change in the future, especially not due to an encounter with him.

But ultimately, after some persuasion by Elke, I capitulated and told my father that I'd be happy to meet him. He came to Saarbrücken. I still remember his taxi stopping in front of our residence hall. I was sitting in my room and looking out the window in anxious anticipation. Together with Elke—at that point she was not yet in the States, and I had asked her not to leave my side during his visit—we sat down shortly thereafter in my small dorm room. I could barely get a word out.

In the end, it was Elke who kept the conversation going. Eventually, though, she had apparently had enough, and she excused herself on some pretext and left the room. I would have liked nothing more than to get up and go, too. But I never would have dared to snub my father like that. Tensely, I remained seated, bracing myself, now that we were alone, for him to reprimand me for having left without telling him.

But I had been mistaken. I had been so preoccupied with myself that I hadn't even noticed how unusually quiet he had been the whole time. Only reluctantly did I acknowledge to myself that he looked sad. He seemed defeated.

As I looked at him like that, it became clear to me that I had nothing more to fear from him. The man who was sitting there before me and from whom I had fiercely struggled to become independent for all those years appeared broken. As I gradually realized that he could no longer determine what happened in my life, he himself must have grasped that he had lost me.

I still remember how soft and sad his voice sounded when he asked my why I had simply snuck out of Kenya without saying good-bye. As always in our confrontations, I went on the offensive. Defiantly, I explained that I had been afraid he would keep me in Kenya. And then I told him what it had been like for me at home at that time. My father just listened, and I saw that my words, my criticism hurt him. What I had done had been no small thing. I had left the country without telling him. In doing so, I had left him, too. Perhaps it was not even clear to him at that time that a huge gulf had already developed between us years earlier. Perhaps he had even thought until recently that I was still his sweet little girl, while I had distanced myself more and more from him.

Suddenly, I, too, was seized by a deep sadness. I simply could not forgive my father. So much had gone wrong in our life together, and I still blamed him for it. I had desperately wanted him to see how much I had suffered from the separation from my stepmother and the breakup of our family. But I had always had the feeling that he didn't really want to know. He had always acted as if everything were fine. He had never asked us—or, perhaps, himself—how we children were really doing.

I told my father all that. He said nothing. He didn't even try to defend himself. And eventually, I didn't know what else to say either. I was mentally and physically exhausted, and he probably felt the same way. He said only, "Do you know that I'm proud of you?" I murmured something and left the room.

We had arranged that my father would spend the night in my room and I would sleep in Elke's room on the floor. The next day, I woke up exhausted from a restless sleep. I made breakfast, and the three of us ate together. Not much time remained; my father had to catch his plane to Moscow. I called us a taxi, for I knew that it would have been impolite not to accompany him to the airport.

The visit from my father had been much too short to work out the difficulties and the many unspoken things between us. Though my fear of him had diminished, the distance persisted. As I saw him boarding the plane at the small Saarbrücken airport, my heart sank. I would have liked so much to be closer to him, but it wasn't possible. The thick skin I had developed a long time ago to protect myself from pain and disappointment could not be pierced.

I felt like crying, but my eyes remained dry. My father, that big man, suddenly seemed small, scarcely larger than I was. Despondently, I left the airport, and knew that it would take me several days to recover.

13.

UP TO THAT POINT, I had not been really interested in the opposite sex. I came from a family in which the men were clearly in the majority, and in my experience women and girls were not treated as equal partners. Undoubtedly, that was one of the reasons why I kept away from relationships with men. On top of that, I knew that if I got involved with someone before marriage and "something happened," my father would disown me. He had threatened me with that often enough. Time and again, he had asked me whether I was still his "good girl." I always murmured something unintelligible. It annoyed and embarrassed me that he tried to find out in that way whether I had already slept with a boy. I would have preferred it if he had asked me directly about it—or, even better, explained to me clearly about sexuality. But like so many fathers, he projected onto me his own anxiety that his daughter could get pregnant, leaving me equally fearful that it could happen to me.

Actually, he didn't have to worry—for I avoided on my own any close involvement with boys. When I began studying at Kenyatta University, I treated my male classmates solely as fellow students. Not only out of fear of getting pregnant, but also because I did not regard myself as particularly attractive.

When I moved to Germany, none of that changed at first. In Saarbrücken there were—besides Peter—a few male students who had their eyes on me. Most of the time, Elke called my attention to it; I myself was apparently too blind to see it. When I did perceive something like an advance, I fended it off. I simply did not believe that a man could be interested in me.

In my case, Cupid was simply taking his time. And when I finally did fall in love one day in Heidelberg, where I had by then been studying for a while, I was completely smitten.

Dieter became my first love.

It began in the usual way. A man took an interest in me, and I didn't notice—as opposed to my friends, who opened my eyes. I didn't take them seriously. But this time the man apparently really had it bad, for he did not give up.

Dieter was nine years older than I and was working on his dissertation. He lived in my student residence hall, but generally had not spent much time in Comeniushaus. Now he seemed to almost never want to leave the place.

Gogo, my Togolese friend, who never left her dorm room unless she was perfectly groomed from head to toe, ultimately took pity on him and invited him from time to time when we got together to share a meal in her room.

"He's really suffering," she said one day with an almost imploring voice when we were alone.

"Who?" I asked, confused.

"Dieter! I've been telling you all along that he's in love with you."

Gogo was a very romantic person. Since we had known each

other, she had been trying to set me up with someone. She simply did not understand why, at almost twenty-two years old, I still didn't have a boyfriend. She was only a few years older than I was, and had long been spoken for. From an earlier relationship, she had a small daughter, whom she had left with her mother in Togo in order to pursue her studies.

"That's impossible," I replied in embarrassment.

In contrast to me, Gogo had a loud, direct nature, not my—as she put it—"prim and proper British manners." She didn't beat around the bush, but immediately called a spade a spade.

"You really are blind, Auma," she said with a laugh. "He can't take his eyes off you for a minute, and you haven't noticed a thing! Didn't you realize that he stopped going home over the weekend? He used to never be in the dorm on those days."

I said nothing. In addition to my shyness toward men, I was also very mistrustful. The idea of belonging to a man—at the time, I equated a romantic relationship with a property relation—repelled me. In my eyes, to have a boyfriend meant the loss of the hard-won independence that had brought me to Germany. I didn't want to take that chance. When Gogo told me about Dieter, I thought only about him inhibiting me in my desire for freedom.

In my rational considerations, I had completely factored out love.

One evening, a veil was finally lifted from my eyes in his presence and I noticed how drop-dead gorgeous he was. He was tall and lean and had pitch-black curls, which fell casually over his forehead. Rather reserved, he did not talk much. I fell head over heels in love with him, and the miracle happened: We became a couple.

Suddenly, entirely unknown emotions welled up in me. I felt something for Dieter that had absolutely nothing to do with the ideas I had previously associated with a relationship with the opposite sex. Being in love gave rise to the fatal need to do everything in my power to make this man happy. He only had to ask me. Today I know that my reservations about romantic relationships were entirely justified—for at the thought of Dieter, my independence and freedom suddenly didn't matter to me at all. I only wanted him to love me as much as I loved him. Everything else was unimportant.

Dieter's love for me did not last long. He had probably fallen in love more with an exotic, romantic idea of me than with the real me. I was much younger than he was, had no experience at all with relationships, and probably often acted a bit awkward.

From Gogo I learned that he had previously been with a woman who had a twelve-year-old child. On the weekends, he had always gone to stay with his girlfriend in their shared apartment, where she had cooked for him and done his laundry. Then he fell for me and broke up with her. Now he stayed in the residence hall on the weekends to be with me—and had to do all his household chores himself.

When I had fallen deeply in love with him, he must have realized that the stranger to whom he had once been so drawn was now too foreign to him. Soon, he again began to go "home" over the weekend. At first, I thought nothing of it. In my naïveté, I didn't notice that my first great romance was heading for its end. Once again, it was Gogo who opened my eyes.

"Haven't you noticed anything?" she asked with a hint of indignation in her voice.

We were sitting in her room. It was the weekend, and Dieter wasn't there. Puzzled, I stared at her.

"He's back with his old girlfriend!" Gogo suddenly blurted out.

"But you told me that he broke up with her when he fell in love with me," I replied apprehensively. I didn't want to hear her suspicions. I couldn't bear the thought that Dieter might not love me anymore. I had devoted myself to him wholeheartedly.

"Listen to me, Auma," she insisted. "I'm sure that he is cheating on you with his old girlfriend. You have to do something about it."

Horrified, I stared at Gogo.

"What?" Suddenly I saw everything around me falling to pieces.

"Ask him. He has to tell you the truth."

"But I don't want to know, Gogo!" I cried desperately.

"You can't be that naïve," she said peevishly. I knew, of course, that her anger was directed at Dieter, but nonetheless her words pierced me like needles. "If you don't ask him, I will. After all, it's my fault that you're together. I have to make up for it."

"Things won't get better," I murmured, trying to imagine a life without Dieter. Pain spread in my chest.

Finally, I summoned all my courage and confronted Dieter myself. He didn't deny it when I asked him whether he still visited his former girlfriend. He explained that he had obligations to her. After all, they had been together for eleven years and bore responsibility for a small child, who was not his but who nonetheless regarded him as a father. He could not just disappear from his son's life.

Even as he was defending himself, I knew that I had lost Dieter. It took me two years to be open to love again.

14.

IF MY FATHER TAUGHT ME anything, it was this: "Always tell the truth, whatever the consequences." What he actually meant by that became apparent to me once on a flight from London to Amsterdam. I was beginning my second semester at Heidelberg University. My father, who was on a business trip through Europe, had invited me to accompany him to England and the Netherlands.

We had last seen each other when he had made a stop in Germany on a business trip to the Soviet Union in order to see me after my "escape" from Kenya.

At the thought of that visit, the terrible jumble of emotions that had seized me when he had called immediately came back to me. Now, months later, I was sitting next to my father with the confident sense that he would not impede me on my path and would not force me to go back to Kenya. We were on an airplane on our way to Amsterdam.

We had just been brought lunch. On the tray was a glass I really liked. In those days, airlines still served their economy passengers drinks in real glasses and not in the plastic cups that are customary today. I decided to keep my glass as a souvenir, and without much hesitation I put it in my pocket, hoping that the stewardess wouldn't notice.

Unfortunately, however, my father saw what I did and reprimanded me with the words: "You don't need to do it secretly, Auma. Just ask whether you can have the glass." Shortly thereafter, he beckoned to a stewardess and told her in his charming gentlemanly way that his daughter—he pointed to me—would like to keep one of those glasses as a souvenir. "Actually, two would be best," he added, before she left.

Other passengers must have heard the deep baritone voice, and at that moment I wished that the ground—or rather, the vast sky around us—would swallow me up. The stewardess had probably noticed how embarrassing the situation was for me, for when she returned with two glasses, she said in a soothing voice, "Passengers often ask us for them."

When she left, my father turned to me.

"Always have the courage to say what you want to say, Auma," he said. "Often you'll be pleasantly surprised by the outcome."

Indeed, that had applied to this situation. But however convinced my father was that you should always be honest and express what you thought, it was, of course, not always a pleasant surprise that awaited him. Still, he remained true to his convictions, and frequently had to accept the negative consequences of his candor—for example, when he had gotten into trouble due to his unconcealed criticism of the Kenyan government, lost his job, and only obtained a post in the ministry again with the utmost effort.

The glass episode would not be the only embarrassing experience during that flight—for my father tried to talk to me about men. It was as if he had suddenly noticed that I had grown up and felt obligated to address the thorny subject.

I let him speak—but suddenly I winced when he proudly declared that when the time was ripe he would definitely find a proper husband for me. In the face of such a statement, how was I supposed to explain to my father that Cupid had already beaten him to the punch? For at that time I had just fallen in love with Dieter and was by no means only *his* little girl anymore, as he probably still believed.

In Rotterdam—after his business appointments in Amsterdam we had gone to the Dutch city on the North Sea—we ate in a Chinese restaurant on the last evening of our trip together. My father ordered wine for the two of us. I had never drunk wine before, and I didn't actually like the taste. But I emptied the glass, because I felt really grown-up for the first time in front of my father.

When we returned to the hotel, a sad message had been left for my father. He had gotten a call from Kenya informing him that his cousin George Were had died in a car accident in Kisumu. Beyond their familial relationship, Uncle Were and my father had been very close, and so his cousin's death was a heavy blow for him—especially as another relative with whom he had felt connected had also recently had a fatal accident.

Along with my father and Uncle Were, this second uncle, a lawyer, had been among the "chosen ones" who had been granted a Western higher education. This privilege was bound up with the lifelong duty to provide for the welfare of those who had remained behind.

All the chosen ones were confronted with these expectations, whether they were financially capable of fulfilling them or not. They were deeply convinced that they owed something to their families. For them it was understood that what belonged to them also belonged to the extended family. Among our relatives, it had therefore become routine, when in financial straits, to go to my father—after all, he was doing better than they were in this respect—or to Uncle Were. But the number of relatives in need far surpassed their capabilities. In those days, the Obama family did not include many educated members with good incomes. Most of them had neither a well-paying job like my father nor a thriving business like Uncle Were. Even if it had been their intention, they could not have helped all the family members in need. Nonetheless, they tried to do everything in their power.

But now Uncle Were, the second supporting pillar of the family, was dead. The fact that two of his closest allies had died within such a short time hit my father hard. I saw him suffering, here in a foreign country, far away from home. But how was I supposed to console him? Although our evening together had been going very pleasantly until we received the news of Uncle Were's death, and I had felt a little bit closer to my father, I was incapable of mustering the necessary sympathy to stand by him in his grief. That would have meant letting him in emotionally, and I was simply not prepared to do that.

I stood in the doorway between our hotel rooms and looked over at my father lying on the bed and weeping, incapable of going to him. The ever-present thick, impenetrable wall of pain and disappointment, undoubtedly mixed with awe and shyness, stood between us. I balked at acknowledging my father's suffering. And what amazed me was that at that moment I even felt an old resentment welling up in me again.

When I saw him there in his grief, I could not help thinking of how often I myself would have needed more comforting. He had never been there for me, I now told myself defiantly. How often had *he* come to console me? And now *I* was supposed to comfort him? I was too proud and too worried about my own emotional equilibrium to feel sympathy.

Ultimately, I was deeply afraid that with one step in his direction I would be overwhelmed by all the pain of the past years that I had so successfully suppressed, and would be left alone and defenseless with those feelings. And yet I suffered inwardly with my father. He looked so helpless and sad—completely devastated. He called me over to him, but I stood motionless in the doorway. I could not go to him. Today, I tell myself that as his daughter it was hard for me to bear seeing my father so weak and hurt—this man, of all people, who was always supposed to be a vital support.

My fears preoccupied me so much that I completely forgot to mourn the person whose death had started the whole drama, Uncle Were, whom I had really loved.

I will always remember the sadness of that evening—in particular because those were to be the last hours my father and I would spend together. The next time I saw him, my father was lying in a coffin.

15.

A YEAR AFTER my father had mourned the passing of the "strong men" in the family, I, too, got a shocking phone call one evening. I was informed—almost fatefully—of another deadly car accident. This time my father was the victim. My father was no longer alive.

I received the call from Aunty Jane. At that point, I had regular contact with her and always found out the latest family developments from her.

"Auma, are you still there?" she asked worriedly.

Her news had rendered me speechless. I couldn't get a word out and struggled for air.

"Can you hear me?" Now she spoke louder and sounded almost frightened.

I began to cry. The most important person in my life was dead. Suddenly I grasped it, and a horrible sense of loss overwhelmed me.

"Yes, I'm still here," I sobbed softly. "I'm coming home."

I hung up and just kept staring at the phone. Unable to budge, I remained in the small telephone booth.

How was it possible that the brief sentence that had just

reached my ear through that small contraption could cause me such boundless pain? Pain I had not even suspected I was capable of feeling. Why did it hurt so much? Hadn't I been angry with my father? Hadn't I experienced as recently as in Rotterdam that I scarcely felt anything for him? Those were all questions for which I had no answers. As I stood in the small, dark booth and the tears ran soundlessly down my face, I knew only one thing: My father was gone.

After his return from the United States eighteen years earlier, his death in 1982 now meant a radical change in my life for the second time. I felt as if the most important organ had been torn out of my body and my air cut off. While I had previously thought of my father only with mixed, mostly defensive feelings, I now felt an irrepressible longing to see him again, to talk to him and tell him that I loved him and understood his woes, which were mine, too.

In a horrible way, it suddenly became clear to me that all the years I had fought against my father and refused him my affection, I had basically only been struggling for his love, and that my own suppression of feelings for him, my early quest for independence, the escape to Germany, and even my striving to get good grades at the university had arisen only from the desire to show him that I was worthy of him.

Years later, long after my father's death, a good friend of his told me that he had been very proud of me and had always told all his friends about his wonderful daughter in Germany.

Eventually I left the telephone booth and went back to my room.

At that time, I was a member of a dance group known as the Afro-Ballet-Ensemble. It included several German and foreign professional and amateur dancers. In our choreography, we incorporated dance styles like Afro dance, modern dance, classical ballet, disco, and break dancing in an idiosyncratic way. Our goal was to combine different dance cultures in order to present their similarities and commonalities and playfully highlight the contrasts.

The dance group had an international character: Jai, our choreographer, was from Peru; Patrice, José, and Felix were French with Caribbean roots; Susanne came from Germany; Elfie from Ghana; and I from Kenya. Now and then, dancers from other countries joined us, too.

With Jai, who was my flat mate for a period of time, I also had a close friendship outside of the dance group. I appreciated her sense of humor and her ability to alleviate difficult situations.

When the news of my father's death reached me, we were in a phase of daily rehearsals, because several performances were coming up. After long months of intense work, the first performance was to take place that week and another shortly thereafter. During the preparations for my trip to Nairobi, I decided not to fly until after these performances.

After a last rehearsal, we all sat together.

"You don't have to dance with us. Go ahead and leave right away," Jai had said with concern when I told the group that my father had died, but I would not be flying home until after the second performance.

"I'll still arrive on time even if I wait until after the performances," I explained. "There's nothing I can do to change the situation anyway, and I wouldn't want to fly home early either." But with these last words, I almost lost my self-control. The thought of being among my many grieving relatives, as they mourned the death of the man who was truly the last and most generous of all the chosen ones in the extended Obama family, was crushing.

Another voice from the group spoke up. "But you don't have to dance, Auma. Really!"

"You're not doing me any favors by saying that," I protested. "Now, of all times, I need to."

I tried to smile. But everyone only stared at me worriedly. They wanted to comfort me, but didn't know how.

"Come on, people—get up! Let's dance."

I gave Jai a grateful look. She had grasped that what I needed now more than anything else was distraction. She went to the cassette recorder, pressed play, and when the music came on, I stood up with relief. All I wanted to do was dance. Forget everything and dance, dance, as if my life depended on it.

I no longer remember clearly the details of my journey to my father's funeral. I remember only that the tears I had so successfully suppressed after the first shock eventually began to flow and did not stop until I was in Kenya.

Someone—I no longer recall who—must have picked me up from the airport in Nairobi. The next thing I see in my mind's eye is myself getting out of the car in the Upper Hill neighborhood of Nairobi in front of the small row house in which my father had lived in the end and entering a room full of people. The whole house was filled with relatives, but I couldn't really make anyone out through the blur of my tears. From that moment on, there is a gaping hole in my memory, extending to the point when my father was to be buried in Alego next to his father.

There I see myself standing at the coffin, and I remember looking at my father's face through a small glass window at the head of the raised coffin. His skin seemed lifeless, very black, but at the same time it was as if there were a sort of gray film over it. Although I recognized my father's features, I knew that he was no longer lying there. He was already gone and no longer among us. For a long time, I remained at the coffin as if in a dream, until someone gently nudged me aside. Others wanted to say good-bye to him, too.

What would my father, who placed so much value on quality and a good appearance, have said about the fact that he would be buried in such an ugly wooden box? I simply could not grasp why he had to die so young. He had been only forty-three years old. I couldn't get it through my head that a car accident had been enough to end his life, especially as he had barely any external injuries. But I shied away from looking into his death in more detail.

When I realized that I had suffered amnesia in the days before my father's funeral, I told myself that I had clearly not been able to cope emotionally with this sudden loss any more than with thoughts about how he had died. Only many years later did I ask my Aunt Marsat, my father's second-youngest sister, what had happened back then. For I had heard during a casual conversation with family members that there had apparently been unanswered questions about the circumstances that had led to my father's death. Indignantly, I asked my aunt why no one had gotten to the bottom of the matter at the time.

"None of us had the necessary money or connections to make inquiries. All of us felt powerless. That's why we didn't do anything, as much as it pained us," my Aunt Marsat explained to me.

At her words, I was beset by a horrible sense of powerlessness. But whom could I blame? At the time of his death, I had already been living far from Kenya and the family for over two years, and had for a long time had nothing to do with my father's life and had made no effort to get to know his friends. I wouldn't have known how to use his influential acquaintances to get help clearing up his car accident.

And what would have been the point? My father was dead. Inquiries would not have brought him back to life. Instead, the struggle for the truth about his senseless death only would have caused me more pain, more hardship. But now I wanted to learn every detail, especially about his funeral. Because I had practically no memory of that event, I had Aunt Marsat tell me everything.

Osumba, as we called Aunt Marsat at the time, had lived with my father until his fatal accident. After the divorce from Ruth, he had not married again and lived alone until he asked Aunt Marsat, who is only a year younger than I, to move in with him. Abongo had moved out long ago and was studying in Nairobi.

My father liked being with Osumba. She is a small, gentle person with a kind face, and her calm temperament was well suited to his taciturn, introverted nature. Her presence certainly helped him not to feel so lonely.

"Shortly before your father died, he had flown to Libya as the leading economist with representatives of the government to a delegation meeting of the OAU, the Organization of African Unity. There, he suffered from eye problems, was examined by a doctor, and returned to Nairobi sooner than planned to get further treatment here. Even though he was on sick leave, he went to the ministry every day for a few hours."

Typical, I thought, as I listened to my aunt with rapt attention.

"At that time he was assigned to participate in a meeting with the president of the World Bank," she went on. "This took place in the Norfolk Hotel, here in Nairobi."

"How do you know all this?" I asked her.

"Because your father told me. He always told me where he was and what he was doing."

She said that so matter-of-factly that I had to believe her. *Strange,* I thought. I did not remember my father as someone who confided in others about his affairs. Suddenly, I saw my aunt with completely different eyes, and I have to admit that I was a little bit jealous.

"He never returned from that meeting," my aunt went on with unmistakable anger in her voice. "At the time, he was already with Jael, and little George was not yet a year old."

Jael had been romantically involved with my father at the time. She moved in with him when Aunt Marsat was living with him. Shortly before he died, Jael bore him a son: George.

I nodded. I wanted her to go on talking about my father.

"As it got later and later and he didn't show up, Jael and I began to worry. We tried to persuade ourselves that he had gone out after the meeting. But the next day he still wasn't there." My aunt rubbed her eyes, and for a second I thought she was going to start crying.

"We waited all day, but heard nothing from him. The next morning we decided to inquire at his office in the ministry."

That day, as Aunt Marsat and Jael made fruitless inquiries at my father's office, the transferred corpse of a student who had died in a gas explosion in India arrived in Nairobi. Like my father, the dead woman was a member of the Luo people. After her family had picked her up at the airport and brought her to the city mortuary, they discovered there the body of my father, who was well known among the Luo.

"They did not believe their eyes, and so they inquired at his ministry about him. But just like us, they didn't find him there. So they called Odima. He then got in touch with his friend Okech. Both of them went to your father's house to ask after him."

Only Jael was in the row house in Upper Hill, for she herself, my aunt went on, had gone to ask her older sister Zeituni for advice. Jael could tell the two visitors only that she had not yet heard from my father. Then Odima and Okech went to my aunt Zeituni.

"I did not believe my ears," Aunt Marsat continued. "What the two of them told me about your father's body put me in a complete state of shock. Confused, I left the house. The servants obviously noticed how disoriented I was, because they followed me. They stopped the bus for me, and I got on and sat thunderstruck in my seat."

Only during the bus ride did Aunt Marsat gradually realize what had happened. She headed to my brother's home, and by the time she arrived there, she had pulled herself together enough to speak with Emmy, Abongo's girlfriend at the time. My brother was not at home. Aunt Marsat delivered the news of my father's death to Emmy and sent her to look for Abongo. Then she headed back to Upper Hill, where she found her sisters Zeituni and Nyaoke, the oldest of the family, who had met there in the meantime.

A few hours later Abongo appeared, too, and shortly thereafter my mother and Aunty Jane. More and more people gathered in the house, and the weeping, regarded by the Luo as the highest sign of respect toward the dead, drowned out all other sounds.

"You know, Auma," my aunt said, "when your father was found at the scene of the accident, he still had his expensive watch, worth several thousand Kenyan shillings, and all his papers on him. He was even wearing his glasses."

She took a deep breath, as if she wanted to give herself and me time to digest what she had just said.

"The car he was driving was labeled as a ministry car. But someone must have taken him out of the car and brought him to the mortuary without informing the family." She sighed deeply. "His body lay there for two days before it was identified."

I swallowed hard. My chest tightened painfully and I could barely hold back my tears. My heart was as heavy as lead, and I felt completely helpless. At that moment I wished that I had been more outgoing a few years earlier and had not avoided associating with the great and powerful in Nairobi. Then I would have known to whom I could turn now to find out what or who was behind my father's death.

"Not until the family of the student from India had raised an alarm was your father's body identified by Odima, Okech, Zeituni, and Nyaoke. Then, on the third day, Abongo went to the mortuary, too."

"Then what happened?" I asked. I couldn't bear the silence that had followed Aunt Marsat's words.

"When the police later began their purely routine investigations, we found out that a Nissan from Kenya Airways, in which employees are brought home from the airport, had passed the scene of the accident. The accident had happened in Upper Hill, on Elgon Road. The passengers in the vehicle saw your father's car. The driver braked, but didn't stop, because there were already people at the scene of the accident. But one of the passengers notified the police."

"But they obviously didn't respond immediately," I remarked bitterly.

My aunt shrugged. "I don't know. I only know that the car wasn't there anymore the next morning."

The working hours of the Kenya Airways employees indicated that the Nissan had passed the scene of the accident around eleven o'clock at night.

"I can show you the exact spot on Elgon Road, if you want. Besides a small tree, there is nothing there far and wide that could have caused an accident. We were told that your father drove into this small tree and the steering wheel crushed his chest with the impact."

"But he didn't have any injuries. I saw him at the funeral," I said despondently.

"Exactly! We said the same thing to ourselves. Apart from a small scratch on his forehead, there was no visible sign. And even more interesting is the fact that the accident happened practically in front of the residence of a minister. The question is what the military guards were doing who normally stand there."

The sarcasm in the voice of my usually so sweet-tempered aunt could not be missed.

"Something isn't right there, Auma," she concluded and left it to me to digest those weighty words.

"Why didn't you do anything to find out the truth?" Again I asked this question, this time reproachfully.

"I told you that we all had the feeling that something was amiss. But what could we do? According to the autopsy report, your father died of internal injuries. The case was not investigated further, but was shelved." In those days, it was difficult to pursue anything. Under Daniel arap Moi, corruption reigned everywhere.

It would have been impossible to persuade potential witnesses to testify in court along the lines of our way of thinking. Everyone was too afraid.

Indeed, the political situation in Kenya in those days was anything but pleasant. Moi ruled with an iron fist. He stood at the head of a one-party system, and all important government posts were occupied by people who were loyally devoted to him. Oppositional figures disappeared. Many rumors of torture and even deaths were circulating. And the corruption had reached a scale that far surpassed all that had preceded it.

Shortly before my father's death, Moi had dismissed the then-governor of the Central Bank of Kenya. My aunt now informed me that my father told her that he had been slated to be the successor, because he was the leading economist responsible for the national budget (he had specialized in econometrics, which not many people had mastered at that time). But he died before he could take up the post. Without being able to point a finger at anyone in particular, Aunt Marsat seemed convinced that his death had something to do with that.

"Your father was too well known to be brought silently from the street to the mortuary like an anonymous accident victim—especially since he had his papers on him!"

I was speechless. For a long time, we just sat there without saying a word, each of us preoccupied with her own thoughts.

"Do you know that you actually refused to accept your father's death back then?" Aunt Marsat asked when we resumed the conversation a few days later.

"How so? I had no choice but to accept it. He was dead."

"Of course, I know. But you withdrew into yourself and blocked out everything going on around you."

"What do you mean?"

I had actually decided not to discuss my father's death anymore. Our last conversation about him had been very painful, and I didn't want to suffer even more than I was suffering already. But I had opened Pandora's box, and now there was no going back. I could also sense clearly that my aunt wanted to talk about my father. And so she just started speaking.

"The mourning went on for four days in Nairobi. Many, many people came to pay their last respects to him. Even Mwai Kibaki, the former Minister of Finance and current President, was among them. He had been his boss in the Ministry of Finance. On the fifth day, we went home with the body to Alego, in a long convoy of cars, buses, and minibuses."

"And me? Where was I?" I asked, gradually becoming curious. She was right. I absolutely could not remember what had happened in the time up to shortly before the funeral.

"You were completely devastated. We rode together in one of the cars in the procession. When we arrived in Alego at the homestead and you started to get out of the car, you passed out."

At first I didn't want to believe her, but I could tell from her facial expression that she wasn't lying.

"You were carried into the small room in the main house." The room was known as "Bobby's room" at the time (Bobby had been Abongo's nickname); today it is called "Barack Jr.'s room," because he slept there on his last visit to Alego before he became famous.

"You came to. But in the days leading up to your father's funeral, you stayed in the room."

I tried to remember, but everything remained a blank.

"The place was teeming with people who had come to mourn," my aunt went on. "Day and night, people arrived. Your mother was there, too."

But I couldn't even remember her being there.

"Like many other relatives, she had been holding a vigil in Nairobi in your father's house in Upper Hill since she had found out about his death. Then she accompanied the body to Alego."

That made sense to me, because as my father's first wife, she was required by Luo custom to be present at the funeral.

"Many important figures came, colleagues of your father's, ministers like Robert Ouko, Peter Oloo Aringo, and Olum Gondi. All people who had influenced his career."

Of all the individuals she listed, I saw none in my mind's eye.

"I can't remember any of them," I noted in frustration.

"The few times you tried to leave the room, you were overwhelmed by such intense grief that you couldn't breathe and passed out again."

My younger brother Opiyo had participated in the funeral, too. Barely two years before the death of his father, Opiyo had returned to the Obama family at the age of fourteen, after he had been separated as a three-year-old from his biological father when Ruth and my father got divorced.

Opiyo's mother, who after the divorce wanted to separate from everything that reminded her of my father, had even changed her sons' names. She called them only by their Jewish first names, and she had their last names changed to that of her second husband. Thus Opiyo David Obama and Okoth Mark Obama became David Ndesandjo and Mark Ndesandjo. That was intended to achieve a final severing between the children and their father and prevent any association with the name Obama.

As a fourteen-year-old, Opiyo was no longer willing to accept that. He sought out his father and was lucky to still be able to spend a little time with him as an adolescent.

The thought that he reestablished a connection with my father of his own accord is a great comfort to me. Despite everything he had heard about him, he wanted to get to know his father and give him and himself a chance. Thus my younger brother, too, got a sense of the love that my father, despite the mistakes he made, felt for his children. Opiyo's participation in his funeral is for me a clear sign of the affection of a returned son, who had the opportunity literally at the last minute to be embraced by his father before his sudden death abruptly tore them apart.

What I most regret to this day about my memory loss at that time is that it also almost totally effaced my recollection of Opiyo. For my brother himself suffered a fatal traffic accident only a short time after our father's death. Once again, I found out about this through a phone call from Aunty Jane. As I hung up the phone, I knew that I would miss him just as intensely as I had when he was taken from me as a three-year-old. And that I loved him just as much as I had back then, even though I had barely gotten to know him.

My father was gone, and the Obama family had to recover and look to its future. That was easier said than done—for immediately after my father's death, a gulf opened up.

Jael had not been married to my father. But because she had a child from him and had lived with him at the time of his death, the Obama family did not want to cast her out. As a mere girlfriend, however, Jael would not have been permitted to participate in the funeral rites, because she would not have been recognized as part of the Obama family. So the suggestion was made to marry my father and Jael retroactively in accordance with a Luo custom.

Not all family members agreed with the posthumous marriage. Supported by Muslim relatives, who were against this custom for religious reasons, they rejected it. They wanted to prevent an imposition of a wife on my father after his death. After long debates, the Luo tradition, which Odima had represented with strong arguments, prevailed, and the opposition was outvoted. Money was raised for the bride price, and my father's younger brother Uncle Yusuf and a few other male relatives rushed off to Jael's family to ask for her hand on behalf of my father. Now Jael could participate in the funeral, and her son, George, was recognized as a member of the Obama family.

Jael, who after my father's death got a job in the Ministry of Finance, was allowed to live for a few more months in the government-provided house in Upper Hill, until she could stand on her own two feet with the help of the new job.

Aunt Marsat stayed in Alego and helped receive the many guests who kept coming long after my father's death to pay their last respects to him. Afterward, she moved in with her sister Zeituni.

As time went on, Jael distanced herself more and more from the Obama family; except through her son, George, there was no real connection to us anymore. Then one day she went away completely, taking her son with her.

16.

IN 1984, MY MOTHER VISITED me for the first time in Heidelberg. I had invited her to spend part of the summer with me. Since I had never really lived with her, except in the first years of my life, of which I had no memory, her visit seemed to me a good opportunity to make up for this.

What connected us was no classical mother-daughter relationship. Though we had seen each other often since I had "reunited" with her at the age of thirteen, it had always been with other people, with my Aunty Jane, her own mother, or other relatives. The two of us had never been alone together.

Now, in Heidelberg, I had the chance to get to know her without constraints and expectations. After my father's death, she had taken up her place as his first wife and was again living with my grandmother on the compound in Alego.

Her visit was planned for a month. I was really looking forward to this time and imagined everything we would do together, all the usual mother-daughter things. If her past attempt—when I was fifteen—to catch up on a "real" family life had failed, she could now at least participate in my life.

We had a wonderful time together. My friends couldn't believe that she was my mother; most of them thought she was an older sister. Because she had had me at the age of seventeen, the age difference between us was not that large—she was only forty-one on her visit.

We often sat in my room and talked. I was no longer living in a residence hall; for some time, I had been sharing an apartment with other students in the Heidelberg old town. There, one of my closest friends, Maria, was a frequent guest. We cooked, danced, or went on walks together.

Maria was thin, had short brown hair, studied Romance languages and literature, and was a dance enthusiast like me. I first met her at a job I got through the employment agency of student services. We were both working on the cleaning and kitchen staff at the university's ear, nose, and throat clinic. For me, the work was new and difficult. Polishing the linoleum floor with a heavyweight buffing machine was a particular challenge. You had to have the heavy apparatus well under control, or else it would zoom all over the floor, crash into the bedposts, and scare the patients.

On breaks, Maria and I groaned about the monster and laughed at near-catastrophes. The hospital experiences bound us together and were the beginning of a friendship that lasts to this day.

I did not give my mother much time to get settled into the apartment before I started asking her questions. I wanted to know more about my parents' relationship and was curious about the details of what happened in those days. And above all, I wanted to know why my mother had left us with my father when we were still so young.

"I had no choice," was her answer, when we were sitting alone in the kitchen at one point. "When he didn't want to have me as his wife anymore, I didn't know what to do. How was I supposed to take care of two small children without a livelihood?"

I refused to believe that that was the only reason she had given us up. The stories a former schoolmate had told me crossed my mind. She had been raised by her single mother, who had sold vegetables at the market to scrape together money for the school fees.

"So was it painful for you to give us up?"

"Those were hard times." She continued to defend herself. "I was so young and completely distraught. I never would have expected that I wouldn't live with your father anymore."

I simply did not understand. Nor did I really want to understand. For at that moment I felt that it was also because of her that I had no "real" family. That it had not only been my father's fault. She, too, could have acted differently, made other decisions back then. I felt an old resentment welling up in me, and sensed myself hardening inside, just as I had with my father in Rotterdam.

"Many things didn't go the way I would have wished, Auma," my mother went on. "There's nothing I can do to change that now. You should only know that I almost went mad when I relinquished you and your brother to your father. Something cracked in me at that time, and after that my life completely changed."

I stared at my mother and tried to comprehend, as hard as it was for me. She stared back at me, her eyes pleading for understanding.

"Your father and I were really in love before he went to the United States."

No tears glimmered in her eyes, but her voice revealed pain and disappointment.

"We were together constantly back then," she went on. "He taught me everything. Even the clothing I wore he had picked out for me. When your older brother was born, your father was so proud of his little family. You weren't there yet." She smiled lovingly at me.

"I was never there in that situation," I replied bitterly. I simply could not fight my emotions. After a while, I asked, "Do you sometimes think about how it might have been if he hadn't left?"

"Not for a long time. What happened, happened. There's no sense in endlessly speculating."

Little by little, I was accepting the idea that it always takes two to make a failed relationship. I probably had to face the fact that only my father and my mother really knew what had happened back then. Everyone else, the victims of their past decisions, had to live with it.

Determined to keep our difficult past from catching up with us and ruining the lovely time we were having in Heidelberg, my mother and I made a silent pact neither to occupy ourselves exclusively with it, nor to take personally everything that came up in our discussions.

One thing was bothering my mother in Heidelberg: the fact that at my age I didn't have a boyfriend. I explained to her that I was still in love with a man who had left me two years earlier.

She couldn't believe that after such a long period of separation I was still in love with a man who didn't love me. "That's not normal," she said with concern, and advised me to forget Dieter immediately and look for a new boyfriend.

It was September, the time of new wine and onion pie. In the old town, people celebrated the Heidelberg autumn. At every corner, music groups played deep into the night. The whole city was astir. My mother and I walked along the main street and stopped here and there to listen to a band. Suddenly I felt queasy: On the stage, a rock band was playing, and at the bass stood . . . Dieter.

When I pointed him out to my mother, she was not particularly impressed.

"That's who is keeping you up at night?" she said somewhat disparagingly. "He's not worth it. And he isn't even particularly good-looking."

At first, I was shocked by her judgment, but then I tried to see Dieter through my mother's eyes. For the first time, I asked myself what it was about him that had such a hold on me. I didn't find an answer.

After that chance encounter, I developed the healthy desire to finally put an end to the Dieter obsession. I had been agonizing over him much too long already. So I decided one day to meet with my ex. My mother was right. I had to find out whether I was really still in love with him or only wanted to cling to something I had once felt for him. I called him and arranged to meet him the next afternoon in his room in the residence hall, where he still lived.

The hours before our meeting were probably among the hardest I had experienced in Heidelberg up to that point. I told my mother nothing about the plan. I wanted to get through the whole thing on my own and tell her about it only afterward.

It was a strange feeling to go back to Comeniushaus, the place where I had fallen so deeply in love. I still had his room number memorized.

Dieter greeted me coolly. I sat down and told him outright that I still had feelings for him. He didn't seem particularly surprised about that, but only answered, "I know." He smiled as he spoke. Oh, that smile! I still remembered it so well. With that smile he had always looked a little shy and embarrassed and at the same time irresistible. But that afternoon I detected in his eyes neither shyness nor embarrassment. He seemed self-confident and superior. And I sensed myself moving away from him inwardly.

Suddenly, I no longer recognized the man sitting in front of me. Had I really pined for him for two years? He showed no sympathy at all for my lovesickness. On the contrary, he seemed to enjoy the fact that I was still in love with him.

When we parted, I knew that I could banish him from my mind. I had done the right thing with my visit. Finally, I could heave a sigh of relief and face forward again.

And when I told my mother about it, she only smiled at me meaningfully. The rest of the time we spent completely lightheartedly. We were enjoying being together and the good mood between us much too much to let sad stories ruin it for us. We spent a lot of time with my friends. I wanted my mother to get to know all of them before she had to fly back to Kenya.

17.

ONE DAY I GOT a letter in the mail with my name and my Heidelberg address written on it in very neat handwriting. The handwriting was startlingly similar to that of my father. And when I turned over the envelope, the name Barack Obama jumped out at me. I will never forget the shock that seized me at that moment. That handwriting, that name—at that point, my father had already been dead for some time. Slowly, I opened the envelope and pulled out a piece of paper covered with writing. The similarity to my father's handwriting was even more striking in those lines.

The letter was from my brother Barack. In our family, he had always only been called "Barry," the unknown brother, who lived in the United States with his mother, Ann, my father's second wife. I had never visited him there, and he had never come to Kenya. He was a stranger to me.

For years, my father had urged me to write to Barry, but I had always gotten out of it with some excuse. The brother in the United States was too far away, too abstract for me to take an interest in him. My reality was limited to my immediate surroundings, and I was sure that Barack felt the same way.

And now, in 1984, in his early twenties, he suddenly got in touch and gave me a huge scare, because his name and his handwriting so unexpectedly conjured up my father. How could it be, I wondered, that the two of them had such similar handwriting, although they had lived together only for a very brief time, when Barack Jr. was just an infant? Later, when I got to know my brother better, I discovered a number of other similarities, which never ceased to amaze me.

But after the initial shock had subsided, I was happy to hear from my faraway brother. Excitedly, I read his letter. Barack wrote in a sober but friendly tone. He asked about my well-being and reported in detail on himself, so that I had the feeling that I knew more about my unknown brother than I had previously learned from my father's stories.

After he had established contact, we wrote to each other regularly, and it wasn't long before we made plans to meet. Thus, Barack's letter was the beginning of a friendship that has always meant more to me than just a sibling relationship.

At that time, Elke was still living in the States. After the end of her scholarship, she had decided to continue her studies in America. As chance would have it, she lived in Illinois just like my brother. So I immediately accepted when Barack invited me to Chicago, for it allowed me to connect this chance to get to know him better with a visit with Elke.

Although Barack and I had been exchanging letters for some time and seemed to get along very well on those terms, I was nervous about our first meeting. *Perhaps we won't even like each other anymore when we're face-to-face,* I thought. I was looking forward to the trip, which would be my first time in the United States, but at the same time I was afraid of being disappointed. So I decided to first spend a few days with Elke in Carbondale, in southern Illinois, and to head to Chicago only afterward. At the end of that trip, I planned to go back to Elke's. That way, if the meeting with Barack turned out to be a flop, I could recover from the letdown at her place.

In the university town of Carbondale, Elke lived in a really nice little apartment, which consisted of a bedroom with a huge double bed, a small kitchen, and a tiny bathroom with a bathtub. I often sat in the tub, for it was August, the hottest month of the year in Illinois, and in the intense heat the smallest movement cost great effort. Elke had no air conditioner in her apartment. When we didn't go to the university, where she studied and worked and I was able to sit in the air-conditioned library for hours and read, I liked to sit in the cold-water-filled tub.

"Why are Americans always so astonished at the tropical heat in Africa?" I asked Elke. We had fallen wearily onto the bed, which during the day also served as a sofa. I stared almost absently through the open door into the small front yard, without turning around to look at her. To move took too much energy in the murderous heat.

"You can say that again. The heat here surprised me, too. When I visited my former boyfriend in Togo, it was never as hot there as it is here in the summer." Elke lay exhausted on her gigantic bed and didn't move a muscle either. "Do you know that there used to be mosquitoes and malaria here?" she asked sluggishly.

"No, but with this climate I can easily imagine it."

Since she had left Saarbrücken, I had now and then visited Elke at her parents' house when she had come home for a short time. Otherwise, we maintained our close friendship by letter and telephone.

During this visit in Carbondale, she, who was usually the calmer one, was almost even more excited than I was about the meeting with my unknown brother.

"Isn't it great that you will finally get to know each other?" she had already said several times since my arrival.

"I hope it will be great." I tried not to show her how nervous I was. "Hopefully he's not a loser. What if we have nothing to say to each other?"

"I doubt that. Judging by his letters, I'm sure you'll get along really well."

Elke had just finished the sentence when she clapped her hands.

"Whoa!" I cried, startled. "What was that?"

"A mosquito! But I got it!" she exclaimed joyfully.

"Eeew! I thought they don't exist here anymore."

"Yes, they do! There's just no more malaria. And they still bite, too. You just don't get sick from them anymore."

I rolled onto my side and sighed. "Well, I don't know where you get the energy to kill mosquitoes in this heat. But tell me what I should do if I don't like my brother."

"Just come back to me. That's the plan anyway."

"And what about the disappointment?"

"There won't be any disappointment. Stay positive. You'll like him, I'm sure of it."

And so we spoke late into the night. The merciless heat didn't let up until the early morning hours.

After two weeks, I headed to Chicago. We had planned that Elke and her boyfriend Robert would join us at the end of my visit with Barack. From Chicago, we were going to travel together to

Madison, Wisconsin, to visit a Heidelberg University friend of mine there.

The train ride to Chicago took about seven hours and was as monotonous as the passing landscape, an endless succession of cornfields. Elke had wisely advised me to pack books, so I read almost the whole time.

Fortunately, the reading had a calming effect. So far, I had successfully suppressed my nervousness. But now the encounter with my brother—the actual reason for my trip—was about to happen. There was no going back. At the end of this journey, Barack was waiting for me. I had spoken to him on the phone one time since I had arrived in Illinois. Now I would be staying with him, the unknown brother, for ten days in Chicago, without the slightest idea how the visit would go.

In the late afternoon, the train slowly rolled into Chicago. The farther we penetrated into the center, the more uncertain—but also excited—I became. I felt overwhelmed by the size and the bustling activity of the city. Hopefully, Barack was really at the train station where he was supposed to pick me up. (He remembers picking me up in Chicago at the airport, but I actually arrived on the train.) Hopefully, we would recognize each other. I had no current photo of him. In my excitement I had forgotten to ask him for one, and I no longer remembered whether I had sent him one of me. *Off to a good start,* I thought nervously.

"Auma."

I looked up and stopped immediately.

"Auma, over here!"

I turned my head to the right and saw a young man standing at some distance, who looked excited and was smiling at me. I smiled back. That could only be Barack. I ran to him and, without thinking twice, wrapped my arms around him. We held each other tight and for a few seconds neither of us said a word. Then we let go and both took a step back to look at each other.

"There you are at last," I said finally.

"And there you are," Barack replied. "Welcome to Chicago, sister!"

Barack held my hands and pulled me to himself again to take me in his arms a second time. And all the while I simply couldn't stop laughing. I had waited so long for this moment with conflicting feelings, and now all tension suddenly drained away from me and everything struck me as so normal and natural. I immediately felt at home with Barack.

"How did you know it was me?" I asked him.

"I just knew."

I didn't inquire further. I understood what he meant—for it had basically been the same for me. When he had called my name, I had already recognized something familiar in the sound of his voice.

On the way to his car, I couldn't help glancing again and again at my brother. He was much taller than I was, had very short hair, and wore classic sporty clothing: a polo shirt and linen pants. I was again reminded of my father, who had favored a similar style for casual dress. And like my father, Barack was very slim, almost bony. When he heaved my travel bag into the trunk of his car a bit later, I noticed how long and thin his hands were. I have hands like that, too. I'm often told that I have the hands of a piano player. So I wondered, as I made myself comfortable in the passenger seat of the small car, whether people also compared Barack's hands with those of a piano player.

In the car, I sat silently at first next to my younger brother and watched him slowly drive south through the dense evening traffic. I looked curiously out the window, impressed by the skyscrapers, their interesting architecture, the elaborately designed structures. The city was teeming with cars, and scores of people, black and white, walked along the sidewalks. Chicago had nothing in common with the small city of Heidelberg—or with Carbondale, for that matter. I was impressed.

Then we broke the brief silence. And from that point on, my focus was only on my brother—and his subcompact car.

"It's kind of scary sitting in your car," I joked.

"Are you really scared?" Barack asked with concern, and slowed down a little.

"No, no," I reassured him. "It's only strange to sit in a small car like this next to all these huge American cars."

"That's true. But this way I save gas and can park almost everywhere. I work in the projects and don't make much money."

"In the projects?"

"Yes, you'll see what I mean soon. It's public housing. But first tell me about your life in Germany."

I had to smile. Barack was like a starving person who suddenly gets something to eat. One question followed another. We talked and talked, as if we were already running out of time. I started to tell him stories and knew that long after our arrival in Barack's apartment I would still not be finished. My brother wanted to know everything about me and our family. Ultimately, we did not stop talking until my departure.

"Do you know that I'm actually a really good cook?" Barack asked me mischievously.

"Of course," I replied. "After all, I've known you my whole life!"

"No, seriously. I can make Indonesian food really well. Wait and see."

Barack was standing at the stove in his small kitchen, and I was sitting in the living room on the couch, from where I could see him through the doorway. Besides these two rooms, his apartment also included a small bedroom.

"Tell me something about my father," Barack asked, when we sat down at his kitchen table to eat. I had already told him about our mutual siblings, striving to describe each of the brothers vividly and bring out their individual personalities. In this way, Barack got through my eyes his first impression of his Kenyan family, whom he had never met, because his parents had separated in his early childhood.

"Do you know that our father always really loved all of us?" I said, as I gazed at my food, lost in thought.

"No, I don't know that, Auma. I didn't actually know him. I only saw him once in my conscious memory, as a ten-year-old. That was too short to learn anything about him." Barack's voice remained calm, but his words spoke volumes. Did my father know back then how much his son missed him?

"He really loved all of us," I repeated. "He just wasn't capable of showing it. And even though it was always clear to me, I felt nothing but anger toward him for many years."

"Why? You lived with him, didn't you?" asked Barack.

"For that very reason," I said, getting worked up. "Whenever things went wrong for him, we children who lived with him—Abongo and I—had to pay the price. There were many things we didn't understand at all, and for many things we never got a proper explanation." I had to pause for a moment. As always when I spoke about my father, a mixture of pain, grief, and disappointment welled up in me. Disappointment because he had died before he had time to answer my many questions. Pain because I had suffered so much on account of him. And grief because I had banished him from my heart and never got the chance to let him back in and openly show him my love.

Suddenly, I felt overwhelmed. I was at a loss. Barack wanted to learn more about his father, understand him better, and replace the phantom that had accompanied him his whole life with a man made of flesh and blood. But I myself didn't know whether I, who had spent my childhood and youth with that very man, had ever grasped him. How was I supposed to explain the contradiction my father embodied for me to Barack in such a way that he, unlike me, would not condemn him but would have the chance to arrive at understanding and perhaps even love?

I took comfort that evening in the thought that we still had several days together. Somehow I would manage in that time to give him a better understanding of his African family, especially his father.

Barack's meal was indeed delicious. I was excited that my brother apparently had a domestic side and was a good cook.

"Our father was someone from whom everyone expected too much," I said when we had finished eating. "He didn't know how to defend himself against the many demands made on him. His sense of duty toward the larger Obama family was very strong. But the reverse was unfortunately not always the case."

"What do you mean by that?" asked Barack. We were now sitting in his living room. While we ate, I had tried to explain to my brother the phenomenon of the "chosen ones," for he just couldn't understand how a single person could be expected to assume responsibility for an extended family.

"I understand that it's hard for you to grasp," I replied. "I basically feel the same way. But it's simply what our tradition requires.

There were times when there wasn't even enough money for my school fees, and I had to watch our father give away everything he had left to a relative. He was always confident that we would somehow get by." Against my will, my words had sounded despondent.

"Did you ever object to that?" Barack asked sympathetically.

"Not really. As an African child, you're brought up not to argue with your parents or criticize them. But even if you dared to raise objections, our father always answered with the words: 'I'll take care of everything.' " I sighed. "It was difficult with him. For just as he helped others, he expected that people would help him, too, when it was necessary."

"And that didn't happen?"

"Not really, in comparison to what he provided," I replied.

"Even relatives he supported for many years were not always willing to help him?" Barack looked at me uncomprehendingly.

"The old man, as our father was always called, was a prisoner of his own principles. He didn't want to back away from his position, according to which you always, whatever situation you were in at the moment, had to provide for the extended family. I found that this could lead too easily to exploitation and dependence. Those who had nothing didn't really feel responsible for getting themselves out of their misery."

It was already pretty late, and Barack had to go to work early the next day. I had the impression, however, that he would have liked best to keep talking all night. But he looked tired. And I, too, was tired from talking so much.

"Let's continue tomorrow, Barack," I said. "We still have several days ahead of us." With those words, I stood up and stretched. My brother showed me how to convert his pullout sofa into a bed.

Before he disappeared into his bedroom, I hugged him once again at the end of that unforgettable day and said good night.

"I'm glad you're here," he said with an earnest expression.

The next morning we got up early. Barack took me with him to his office to show me where he worked. He also wanted to introduce me to his colleagues.

We entered a rather bleak-looking neighborhood. Flat-roofed, bungalow-like houses stood close together. Not far from there were apartment buildings with gray facades and dark entrances. Everything looked run-down and impoverished, entirely different from the part of Chicago I had seen on my arrival. Barack explained that we were "in the projects."

"These are residential areas in which affordable housing is built for the lowest income groups and for welfare recipients. The people who live here have only a very low income or none at all and rely on public assistance."

"It looks really poor here," I remarked, surprised. I had a somewhat naïve idealized image of America in my head, the cliché of wealth and prosperity in the States that is widespread in my native country—but not only there.

"The people are poor, too. And unfortunately, most of them are black," Barack went on. It pained me to hear that. In Germany, I fought daily against the many prejudices toward us black people, particularly against the idea that we were all in need of help. So I was not happy to hear now that this was actually how things were for a lot of black people in the United States.

"And what do you do here?" I asked Barack, eager to hear what solution he offered these people with his work.

"I try to help the poor people in this area deal with the authorities so that they receive the support they're legally entitled to."

We had parked in front of a building that looked like a church community center. Barack explained to me that he worked for a priest and that his office and his colleagues' offices were in this community center. We went in through a side entrance, and shortly thereafter we stood in a large, very simply furnished room teeming with people. Barack went from one person to another and introduced me to his colleagues. Everyone greeted me very warmly. Afterward he led me into a room. He wanted me to meet his boss, an older white man with a charismatic aura. Finally, he showed me his own small workstation.

I liked the atmosphere in the community center. Everyone gave the impression that they believed in what they were doing. Their commitment was palpable. After we had stayed there for a while longer so that Barack could take care of a few things, he showed me the projects and described his work to me in detail. Meanwhile, we kept returning to the subject of our families. He told me about his little sister, Maya, his mother's second child. Maya's father was Indonesian, and she lived with her maternal grandmother in Hawaii.

"You'll like her," he said. "She's charming." It sounded as if he loved her. *Might he talk about me the same way one day?* I thought fleetingly.

"My mother lives in Indonesia. She's diligently doing research there for her dissertation," Barack went on with a laugh. "And I think she'll stay there for a long time. She loves the country and simply can't stop pursuing her research. Anthropology is her life." As he said that, he shook his head with amusement, as if he had long ago given up the attempt to understand her.

"I'd like to meet her. I've heard a lot about her from our father."

"Did he talk about her? What did he say?" Barack asked with curiosity.

"Only good things. After Ruth left, he kept promising us that you and your mother would come visit us in Kenya." I smiled somewhat wearily. "I believed him and waited a long time in vain for your visit."

Barack looked at me with astonishment. "I knew absolutely nothing about that," he replied after a brief silence.

"They wrote to each other. But you know that, right? Your mother always sent him your school report cards and regularly told him how you were doing. He always knew what was going on with you. He told us and anyone who would listen about you. From his descriptions, I knew you pretty well. So I thought at the time anyway."

I couldn't interpret the expression on Barack's face, but I nonetheless had the sense that what I had just said moved him.

"But that wasn't enough," he said finally.

It was evening and we were back in Barack's apartment. The day had gone by fast. We had done a lot, and my brother had shown me his neighborhood so that I would find my way around on my own while he had to work. He showed me the small shopping center and explained to me how to get to the city center and to nearby Lake Michigan, on the shore of which there were several museums.

We were again sitting on his couch and continuing to talk about our complicated family.

"Maybe you were even lucky that you didn't grow up with him. You missed his presence, but on the other hand, precisely because you didn't know him, you could also imagine him however you wanted. You didn't have to deal with him." I began our conversation with a bold hypothesis.

"You're right." Barack laughed. "Instead, I had my grandfather, my mother's father. I always called him Gramps. He assumed the role of father." He paused briefly. "Do you have photos with you?" he suddenly went on.

"Yes." I nodded and went to get my bag. In all my excitement, I had not forgotten to pack photos of our family to show my brother. Among them were some of our father. For fun, I had also brought old pictures of Barack himself, which his mother had sent our father. These were from the time he was studying at Occidental College in Los Angeles. One photo showed a serious-looking young man with a full Afro in a white blazer and a dark shirt with a wide collar, entirely in the style of the 1970s. He smiled confidently at the camera. It was probably taken for the school yearbook. Another showed him playing basketball. It had been taken at the exact moment he jumped up to shoot.

Barack smiled as he looked at the photos.

"That's right. I sent these photos to my mother."

"Imagine," I said, for I had suddenly remembered something amazing. "When I was studying German in Saarbrücken, a German city on the French border, an American exchange student was living with me in the residence hall. She happened to study at Occidental. One day, we were looking at my photos, and suddenly she pointed to this photo with the Afro. She recognized you as one of her classmates. Crazy, right?"

Barack nodded as he continued to look at the picture.

"Back then the old man was still alive," I added, without knowing exactly why I did so. I suddenly wondered why I hadn't sought out Barack back then. I could have given the exchange student a message to pass on to him. Somehow it now struck me as strange that I always proudly had the picture of this younger brother by one year with me but hadn't done anything to get in contact with him when an opportunity arose. The only explanation that occurred to me was that I viewed Barack at the time as my father's business and feared opening another Pandora's box with the attempt to get to know him.

"You wanted to explain to me why our father was so complicated, at least from your perspective. Last night you started to go into it." Barack put aside the pictures and leaned back on the couch. "I'd like to understand what drove him."

I took a deep breath. It wouldn't be simple to explain who Barack Obama Sr. had been, especially to a son who had never lived with him for an extended period of time or had more in-depth experiences with him. It seemed to me that I had to go back a long way. I began to explain.

"Our father lived in two cultures. He was always straddling two worlds. Like almost all Africans, he was a victim of colonialism. This had destroyed the established tradition, and our father, in order to have a chance in the changed society, had been forced to adapt to a foreign, Western way of life, which was opposed in many ways to his customary existence. That intensified when he married Ruth, who represented this Western world in every respect. And although he was exposed to her lifestyle and even practiced it himself for a long time, our father was at the same time thoroughly Luo. He respected the traditions and adhered to them. Ruth, on the other hand, did not manage to adapt, might not have even tried to grasp his African roots. She had married the man she had met in her country, in America, who was a scholar, had the charm of a Romeo, and had assimilated so wonderfully, as far as her culture was concerned.

"I imagine that Ruth's ideal image of a happy marriage did not include another woman's two small African children, an extended family that constantly needed financial help, and all the African friends who took her husband away on many evenings to go out for a drink and sometimes stay out until the early hours of the morning. In his own house, these two worlds collided with full force, and the old man didn't know how these differences could be reconciled. It almost tore him apart. There was his old African identity, his new one as the husband of an American woman, and his traditional obligations."

Barack looked at me inquisitively.

"As for why things didn't work out between our father and Ruth," I continued, "one of his friends at the time once said something interesting to me about that: 'To make Ruth happy, your father would have had to turn his back on his family and all his friends.' Yes, and I remember that during school breaks in those days Abongo and I were always sent upcountry to visit our grandmother Sarah. Probably so that Ruth, even if only temporarily, could have the semblance of a small nuclear family with her husband and the two sons they had together."

I talked on and on, completely transported back in time.

"I will never forget the day when, after Ruth was gone, I found in a closet somewhere an unfinished letter she had been writing to her sister in the United States. In it, she had complained to her sister that she just couldn't relate to us, her husband's black children. She described to her, for example, how hard it was for her to bathe us, because she so disliked touching us. Imagine how awful it was for me to read that.

"Our father must have known what was going on and what Ruth thought of his family and friends. How could he have accepted that, without denying himself? His disappointment and bitterness must have been really intense, probably as intense as Ruth's.

"On top of that, there were his difficulties with work. As a young man, he had gone to America to complete his studies, which would enable him to help steer the development of his country. After he graduated, he was brimming with enthusiasm and devoted himself to his new duties full of optimism. And then, after a short time, he already had to face the fact that in Kenya one dictatorship had replaced another. And it seemed to continue the work of the colonial rulers: Through nepotism and favoritism, those in power divided the various ethnic groups and played them off against each other. With his work ethic and idealism in the ministry where he worked, our father made some enemies. Among them were colleagues as well as superiors, who mistrusted him. They could not understand why he didn't try as they did to enrich himself—according to the principle: 'Now it's our turn.' I think he was basically a very lonely man."

After my long explanations, I briefly paused for breath, but only to resume my reflections immediately.

"I could imagine that in his personal life our father tried for a long time to make the best of his difficult situation—and also that he and Ruth noticed very early on that their relationship wasn't working. But instead of ending it, they stayed together until nothing was salvageable. When, after those hard times, our father also had the serious car accident and lost his job, we were all in tough straits. Though distraught at the collapse of our family, I could take refuge at boarding school, but Abongo, who was a day student, was completely derailed by the events. I don't think that he ever forgave them for putting him through all that."

"Forgave whom?" Barack asked. He had sat there silently and pensively the whole time. I was startled. His voice brought me back into the present. I had been so absorbed in my father's story that I had almost forgotten my brother's presence. As I was talking, it had dawned on me that I was trying to explain Barack Sr. to myself, too.

"His father, his mother, Ruth, and even me," I answered sadly. "The relationship between Abongo and me was always difficult."

"What a shame. One might have thought that going through all that together would have brought the two of you closer."

"True, but unfortunately that wasn't the case. We never managed to share our pain." It hurt to say that. I had tried for years to get closer to Abongo, but he had never allowed it. Although we remained in contact and now and then got in touch with each other, there was no close relationship between us.

I looked at Barack Jr. sitting opposite me, and suddenly my heart warmed. Thank God I had found him. He seemed to understand me instinctively, my longings and hopes, my motivations and my disappointments. He listened without evaluating or judging and took each of my words seriously. It felt good to know that this was only the beginning, that he was now part of my family, of my life.

During the time with him we spoke daily about our family, but also about his work, about my studies and my experiences in Germany, and I sensed that he grappled intensely with many things. For the first time, I had found someone in my family with whom I could really talk about anything that was important to me without having to constantly explain and justify myself. Our encounter was an enormous gift for me.

When we weren't sitting together and talking, Barack showed me Chicago. We visited museums together, took walks, and went shopping. I posed in front of the Picasso sculpture and Barack took a photograph of me.

I also did some things on my own while he was working. I wandered through Chicago's streets and looked at the beautiful buildings.

The days went by really fast. Soon, Elke and Robert arrived in Chicago, as we had planned before my departure from Carbondale.

We all spent one night in Barack's small apartment and had a big breakfast the next morning before we headed to Wisconsin.

I was sorry to have to say good-bye to the new brother I had gained. I had only just discovered him and was reluctant to let him go. The visit had exceeded all my expectations. I not only liked Barack as a person, but I also immediately felt incredibly comfortable with him. In the brief time we had spent with each other, we had gotten so close that we had actually managed to bridge the years of separation between us.

We didn't even need to promise each other to stay in touch. For both of us, that went without saying. When I hugged him tightly in parting before getting into Elke's car, I said only, "Now it's my turn to show you my hospitality. Next time we'll see each other in Kenya."

18.

I LEFT MY BROTHER and my best friend behind in the United States with a heavy heart, but at the same time I was really looking forward to seeing Karl again.

Karl studied law. We met through a carpool. I fell in love with him. Shortly after my return from America, we saw each other almost daily. I told him in detail about my moving journey to visit my brother.

Karl was tall and athletic. He played handball, a sport with which I hadn't previously been familiar. He was also a passionate fan of the German rock band BAP. I liked his energy and charisma, his cheerful nature. To this day, I can see his dimples in my mind's eye, when he smiled at me or burst out laughing.

Shortly after our relationship had begun, he invited me to his home. He was still living with his parents in a village near Heidelberg. I was excited about the visit with his family. Karl had a younger sister, Gerda. His father, who had since retired, had been a baker, and the family lived in the house in which the bakery had once been.

When we got out of the car and his parents came toward us, I looked into two astonished faces. I sensed how both of them almost imperceptibly but instinctively recoiled. *Oh no,* I thought, *Karl forgot to tell them that I'm black!* My boyfriend approached his parents with a smile and introduced me. Hesitantly, I held out my hand to his father, who stood directly in front of me. He, too, hesitated, but then took my hand and shook it vigorously.

"Guten Tag, Fräulein Auma," he said. *"Guten Tag."*

The mother stared at me and also said, *"Guten Tag."* She gave me her hand only reluctantly. Immediately, I knew: It bothered her that her son was with an African.

However, the visit with Karl's parents did no harm to our young love. Not long after, my boyfriend moved out of the house, but continued to insist on us visiting his parents together. In his view, they had to accept me. He didn't want to have to choose between us. I respected that. As an African, I set great store by family, and didn't doubt that, if I loved Karl, I would have to accept his, too. Still, each time I noticed how much trouble his mother had with me. I simply did not fit into the picture. That became clear to me when Karl's sister got married.

The upcoming wedding was a constant topic of conversation in the family, because Karl's sister's fiancé was the owner of the largest company and thus also the most important employer in the village. Of course, I assumed that I would be invited together with Karl. I was the girlfriend of the brother of the bride, after all. I had also already met the groom. So I was all the more surprised one evening when my boyfriend, somewhat embarrassed, said, "Unfortunately, I have to go to the wedding alone."

"What do you mean?" I asked, taken aback. I noticed how he shifted on his feet and searched for the right words.

"It's because . . ." In his embarrassment, he could not continue speaking.

I looked at him expectantly.

"Uh, um . . . Not many guests are being invited, so I have to go alone."

"What you actually mean is that your parents are embarrassed to introduce a black woman to the guests as their son's girlfriend, right?"

Karl looked at me helplessly, and I didn't want to make it easy for him. I was angry about his behavior. He had simply accepted that his family excluded me from this event. So now it had happened, after all: He had been forced to choose between me and his family. And he had chosen the latter.

"What am I supposed to do?" he pleaded with me. "I can't abandon my sister on that day. But my parents are afraid of what people might think when they see you. They haven't really accepted yet that we're together."

"And you?" I asked him. "What do you think about it?"

"You know the answer. I stand by you!" Karl sounded distraught. "But I have to participate in the wedding. Please understand."

But at that moment I didn't want to understand. I wished that he had made a different decision, if only to make his position clear. But deep inside I knew that I was neither able nor willing to compete with his family—especially since I was always telling him to respect his family. In the beginning of our relationship, I had witnessed a few times how harshly he could behave toward his parents. The first time, I was really shocked. If I had spoken that way to my parents, I would have regretted it forever! Even when I had not agreed with something and was right, as was also sometimes the case with Karl, I had always had to find a way to make it clear to them without being disrespectful or even sounding annoyed. I told my boyfriend that in my whole life—and I was already twenty-five years old at the time—I had never really argued with my parents.

Despite the unpleasant family situation, we spent wonderful times together. One of the high points was our ten-day trip to Italy in the summer of 1985.

We planned to drive to Tuscany and spend the nights at campgrounds there, which I could not really imagine. Previously, I had only gone camping during my school days, and it had always been in the wild and without any comforts.

Our route was to take us to Lake Garda and then through Tuscany. We wanted to visit Assisi, and, of course, Florence and Pisa were on the agenda.

We reached our first campground in the evening, checked in, paid, and picked out a site to pitch our tent. That night, Karl got to know me as a city dweller who was afraid of the dark. Later on in the journey, we even had to spend the night in the car a few times because I simply felt too uneasy in the tent. In Tuscany, I was actually more afraid of people who might mug or abduct me than I had been of dangerous animals in the Kenyan wilderness.

In Florence, we viewed the cathedral of Santa Maria del Fiore with its beautiful dome, visited the Uffizi Gallery, strolled through the narrow streets of the city. There were swarms of tourists everywhere, and we kept coming across Senegalese and Ghanaian street peddlers. We liked it there so much that we extended our planned stay.

We had decided that Florence would be the southern boundary of our trip. On arriving in Pisa on our way back, I was disappointed to discover that the famous leaning tower was much smaller than I had imagined it.

Finally, we reached Milan, the last Italian city we wanted to visit. The first stop was the cathedral, the Duomo di Santa Maria Nascente. No sooner had we entered the magnificent church than we saw a monk slowly approaching us. We smiled politely, and he spoke to us softly.

"Miniskirt is not permitted here," he whispered.

"Miniskirt?" we asked, surprised.

He nodded toward me and said to Karl, "The lady. She is not allowed to show her legs like that."

I couldn't believe my ears. The denim skirt I was wearing reached down to just over my knees. For me it was anything but a miniskirt. Karl, the Catholic and former altar boy, seemed to understand immediately. He apologized profusely, promptly took my hand and directed me toward the church gate. He knew me all too well and was aware that I would not yield without a good explanation. In his mind, he undoubtedly already heard me protesting. "But why? That's hypocrisy! What matters is what is in people's hearts, not how long their skirt is." But before I could open my mouth, we were already outside again.

"It wouldn't have been worth it to argue with them about your skirt. They still would have thrown us out," Karl said. "There wasn't much to see anyway."

The vast cathedral square lay before us, lined with the expensive boutiques for which Milan, the city of fashion, is so famous. In the shop windows, mannequins presented the latest fashions, among them clothes that barely covered the most intimate body parts.

"What hypocrisy!" I said with a strained voice. Milan was ruined for me. We didn't stay longer in the city and set off again on our return trip to Heidelberg. There, I faced new challenges.

The discovery of my "African identity" in Germany went hand in hand with dealing with the Germans and their view of us Africans. It shocked and disappointed me that most of the Germans I met knew so little about Africa. They talked about it as if it were not a continent with fifty-three states, but one big country. Time and again, I had to correct my conversation partners, "Africa is not a country, Africa is a continent!" And then I would often just get the reply, "Yeah, yeah, but as I was saying . . ." And the person in question would go on speaking as if my remark had been merely a trifling interruption of an important statement.

The fact that our massive continent in all its diversity was given such little regard moved me to deal more intensively with the prevailing image of Africa in Germany. For me, the question of how this could be changed became central.

One day I met Ali, who had studied economics and was actually named Alfons. He had very light skin, curly, almost ash-blond hair, and was a typical "alternative" German. To my ears, his Arabic-Muslim sounding name did not at all fit with his appearance.

Ali and I decided to work as a team. We organized a series of seminars with which we intended to portray Africa and the Africans more realistically than we felt the media did. In doing so, we also wanted to emphasize the connection between the prevailing clichés and Germany's Africa policy, and make clear to what extent these false images also influence government decisions in matters of development aid.

In the beginning, it was great fun to hold these seminars with Ali. From Heidelberg, we traveled to the various places where our events were planned. Usually, the seminars took place on the weekends and extended over several days. The participants arrived on the first evening, and then spent two days discussing Africa, its individual countries, the diverse cultures, languages, and people—all this against the background of the preconceptions of Africa that the participants brought with them. We also employed film footage, presenting documentaries and feature films made by Africans or Germans in order to convey a multifaceted, nuanced image. Our work was so well-received that we got further engagements, particularly from the Friedrich-Ebert-Stiftung, a foundation for political education that was closely associated with the Social Democratic Party.

We gave our talks in a lively fashion and complemented each other really well. Ali, the German, made many jokes and mocked his own prejudices, which made it easier for the participants to speak about their resentments and stereotypes. I myself lent the portrayals a certain intensity through my firsthand experience as an African. And from my perspective, I could describe the impact of the Germans' view of Africa on the life of an African in Germany. At these seminars, I often said jokingly that this time I was the one providing development aid. However, I was repeatedly confronted with the objection that as an African I could not view the situation of the "black" continent objectively. I was simply too personally affected. It bothered me that I was frequently considered incapable of forming an evaluation for that reason. If those people then participated in the seminar a second time, they often became unpleasant know-it-alls. They no longer engaged in discussion, but stuck rigidly to their assertions, argued with us, and even seemed to enjoy these confrontations.

At first, I tried hard to convince them of the importance and rightness of our message. But over time, I sensed more and more strongly their arrogance and stubborn refusal to accept our judgment of things. They had acquired their knowledge from books, newspapers, and television and believed that it corresponded to the facts. It became particularly clear to me in these confrontations what enormous power the media possess.

The more these disputes repeated themselves, the more I lost patience, and finally my impatience turned into frustration. I sensed an ever-widening gulf between me and the participants.

In the period that followed, I accepted offers to hold seminars less and less frequently. Instead I gave talks. I traveled to the place to which I had been invited, gave my lecture, answered questions, and left. Here there were none of the repeat encounters that had so demoralized me.

I studied in Heidelberg for four years. In comparison to the Kenyan university system, the German one was substantially more open—at least in the humanities—and had given me the freedom to choose my own classes and even exam dates. I had really enjoyed assuming the responsibility for designing my own course of study and now it was approaching its end. My thesis had to be written. I had chosen a literary topic. And from that point on, I sat for entire days in the university library or at home, where I discussed with my friend and then-roommate Maria her corrections of my German writing. I enjoyed this time of research, writing, and discussion. Then came the final exam—and at last I held my diploma in my hands.

But my university days were not over yet. I wanted to pursue a doctorate. For me, this wasn't about attaining a higher academic title. My love for Karl was the decisive factor. To leave Germany for good and go back to my native country alone was inconceivable to me at that time. For Karl, too, a separation was out of the question, and so a doctoral program was a way to stay with him longer.

I applied for a doctoral scholarship from the DAAD. But the foundation wanted me to return to Kenya and teach German at the university there. Nonetheless, I was able to convince the decision makers that a doctorate was necessary for an academic career in German studies. Thus, I was granted a scholarship, but under the condition that I work for a year in Nairobi as a tutorial fellow at the university before continuing my studies in Germany. The DAAD remained adamant about that: Kenya or no new scholarship.

After I had come to terms with the fact that I had to leave Germany for a while, Karl and I discussed what would happen with our relationship. He had just passed his first state law exam and was free to do what he wanted with the six months before his second state exam. He decided to do an internship in Kenya during that time. After some searching, we found an internship for him with UNEP, the United Nations Environmental Programme in Nairobi. But because he could not come with me right away, we would nonetheless be separated at first.

19.

MY RETURN TO KENYA was truly a challenge. Though I was looking forward to seeing my native country, I was also afraid of all the uncertainty that lay ahead of me.

Immediately after my arrival in Nairobi, I had a lot to do. I had to get all my belongings, which I had shipped from Germany to Kenya, at the port of Mombasa and bring them into the capital. Among my things, there was also a car, for as a returning Kenyan with permanent right of abode I was permitted to bring my own car into the country tax-free. That might sound simple, but it entailed a huge bureaucratic effort. I had to go from one ministry to another, fill out numerous forms, and submit them at all sorts of agencies.

When Karl finally arrived, all this still wasn't done. He was astonished when he saw how many bureaucratic hurdles had to be overcome in Kenya. He said that he could never live permanently in this country—the bureaucracy and corruption would make him crazy. At the time, I thought nothing of it and just laughed. After all, both of us wanted to go back to Germany.

At first we stayed with my Aunty Jane in Kariokor, an old,

somewhat run-down neighborhood near the center of Nairobi, where the Carrier Corps had lived during the colonial era. She provided us a room in her apartment. But we were not her only guests. People were constantly showing up, usually relatives, who wanted to stay for one or two days, but then ended up staying with my lively aunt for weeks or even months. She threw none of them out, even though they not only lived with her for free but also ate with her without contributing a cent. Sometimes there were so many people there that some slept on the living room floor, in the kitchen, or in the storeroom.

Somewhat annoyed about all the self-invited guests, I asked Aunty Jane one day why she took in all these people. She just looked at me with a smile and said, "You're here, too. Should I send you away?"

I found this comparison unfair, because we had gotten in touch months earlier and arranged the time of our stay. We also shared in the household costs and the chores that came up. But I didn't say anything. For my mother's sister, it was always natural to share everything she had with her relatives. What we gave her thus benefited everyone. It reminded me of the discussion I'd had with Barack in Chicago about my father.

What might partly explain her behavior is the fact that my aunt had no children of her own. For her, we were all her children, and probably she was also afraid of being alone after her husband had left her. On top of that, Aunty Jane adhered strictly to Luo customs and was extremely superstitious, especially in her attitude toward death. She had always been terribly afraid of dying alone. She once told me that she chased no one away because otherwise no one would come to her funeral. At first I thought that she was joking, but she was, in the truest sense of the term, dead serious.

My father's farewell photo just before he left for the United States to study. Seated are my grandfather and mother (who was pregnant with me at the time.) Uncle Were, an aunt, and my father, who is holding Abongo's hand, are standing.

Me with my mother and Abongo.

My father with Abongo and me in our house in Roslyn shortly after we had moved in with him and Ruth. Uncle Were is standing in the background.

My grandmother Sarah at her homestead next to her water tank.

Me with grandmother Sarah on her compound.

My older brother Abongo and I (at around fourteen) at a friend's house.

Me in front of the school library at Kenya High School.

Me at nineteen with grandmother Sarah.

Me cooking in the communal kitchen of our shared student flat in Heidelberg.

Me and my mother during her visit to Heidelberg.

With Barack in his kitchen during our first meeting in Chicago.

Barack and Michelle with family members—I'm in purple—on their first visit to Kenya and our homestead in Alego.

A studio shot with Samson, Abongo, Barack, and Ben. My mother and I are seated.

Barack and family members during the inauguration of the new Obama homestead.

Barack and Michelle at my mechanics in Kibera, waiting while I get my Volkswagen (in the background) fixed.

Akinyi, age eight, and I in England.

So we lived with Aunty Jane among various relatives. Karl started his internship and took a UNEP bus across the city to his workplace every day. After a few weeks, my job at the University of Nairobi finally began, too, and now that I was an employee of the university, we could move into our own apartment. It was in Kileleshwa, one of the nicer neighborhoods in Nairobi. Behind our apartment building stretched a lush, inviting garden, along the end of which a stream flowed. The tall trees that stood in the small park attracted several little monkeys every evening, who climbed around in their branches. If you ever forgot something edible on the balcony, you could be certain that the animals would make off with it.

Despite his reservations about the Kenyan bureaucracy, Karl settled into his new surroundings very quickly. Because I had sold the imported car early on, we bought an old blue VW Beetle after a few months. Now we were mobile again.

At the university, I taught German to a group of very pleasant Kenyan students, but because they could barely get out a sentence due to sheer shyness, I constantly had to encourage them to participate. That was more of a strain for me than the teaching itself.

At that time, I often thought back to my German teacher Mrs. Kanaiya at Kenya High School, in whose lessons we had always had substantial discussions. My students, however, lacked the courage to participate in class. But I did not accept their insufficient language skills as a reason for their timidity. How else would they learn German if not by speaking? If necessary, they could even complete sentences in English, as long as they participated actively in class. But because this rarely happened, I became bored with the work pretty quickly.

Alongside the job at the university, I taught German at the

Goethe-Institut in Nairobi and gave private lessons, in order to supplement my income. With the extra money, Karl and I could take trips through the country, since he received no salary from UNEP and had to live on his savings.

One day, on the spur of the moment, we drove the old Beetle to Lake Turkana in the north of the country. Because I didn't think myself capable of driving alone with Karl to the lake over four hundred miles away, I asked Patrick, the younger brother of my friend Trixi, who was now studying in Munich, whether he wanted to come with us. He immediately said yes, and without extensive preparations, we set off. We took with us additional gasoline, a very simple three-person tent, and some canned beans and meat. We planned to buy everything else on the way.

After we had driven almost all day, our bones somewhat stiff from sitting for so long in the cramped Beetle, we reached the lake in the late afternoon. There we followed a sign that said TURKANA LODGE. Although we had only very little money with us, we thought that we might be able to spend the night there. After the drive, a bed seemed more pleasant to us than the hard ground in the tent.

The lodge on the shore of the great lake that stretched out before our eyes looked deserted; in general, the whole area made a rather lonely and desolate impression. But as we approached the lodge, we saw that it wasn't closed. We sat down on the porch and enjoyed the tranquillity and the impressive view of the endless surface of a body of water that is about fifteen times the size of Lake Constance in Germany. Shortly thereafter, a waiter approached from the bar and brought us a menu.

"Let's see," I said, taking the menu and asking the waiter to give us some time to choose. He nodded and went back to the bar, from where he nonetheless did not stop looking at us.

"He probably thinks we have no money," I said to Karl, slightly annoyed.

"And he's right about that," Karl remarked, grinning.

"But he can't know that. He's tolerating our presence only because you're here. Otherwise he would have sent us away a long time ago."

"Why me?" Karl asked, confused.

"Because you're white. So you must have money. That's what the people here think anyway."

"If only he knew!"

"Yes, if only he knew!" I didn't find the situation funny at all.

It was not the first time that we ended up in a situation like that. Time and again it had happened that we went into a restaurant and the waitstaff completely ignored me as a hanger-on to a white man, until it was time to pay and Karl pointed to me. But at that point, the embarrassed faces were no comfort to me.

"Okay, let's see what we can even eat here," said Karl. "Because we're definitely not spending the night here. Have you seen the room prices? For that we can buy our groceries for a week."

"How do you know that?"

"I saw it at the entrance, on the way to the bathroom."

Ultimately, Patrick and I ordered Sprites and Karl a Coke. The waiter seemed less than thrilled about our lavish order.

Besides the superb panorama, Lake Turkana had nothing special to offer. I went to the shore and dipped my hand in the water—carefully, because the lakeside vegetation looked like a favorable stomping ground for crocodiles. I knew that those hungry reptiles lived here. The water looked very clean and shimmered silvery blue. I marveled at how soft it felt, almost like hand cream.

We had quickly emptied our glasses. The unfriendly waiter was still standing nearby, as if he wanted to chase us away, which irritated me even more in light of the fact that the lodge looked so deserted and we had ordered something, after all. *He should at least be happy to have the company,* I thought, and I didn't leave him a tip.

We set off, because we still had to find a place to spend the night before dark. Pitching the tent was itself an adventure, because the ground consisted only of sand and tufts of tall grass—and was thus extremely ill-suited to the task. But we didn't want to change the site and search for more solid ground, because we preferred to stay near the lodge in case of any danger.

Somehow, we managed to pitch the tent between the tufts of grass. Even in retrospect, I still shudder at the thought that not at all far from our scarcely protective shelter crocodiles were undoubtedly prowling around.

The night was an adventure in itself. For hours, the wind howled outside, and I had the feeling that any moment the tent would be lifted off the ground and carried out into Lake Turkana. A few times, Karl or Patrick had to leave it to hammer down the stakes again. As soon as they unzipped the flap, the wind blew sand into the tent, which settled in every fold and crevice. The only good thing about the sandy ground was that it provided a relatively comfortable bed, even if sleep was unthinkable for half the night due to the wind.

The next morning we made a small fire, as we had the evening before, warmed up a few cans of baked beans, and consumed the contents with some bread. Shortly thereafter, we set off again toward Nairobi. We had covered the long distance to see the lake, had drunk a Coke and two Sprites, slept miserably in a wind-lashed tent, and felt as if we had been on a great adventure.

That's how we were in those days: For a small pleasure, we didn't shy away from even the greatest effort.

On the way back, the mostly straight road was as empty as it had been on the way there. To the right and left stretched a dry landscape with low bushes. They would have looked dead but for their small, bright-red flowers, which blurred on the horizon and resembled a blazing fire—an eerily beautiful sight.

But our adventure was not yet over. After a few hours' drive, the Beetle began to sputter and finally stopped completely. We got out. Karl and Patrick looked for the cause of the breakdown, and I sat down on a rock and stared into space. We weren't in a hurry.

It wasn't long before the two men had discovered the reason for the problem. Sand had jammed the engine. But no settlement or village, let alone a repair shop, could be seen far and wide. Nor had we encountered another car. We were completely on our own.

To this day, I am amazed that I wasn't worried at the time. I was certain that we would somehow overcome this difficulty. And Patrick actually did find the solution. He had once helped out at a car repair shop and knew that in order to continue driving, we only had to find a way to clear the carburetor of sand.

The two men stuck their heads under the hood and dealt with the innards of the Beetle.

"We have no choice. We have to clean everything with gasoline," Patrick asserted.

"How do you intend to do that?" I asked. "We don't have any real tools with us, let alone a siphon."

"With our mouths," Patrick answered resolutely.

"What? Is that even possible?" Karl asked.

"It's possible. We have to suck the gasoline out of the tank with our mouths and then clean the individual parts with it."

Karl did not look all too thrilled. Nor was I.

"Are you sure?" I looked first at Patrick and then at my boyfriend.

"We have no choice," the two men said, almost simultaneously.

"Otherwise we'll have to stay here until someone finds us," Karl added.

"But that could take days!" A tiny sense of panic flared up in me. In the past two days, we had seen at most one or two cars.

"Exactly," Karl said soberly.

I didn't say anything else.

"So let's get to it!" Patrick said with gusto.

"Can I do something?" I didn't want to just sit there and watch my companions swallow gasoline.

"No. Just keep an eye out for a car."

A big job indeed! So I watched helplessly as Patrick and Karl removed the carburetor and began to clean it with the sucked-out gasoline.

The whole thing took over an hour. Finally, the men raised their heads and looked at each other.

"I think that's it," Patrick said. Everything stank of gasoline, and I was glad that none of us smoked—who knew what danger we would have exposed ourselves to.

At that moment, the roar of the engine sounded to my ears like the most beautiful melody. We sighed with relief. As we drove on, I could not rid myself of the thought that we had been damn lucky.

20.

SINCE MY TRIP TO CHICAGO, the exchange with my brother had remained lively, as I had suspected—no, had known it would. And when he learned that I would be spending a year working in Kenya, he wanted to visit me there and take the opportunity to see his father's country for the first time. But Barack did not intend to stay for only a few days; rather, he wanted to devote a whole month to discovering his roots. His desire was to meet as many relatives as possible and to continue with me the conversation we had begun.

After a painful good-bye, Karl had returned to Germany, and it had gotten very lonely in my small apartment in the beautiful neighborhood of Keleleshwa. So I was all the more excited to have Barack as a guest. The apartment was not very big, but it would suffice for my brother and me. I borrowed a cot from a friend and stowed it in the living room behind the large couch. It would serve my brother as a guest bed during his visit.

When I expressed my reservations regarding the comfort of the apartment to Barack, he said he was "very low-maintenance." He explained to me that as long as he had a place to sleep, could jog, and got something to eat, he was happy. But the last of the items he mentioned meant a slight challenge for me. I had never been very domestic, and I knew it would be hard for me to guarantee Barack a warm meal each day. Usually, I ate in the university cafeteria, rarely at home. When Barack came, I tried to shift gears and made an effort to put food on the table every day. But often I forgot to cook or buy groceries, and then my brother had to make do with peanut butter sandwiches and salad.

Aunt Zeituni and I picked up Barack at the airport in my blue Beetle. I was excited; after all, it was only our second meeting.

He himself had arrived smoothly, but apparently not his suitcase. The next day, we had to drive to the airport again to inquire where his luggage was. I can still see us standing at the Kenya Airways counter, where Barack spoke with one of the members of the ground personnel, a young woman, tall, with a pretty, well-proportioned face and wonderfully smooth, brown skin. Her good looks had definitely not escaped my brother's attention, for when we finally got his suitcase and had stowed it and sat in the car, he made a remark about her attractive appearance.

I still remember that we then got into a conversation about relationships in general. He told me that he had just broken up with his girlfriend. They had studied together, but had drifted apart and finally separated—among other reasons, because Barack was planning to leave Chicago to continue his education at Harvard University. He would no longer be returning to America's West Coast, preferring to stay in the east.

Of course, Barack asked me how things were going with my German boyfriend. Since Karl had only recently returned to Germany and I really missed him, I wore my heart on my sleeve.

"You've really got it bad," Barack said, after I had raved to him about Karl.

"That's how it should be when you're in love," I replied. "I'm definitely happy, apart from the fact that I miss him."

Barack laughed. "It's true, you're really beaming!"

Again we spoke almost without cease. My brother was preoccupied with many questions, and as the days went by, there were more and more.

During one of our conversations, he explained to me why he was planning to go to Harvard. He had already studied political science at Occidental College and at Columbia University in New York. Now he wanted to earn a law degree, though he was still working in the projects in Chicago.

"What I'm doing now is far from enough," he said resolutely. "There's only so much I can achieve through my current work. I accompany the people I advocate for to plead their cases to the city authorities. I comfort them when they lose a child to violence or complain about the state of their schools, poor health care, or lack of a pension. But in the position I am in, I cannot ultimately bring about significant change in their lives."

I didn't fully understand. "But you are changing something. You give the people hope for a better future."

Barack looked at me seriously. "But that's not enough. I don't want to just give them hope. I want to make a better future possible for them or at least for their children."

"And how do you plan to do that?"

"By working within the system to influence legislation and the policies that govern these people's lives."

"But is studying law enough to be able to do that?"

"No. But I don't want to study law in order to work solely as a lawyer afterward. I want to become more politically active. I hope that with a background in law I will be able to have an impact on policy makers."

I looked at my brother. He spoke so earnestly, his voice firm and committed. I didn't doubt for a moment that he meant every word he said.

Our conversation led us to the subject of world politics. We discussed Africa and the continent's relationships to the rest of the world, and talked late into the night. Barack listened with interest when I told him about my "development work" in Germany and about how I had ultimately stopped doing it out of frustration.

"You shouldn't have quit, Auma," he said. "I'm sure you were doing good work."

I smiled sadly.

"I was probably in over my head. I always got too worked up."

"You can't do that. You always have to keep your eye on your vision. Sometimes people take longer to understand, but eventually they get it. I believe firmly in that."

"Maybe you're so optimistic because you come from a country where it's possible to dream. Here you can dream as much as you want, but in most cases it doesn't go beyond hope. Just think of our old man," I said.

"He just didn't try to become a decision maker, someone who determines what really happens."

"Oh yes, he did," I protested. "Only no one wanted to listen to him. He was the leading economist in the Ministry of Finance and advised the government in all economic matters. Wasn't that enough?"

"No, because his proposals were not backed by legislation."

"Does that mean that only legal experts can change the world?"

"Of course not." Barack laughed out loud. "It takes much more than legal skills to do that. But laws have a significant impact on people's lives. If you want to make a difference, you have to put yourself in a position from which you can influence events. Our father apparently didn't know how to do that."

My brother's argument did not entirely persuade me. My view was more that the possibility of bringing about serious and meaningful social change very much depended on what type of person one was. There were people who could carry others along with them. They could convince others with their visions—my father was not one of those people. He was too much a loner, too much a man of ideas. Though he was forward thinking, he was not necessarily the best person to realize his visions.

To Barack I said, "What you are trying in the United States would be much more difficult in Kenya. But knowing you, you'll definitely accomplish it."

Shortly after his arrival, we decided to visit our grandmother Sarah. We chose to take the train, because in those days it was still reliable, and comfortable, too. In the early evening, the train slowly rolled out of the station and departed Nairobi's center with increasing speed. It headed toward the Great Rift Valley, which became world-famous through the film *Out of Africa*. Unfortunately, we saw nothing of the East African Rift, because by the time we passed through the valley, it was already dark. While the train crew made our beds, we went to eat dinner in the dining car. The old car with its colonial flair seemed like a museum piece.

The waiter proudly showed us the royal coat of arms of the British Empire on the knives and forks and huge soup spoons that lay on the small dining tables.

"We still praise the British here and are proud of our colonial heritage. People don't think about how much was destroyed back then in this country." I had to get this comment off my chest.

Barack shrugged and said with a smile, "Ignorance is bliss."

The next morning at sunrise we approached Kisumu, our first stop. There were green fields everywhere, in which various types of grain were growing. The sight conveyed an impression of wealth and abundance.

It was as if Barack had read my mind, for he said with astonishment, "The landscape is completely at odds with the image of starving Africans that we have in the West."

"Our reality is at odds with Western preconceptions in many ways," I replied. "But we're not the only ones who see this; others do, too, though they don't register it. I'm talking about fellow Africans. It's as if we are blocked. Many of us flee the rural life, only to end up in slums in the city. And we ourselves reinforce the image of poor, starving Africans. It reminds me of my experiences in Germany. The people there often didn't perceive me as I really was, but rather according to their own preconceptions. Even when I had discussions with them for hours and explained to them that I was different from the preconceived image in their head, most of the time they refused to believe it. Even the fact that I spoke German almost fluently usually didn't change anything. Some went on speaking to me in that strange Tarzan German. And if I wore traditional West African clothing—in Kenya, we don't have a traditional national dress—they would comment that I now looked like a 'real African.' "

Leaving the Kisumu train station, we took a taxi to the central bus depot. There we boarded a minibus that would stop in Alego Nyangoma. Finally, around noon, we got off the bus and stood, exhausted from the bumpy ride over bad roads, in front of the "shopping center" of Nyangoma, which was actually nothing of the sort. It consisted of only a few tiny shops, a small marketplace, and an outdoor bicycle repair shop, where a man fixed punctured tires under a huge tree.

My grandmother was already approaching when we reached the top of the hill that formed the edge of the upper part of our land. I ran toward her. Barack followed somewhat more slowly.

"*Nyar Baba!*" said Granny Sarah, laughing out loud. In Luo those words mean "Daddy's little girl." My grandmother always called me *Nyar Baba* when she was especially happy about my coming. She lavished other pet names on me, too, but with "Daddy's little girl" she expressed all her love.

I hugged her and greeted her warmly. *"Nadi, Mama?"* I asked. ("How are you, Mama?") From an early age, I had called my grandmother "Mama."

"Very well. And whom have you brought with you there?"

I had intentionally not "warned" her. The visit was supposed to be a surprise.

Barack, who had stood patiently behind me, now held out his hand to our grandmother.

"Nadi?" he said with an American accent.

Our Granny burst out laughing.

"And he even speaks Luo!"

In the meantime, other family members from the compound, attracted by our voices, had joined us, too.

"I'm Barack," my brother introduced himself. "Barack Obama."

My grandmother threw her hands in the air and let out a cry that cut me to the quick. It sounded as if she had hurt herself terribly. I looked at her worriedly, and from her facial expression I could tell that she didn't know whether to weep or laugh. The surprise had been a success.

"Barry? Is it really you? How lucky I am to have lived long enough to meet you! Auma, have you really brought Barry home?" She was beside herself with joy. "If only your father were still alive!" With the edge of her *leso,* a wraparound garment that Kenyan women wear around their hips, she wiped the tears from her eyes. Then she pressed Barack tightly to her ample bosom and pulled him by the arm to the main building on the homestead, my grandfather's house. The relatives who had come over had in the meantime taken our luggage from us and walked ahead toward the house.

"We have to slaughter a rooster immediately," my grandmother exclaimed excitedly as we walked. "The occasion must be celebrated. My grandson has come from America. Osumba, Guala! *Bi uru,* come here!" Osumba and Guala were my grandmother's younger children, who still lived with her.

She spoke quickly and loudly, literally breathless with happiness about Barack's appearance. I followed the two of them, smiling, for I had expected this reaction to Barack's "homecoming."

Most of the time we spent telling stories. Barack thereby learned some more about our father—for example, how he had refused as a small boy to go to the local primary school, because a woman and not a man taught there. In those days, the teachers were permitted to cane children, and our father vehemently resisted being beaten by a woman. He even managed to persuade his parents to send him to school in N'giya, a small village two and a half miles away.

Barack also met new relatives and participated enthusiastically in the rural family life. My brother observed everything closely; despite the fact that on our grandmother's homestead he got only a glimpse of traditional Luo life, he wanted to experience it as fully as possible. He went into the fields with our grandmother and watched how they were tilled. Together we accompanied her to the market. There she brought the cabbage and other vegetables grown in the garden, and Barack helped her carry the large sack. All the people eyed him with curiosity, and Granny Sarah told them excitedly about her grandson who had come all the way from America to Kenya to visit her. Unfortunately, Barack spoke no Luo, and my grandmother could barely converse in English. Nonetheless, they managed to communicate wonderfully with gestures.

After several days, we left my grandmother to travel on to Karachuonyo. In this village on the shores of Lake Victoria lived additional members of the Obama family. It was also where my father and my mother had fallen in love at a dance. Though the Obamas originally came from Alego, our great-grandfather, Obama Opiyo, left Alego to take up residence in Karachuonyo, where land was allotted to him. There his sons and daughters were born. One of these children was my grandfather, Onyango Hussein. Grandfather Onyango was a very community-oriented young man, who liked to participate in political events in Kendu Bay. But it was made clear to him that he was an outsider and thus had no say in decisions. Because he was a proud man, he didn't want to feel slighted anymore, and so he set off with his family to return to his father's home. His siblings remained behind and settled in Karachuonyo, where they established their families.

Grandfather Onyango was accompanied on his return by my biological grandmother, Akumu, his second wife and my father's mother, as well as Sarah, his third wife, at that time his young bride. His first wife, Halima, refused to come with him. She had heard that Alego was very primitive and backward, and she did not want to live there. Ultimately, Akumu didn't last long in Alego either. After only a brief stay she departed the compound and left her three children behind, my father and his sisters, Nyaoke and Auma. Nyaoke, the oldest, was twelve at the time, my father nine. Auma was still a baby. They all grew up with Granny Sarah. Although she was not their biological mother, Granny Sarah was nonetheless considered their mother by tradition and years later became the only grandmother I really knew. When I introduced her to Barack, he, too, embraced her as our Granny.

In Kendu Bay, we were welcomed as warmly as in Alego. The family was happy to meet Barack. They asked almost as many questions as he did. For me, it was not always simple to introduce Barack to his relatives without getting lost in the confusion of the familial relationships.

Back in Nairobi, we were invited to dinner by more family members. In some cases, I would have preferred it if Barack had gone alone, but my brother insisted that I accompany him. Uncle Odima was among those I didn't necessarily want to see. I had mostly unpleasant memories of him and his family and had not been in contact with him for many years. But now I had made Barack curious about this uncle with all my stories.

"Odima lived with you, with our father. I have to meet him and his family." My brother looked at me imploringly.

"You should do that. I just don't want to be there."

"That would be impolite. They must know that I'm staying with you."

I didn't want to tell Barack that I didn't care about that and that I didn't owe that family anything. Only because I saw his disappointed expression, I gave in.

The visit with Ruth was also difficult. I had run into her in the city and told her that Barack was with me. She invited us to lunch and mentioned that Mark (Okoth) was also staying in Nairobi at that time. I accepted the invitation, for I thought that Barack should meet this younger brother, too.

We arrived on time at the home of our father's third wife. Her house was not hard to find. She lived on the large street that leads from Spring Valley to Gigiri, a beautiful area of the capital. She had sold the house in Lavington a long time ago. With the proceeds, I had been told, she had opened a preschool.

After we had turned onto her property, I parked my old Beetle in the gravel driveway. Even before we had climbed out of the car, Ruth was already standing at the front door, a broad smile on her face.

"Welcome!" she said heartily as we got out. She was looking warmly at Barack. "And you must be Barry."

"Barack," he corrected her. I knew that my brother didn't like being called Barry; only with our grandmother had he taken no exception to it.

"Come in, Rita," she said, turning to me. Although I had told her several times that I wanted to be called Auma, she stuck with Rita. To avoid any friction, I resigned myself to it.

Another person was standing at the door, too. It was not Mark, whom I had not seen since he was nine years old, but Juliana, the domestic help my stepmother had taken with her when she left us. I greeted Juliana with a somewhat reserved smile—too many years had passed, too much was unresolved, and too much still hurt.

Shortly thereafter, we stood in a living room with a dining table that was already set. The middle of the room was dominated by a seating area, and next to glass doors that led onto a terrace and into a large garden, there was a piano. I looked out the window and thought of my only previous visit to this house. That time I had come to stand at Opiyo's graveside. Family members had told me that only Ruth knew where he was buried. After his death, they had tried to bury him in Alego in accordance with Luo tradition. But Ruth had resisted that vehemently, even though according to the old customs she had no authority to decide about Opiyo. Nonetheless, she had managed to retain control over the son she had only called David. She had his body cremated—the Luo are unacquainted with such a funeral rite—and his urn buried in her garden.

I looked at that part of the garden where I had said farewell to my brother almost six years earlier. *Too bad that Opiyo is not with us,* I thought. He would have been so happy about Barack's visit.

"I'll get Mark," Ruth said, and left the room. My brother and I looked at each other, but said nothing. My look must have revealed that I found the situation extremely uncomfortable. *Patience, patience,* Barack's eyes seemed to reply. I smiled faintly and was about to make a sardonic remark when Ruth entered the room again, followed by a young man with an Afro and a defiant face.

"This is Mark," she announced proudly. The sentence was directed at Barack, who had taken a seat on the sofa. He stood up and said formally, "Hi, Mark. How are you?"

"Fine, thank you." Mark's answer was no less formal. It was clear that he wasn't particularly interested in the brother who had suddenly turned up. He probably remained in the room only because his mother had told him to.

"Mark is a great pianist," said Ruth, when we had all sat down and there was a lapse in the small talk. "He should play something for you.

"Come on, Mark, play something," she implored him. "The two of them would definitely enjoy it."

Mark did not look thrilled. But when he replied that we probably didn't feel like listening to him play anything, we protested politely, of course. I wondered whether his mother's demand might have embarrassed him a little. But during the brief, stiff exchange with Barack, he had not struck me as shy. He had seemed confident, almost arrogant. Mark wasn't shy. He just didn't want to be shown off.

I have to admit that he elicited beautiful sounds from the piano. He played outstandingly. When the piece was over, I applauded not only to be polite, but also because I was truly impressed.

Mark stood up from the piano stool and accepted our compliments as if they were the most obvious thing in the world. But without music we again had to cultivate the conversation ourselves. We were at the mercy of the melodrama that I had in the meantime silently dubbed *The Reluctant Meeting of Two Brothers.*

At that moment, Juliana appeared and asked whether she should serve the food. Ruth stood up and followed her into the kitchen. She looked satisfied—no wonder, with her son's musical abilities.

Whether Ruth's two sons from her second marriage—she had gotten married again, to a man from Tanzania—ate lunch with us, I no longer recall. I can see only Barack and Mark in my mind's eye, trying out of respect for Ruth to show a certain interest in each other. Before we said good-bye shortly after eating, my stepmother urged the two of them to exchange addresses. That way they could stay in contact in America. They did as she said, probably in the certain knowledge that neither would continue the brotherly contact.

"The things I do for you!" I groaned, when we were back in the car.

"It went well, don't you think?" Barack grinned mischievously.

"But of course. Mark this, Mark that. Did you hear the way they talked about our father? It was as if he never meant anything to them. Ruth I can understand—that is, I can't really understand her attitude, only accept it. But Mark? What reason does he have? And he's so full of himself!"

"Maybe he's a bit insecure. And our father didn't exactly leave them with the best impression."

"Always the diplomat. Typical, that you interpret Mark's snootiness as insecurity. For me, he was just plain arrogant." I knew that I was perhaps being unfair to Mark, but I couldn't help myself. I was simply angry that he had received us without any sense of joy or warmth. And after I had heard nothing but disparaging remarks about my father during lunch, I was not willing to give him the benefit of the doubt. Today I think that Mark's standoffish facade concealed much that remained unresolved from his childhood. After all, the memories were still vivid for me, too.

Before Barack and I left Ruth, we had visited Opiyo's grave in the garden. Neither of us had spoken a word. And inwardly, I had again regretted that Opiyo was not with us. Perhaps he would have managed to bring us all together again.

Our complicated family situation fueled another desire in Barack: He asked me to introduce him to George, our father's youngest son.

Because I was no longer in contact with George and his mother, Jael, I did not know their new place of residence. But eventually I found out where our youngest brother went to school. So Barack and I decided to go there and greet him briefly during a break between classes.

At first, everything went according to plan. We visited the school principal and told her our request. She asked us to wait a few minutes, for soon the bell would ring. She showed us the door to George's classroom; we could wait for him outside in the hall. But on her way back to her office, the principal must have thought twice about our plan and called Jael to tell her about us. For when the bell rang, and the doors of all the classrooms flew open, filling the school with loud children's voices, she rushed toward us from the end of the hall. We had just begun to ask a few boys and girls about George. They pointed him out to us, and we approached a lively eight-year-old.

"Hi George," said Barack. The boy looked up at him with curiosity, and then glanced at me.

"I'm Auma, your sister, and this is Barack, your brother," I explained, but by then the principal was standing next to us.

"I'm sorry," she broke in. "But you can't talk to George."

"Why not?"

"I spoke to his mother on the telephone, and she did not allow it."

"My brother came all the way from the United States and

would like to meet his family, and George is part of it, too." I tried to soften up the principal, but she remained firm.

"Nonetheless, that's not possible. You really have to leave the school now."

George stood there uncomprehendingly and looked from one of us to the other. He didn't know us, and so he didn't grasp the meaning of all this.

"Okay, let's go," said Barack. He sensed the combativeness awakening in me, but he didn't want to make a scene. "We've seen George, after all."

Then he turned to the boy. "It was really nice to see you, little brother. I would have liked to exchange a few more words with you, but that's not possible right now."

"See you soon, George," I said, giving him my hand.

"Bye," the little one replied politely. His facial expression revealed nothing.

What might have been going through his young head at that moment? Suddenly two strangers appeared claiming to be his brother and his sister. That must have been confusing!

"Does Jael have reasons to behave like that?" Barack asked, scarcely able to conceal his disappointment.

"She had a quarrel with my mother. It was about our father's inheritance. Since then, she doesn't talk to us anymore. I'm really sorry for you."

A bit later Barack and I sat silently side by side in the car. Our father had not made it easy for us.

When no family visit was on the agenda, we took excursions, once to the coast, another time to the Maasai Mara game reserve. I wanted Barack to see how beautiful his father's country was.

To visit the national park, we joined a three-day safari tour. The driver chose the route along the ridge that led down into the Rift Valley escarpment. I knew this stretch well and told Barack every few minutes about the spectacular view that had eluded us on our train journey to Kisumu.

When I was a child, my father had often chosen this route when we visited our grandparents in the country. It had once been the main connection between Mombasa and Kisumu. Usually, we stopped along the way at a tiny church, which had been built by Italian POWs during the Second World War.

The journey went steeply uphill, and I remembered that I got dizzy when I looked through the car window into the depths. Now, this winding street was riddled with potholes, but then we finally came around the last curve—and before us lay a breathtaking panoramic landscape. Awestruck, I stood next to my brother and viewed the land of our ancestors.

After that, it took another five hours before we reached the national park. Our group consisted of Europeans and Americans. I explained to Barack that we Kenyans usually couldn't afford the expensive safaris.

"Look, a Thomson's gazelle," the Italian sitting next to me suddenly exclaimed.

"What does Thomson have to do with it?" I objected didactically. "We've always had these animals here. Just because this Scottish explorer, Joseph Thomson, discovered with astonishment an animal that did not exist where he was from, now it's named after him? The Kenyans call it *swara*."

The Italian looked at me with surprise. Barack had already gotten used to me and my Kenyan pride and just smiled. He probably also suspected that I was not yet done with my comments.

"Don't you think that's offensive?" I asked seriously.

The man didn't know how to answer my question. He looked around in confusion.

"I don't want to be impolite, but many other things here were renamed by Europeans, as if they were the first human beings to discover them. I just wonder what the Africans were for them, then. Apparently not human beings."

Over the next two days, we saw many more animals, and what had initially been a very serious discussion turned into a game, in which we debated which name fit best, the official one or the traditional one.

Mombasa, the city on the coast, was an entirely different experience from Maasai Mara. Once again we took the train to reach our destination. We headed eastward. Early in the morning we arrived in the lively port city, then we took the ferry and finally a *matatu,* a local minibus. Barack, curious about the countrymen of his Kenyan family, tried to have a conversation with the driver in English. But the man answered him in Kiswahili, the customary language on the Kenyan coast. He refused to believe that Barack, who looked like many of the coastal dwellers with his light brown skin, spoke no Kiswahili.

"I'm an American," Barack tried to explain, when he saw the man's puzzled look. I nodded affirmatively.

"If he's an American, then why is he taking a *matatu*?" the minibus driver asked me in Kiswahili.

"Because he's a poor American. He's a student," I answered. I immediately translated the conversation into English, so that Barack knew what it was about, too.

"There's no such thing as poor Americans," a fellow passenger from the back of the bus interjected in English.

"Yes, there is!" Barack replied. "You're looking at one right now."

"But he's also Luo," I added proudly.

"Well, that explains a lot," said the driver, and laughed out loud. I wasn't sure whether the remark alluded to his inability to speak Kiswahili or his poverty.

The other passengers now wanted to know more about the strange American and asked him many questions. When we got off the *matatu,* we felt as if we were saying good-bye to good friends, even though passengers had been getting on and off along the whole way.

At the entrance to our hotel, we were greeted by a surly guard. But we didn't let that spoil our good mood. The weather was magnificent and the sea was invitingly blue. We swam and lazed about. I showed my brother the Mombasa old town and Fort Jesus, which had a checkered history. During their colonial period, the British had used the fortress as a prison, among other things.

"Not many Kenyans vacation here," I explained to my brother, when he called my attention to the fact that there seemed to be scarcely any black tourists.

"That's a shame. It's really beautiful, and for the history alone more Kenyans should come here," Barack replied.

"Unfortunately, it's too expensive for most of them. And even if they have money, they are not always welcome," I said.

"Hopefully, that will change soon." My brother looked at me thoughtfully.

I had already warned him that Africans were not readily accepted as guests in most of the hotels frequented by foreign, predominantly white tourists. Black women in particular frequently encountered that reaction, for they were typically regarded as prostitutes.

Years later, that changed, and I witnessed how the people who ran tourist establishments on the coast were forced by the political unrest to solicit native vacationers. Because foreign tourists stayed away, the hotels had to reorient themselves and seek to attract clientele in their own country.

When it was time to say good-bye, Barack had become for me a brother with shared experiences. For the two of us there was no question that we would remain in close contact.

21.

IT WAS LOVE that made me leave Kenya after a year and return to Germany. Certainly, I also wanted to pursue my doctorate—but if it hadn't been for my longing for Karl, I might have remained in my native country. In the previous twelve months, I had felt really at home and achieved more professionally than I had initially expected.

In any case, now I was back in Germany. I wanted to write my dissertation under Professor Alois Wierlacher, but because he had gone to Bayreuth during my "time-out," I could no longer stay in Heidelberg—I, too, had to move to the Wagner city. Fortunately, Karl had been living in Nuremberg in the meantime to finish his law studies there, so that he was only an hour away from me by car or train. As often as possible, I visited him. But unfortunately, he visited me less frequently, which meant that I spent much more time in Nuremberg and as a result did not make many friends in Bayreuth. I often felt very lonely when I was there. Almost imperceptibly, this—among other things—led to my increasing dissatisfaction with our relationship. I felt as if I were pulling on a rope that would not give.

To top it all off, not everything in my studies was going the way I had imagined, either. My dissertation topic, which dealt with the perception of work in German literature, was not among my professor's major interests; at that point he was more interested in the subject of food in German literature. Therefore, I constantly had to vie for his attention. During that time of disillusionment, Barbara and Donald and their two daughters, Roma and Sandra, came into my life and saved the day. Donald was Kenyan. We unexpectedly became acquainted, and he invited me to his home. His Polish wife, Barbara, and I became close friends. Their family became my refuge whenever I sought a place of warmth and wanted to talk in depth about things.

In my own family, a lot happened in that period. In 1990, Karl and I had flown to Abongo's wedding in the United States. He had been living for several years near Washington, D.C., where he had met Sheree, an African American. A few days after the celebration, Karl and I drove a rental car to New York to meet up with Ann and Maya, who had also been at the wedding but had left earlier. Maya was still a student and lived with her mother.

New York did not disappoint us. The metropolis entirely lived up to its reputation; it was loud, fast, exciting, and truly never slept. We strolled along Fifth Avenue and looked at the display windows of the expensive shops. From the Twin Towers and the Empire State Building we viewed the city, and one evening we ate dinner in a high-rise restaurant. In Times Square, we admired the colorful scene of the neon advertisements that lit up the city as bright as day. A trip to the Guggenheim Museum was a must, and, of course, we also paid the obligatory visit to the old lady: the Statue of Liberty.

Our days were completely filled with activities. And when Maya celebrated her birthday at one of the many clubs in downtown Manhattan, we also got to experience New York nightlife.

After that trip, Bayreuth struck me as even more sedate, and despite my brief absence it took a while before I had accustomed myself again to the leisurely rhythm of the small city.

But there was one exciting development: Before Karl and I flew to the United States, I had applied to the German Film and Television Academy in Berlin (Deutsche Film- und Fernsehakademie Berlin, known as DFFB). The solitary work buried in books had become more and more difficult for me. That is why I had recently done a three-month internship with WDR, the West German broadcasting company. The media experiences I gained at that Cologne station fostered a desire in me: I wanted to tell people more about the life of Africans, though no longer in seminars and lectures, but in visual images.

I was thrilled to find out that I was among the few selected to take the entrance exam for the DFFB. The first hurdle was cleared. The exam process took four days—and in the end I could hardly believe it: Among the roughly five hundred people who applied to the academy in 1990, I was accepted with nine other candidates to the three-year film and television program. *I'm in! I'm in!* I kept thinking, as I read my name on the bulletin board of the academy. Now I will finally learn how to tell my stories in image and sound and will receive professional support for it.

Karl, who was done with his studies, was now even farther

away from me geographically. He had moved to Lake Constance, where he had gotten a job in Koblenz. I really liked the area, especially the fact that the winter months there were relatively warm in comparison to other German regions.

But due to the many miles that separated us, we saw each other even less than before. Increasingly, I had the feeling that we each led our own lives and were not necessarily willing to make compromises for each other. I vaguely sensed that the end of our relationship was approaching.

In this state of various emotions I flew to Kenya again. Wanjiru, a fellow student at the DFFB and also a Kenyan, was shooting her graduation film there and had asked for my assistance.

And there was another reason for the trip: Barack and I had arranged to meet again in my native country. Since our brother Abongo's wedding, things had gotten more and more serious between Barack and his girlfriend, Michelle. Now she was his fiancée, and he was eager to introduce her to his Kenyan family. Because I still didn't know Michelle very well, I was really looking forward to the time with her. She exuded a calm and composure that made it very easy to talk to her.

In accordance with Luo tradition, Abongo planned at that time to move the immediate Obama family, meaning my mother, out of our grandfather's compound (Konyango) and to establish our own homestead (Kobama) directly adjacent to it. For this custom, particular rites had to be performed. Among them was the requirement that the oldest members of the Obama family be present—that meant my grandfather's brothers, who still lived in Karachuonyo. We, too, wanted to take part in the ceremony.

Due to complicated flight connections, Barack, Michelle, and I unfortunately did not arrive in Alego until a day after the end of the ritual and found there only a few of the relatives who had come. The new homestead was bare; there were only two hastily erected mud huts, one for my mother and one for her oldest son, Abongo. So I was glad that my grandfather's compound was not many yards away. There, I could—as always since my childhood—spend the night at my grandmother's, this time with Barack and Michelle.

During the few days of our stay in Alego, we shuttled back and forth between the compounds. Since Abongo lived in America, he had become very traditional. In contrast to what I had known of him previously, he now seemed to attach great value to following the Luo ways and customs. And so he also wished for us to spend as much time as possible on the new homestead of the Obama family.

Against the background of the inauguration of the compound, Barack introduced Michelle to the family as his wife-to-be. Everyone welcomed her warmly, and our grandmother insisted on serving only the best food to celebrate her visit.

Michelle's visit upcountry to our ancestral home meant a lot to the family. As I watched her interact comfortably with everyone, eating with her hands—as is customary for our traditional dish of *ugali,* fish, and greens—I was filled with fondness for her. I imagined that many Americans would have found it difficult to fit into our rural routine, which included sleeping in a thatched hut with no running water, electricity, or modern comforts.

The general feeling in the family was that Barack had chosen well. Our grandmother, who could speak only the most rudimentary English, firmly shook Barack's hand in a congratulatory gesture as she pointed at Michelle and happily uttered the words, "Is good! Is very good!" She proceeded to give him a big hug, which he returned, laughing.

From Alego we returned to Nairobi. Through friends I had rented an apartment for us, which must have struck Michelle as very "alternative," because it was completely unfurnished. Barack had already been with me in Kenya and better understood my circumstances. Everything we needed we had to borrow or buy. Another option would have been a hotel, but none of us could have afforded that for four weeks, which was to be the length of our stay.

While Barack and Michelle calmly accepted all this, there was, however, an experience both of them would have gladly done without.

I had sold my old Beetle to Aunt Zeituni when I returned to Germany after my one-year stint teaching at the University of Nairobi. Now she lent me the car so that Barack, Michelle, and I could get around on our own without public transportation. There was only one problem: The car was in need of a lot of maintenance.

One day, when we were driving along the three-lane Uhuru Highway, Barack next to me, Michelle in the backseat, I suddenly found myself forced to stop abruptly and get us all out of the Beetle.

"Get out! Get out!" I shouted, as I flung open the driver's door and jumped out of the car. Then I folded forward the driver's seat so that Michelle could climb out. The two of them just stared at me uncomprehendingly.

"Get out! It's on fire!" I shouted.

With the word "fire," they immediately rushed out of the car. Together we ran to the roadside.

"The car's on fire," I repeated. "I can smell it!" However, no smoke could be seen.

Suddenly, out of nowhere, two mechanics with tools were standing next to us.

"Where's the fire?" one of the two men asked in a friendly tone.

"Under the hood," I said, my heart still pounding.

"We'll fix it."

The two men went to the car, opened the hood, and looked at the engine. In my excitement I had left the key in the ignition.

"What was that?" Barack asked in horror.

"I don't know," I answered.

Barack sat down somewhat apprehensively next to Michelle, who had taken a seat on the curb.

"These things happen," said Michelle, who had long since regained her composure, and put her arm around my brother.

"I have to go back to the car," I said to Barack. "I don't know what the two mechanics are doing there. If we don't pay attention, they might steal car parts. Then we'll really have a problem. Who knows whether they're even mechanics!"

Barack immediately stood up when he saw that I wanted to deal with the car. He was torn. He didn't want me to be with the strangers unaccompanied, but he didn't want to leave Michelle on the roadside either.

"Go ahead. I'll be fine," she said calmly.

The two mechanics who had appeared out of the blue were not thieves; they actually repaired the car. As soon as we were able to start it up again, I dropped off my two companions in front of our rented apartment and then drove to a repair shop. I would not feel at ease until it was checked out again there.

"We shouldn't get into a situation like that again, sis," Barack said to me when I returned. "I'm trying to impress my bride here."

I couldn't help laughing out loud. He was making a dead-serious face, but I could tell by looking at him as well as Michelle that in retrospect they actually found the experience funny.

"Where did those mechanics come from so suddenly?" he asked in amazement.

"No idea. Probably they're unemployed, stand on the side of the road, and hope for people like us."

"There really was something surreal about it. If I tell the story at home, no one will believe me. I've never gotten out of a car that fast." Barack shook his head with a laugh and reached for a pen and his notebook. I wondered whether he might be planning to record this event for his book. Barack, who at Harvard had been elected president of the renowned *Harvard Law Review,* had received an offer from a publisher to write a book about his life. It appeared in 1995 under the title *Dreams from My Father.*

Together with Michelle, my brother and I visited other relatives who lived in Nairobi. And after Michelle had departed—she had to head back earlier—Barack and I went to visit our grandmother again. He wanted to ask her some more questions that had to do with his book. I acted as an interpreter. Afterward, he spent a lot of time sitting over his notes and writing.

When I returned from Kenya, Karl met me at the Frankfurt Airport with a huge bouquet and we drove from there to his place in Konstanz. While we ate and talked, we came around to the subject of my application for an extension of my residence permit, which was due. Every few months I had to reapply for it, and each time I came out of the office with the feeling that I was tolerated only temporarily. It had gone on like that for several years already, and gradually it was beginning to bother me.

"Shouldn't we get married?" I suddenly said. "Then I wouldn't have to keep asking for an extension from the authorities."

His answer came promptly and knocked the wind out of me.

"When I get married, it will only be for love."

For a moment I was speechless. Finally I asked slowly, "And us? What is between us?"

Karl looked at me uncomprehendingly.

"What do you mean?"

I sensed panic gradually and unstoppably welling up in me.

"You say you only want to get married for love—so what is this between us?" I asked, agitated.

"Why are you getting worked up?" Karl still hadn't grasped what I was driving at.

"You only want to get married for love, right? So what is between us isn't love. I came back to Germany because of you. Because of you I am repeatedly humiliated at the immigration office, and you're telling me that you only want to get married for love!" Now I was really angry.

Karl winced. Then he tried to limit the damage he had done.

"I meant that we should plan it first, if we really want to do it. We . . ."

But I was no longer listening. What he had said had sounded so conclusive that I knew: It was over between us.

I wanted to cry, but no tears came. My eyes were so dry that it hurt.

I had been with Karl for six years, and now our relationship was over with a few words! I had, as the song goes, "lost my heart in Heidelberg." On Lake Constance, it broke.

22.

I got an opportunity through Mr. Odengo from the Kenyan embassy in Bonn to work as an interpreter for businesspeople from back home who had been invited to a trade fair in Frankfurt. I had met Mr. Odengo through my mother when she visited me a year after my father's death. Subsequently, I received a trade fair translation job with the Philippine embassy. The work was very well paid, which enabled me in the period that followed to fly to Kenya at least once a year.

One day, I got a phone call in the student residence hall in Bayreuth. "Hello?" Judging by the static on the line, someone was calling me from abroad. For a moment I thought that Aunty Jane was on the phone.

"Hello, am I speaking with Auma Obama?" asked a voice, which could not have belonged to Aunty Jane, however, for it was clearly male.

"Yes. With whom am I speaking, please?"

"Ian Manners from Zenith Promotions. We're a British company and are coming next month to a trade fair in Düsseldorf. We're looking for an interpreter, and you were recommended to us."

He sounded very matter-of-fact, and completely contrary to my habit, I said, "But you know that I'm African, right?"

As I said that, I tried not to sound sarcastic or condescending. I just wanted him to know. In situations like that I often had to think of the Nigerian writer Wole Soyinka. "Telephone Conversation" is my favorite poem on the theme of racism. It's about an African who contacts a landlady on the phone because he is interested in a room she is offering. He tries to prepare her for the fact that she is dealing with a black man. The poem goes:

The price seemed reasonable, location
Indifferent. The landlady swore she lived
Off premises. Nothing remained
But self-confession. "Madam," I warned,
"I hate a wasted journey—I am African."
Silence. Silenced transmission of
Pressurized good-breeding. Voice, when it came,
Lipstick coated, long gold-rolled
Cigarette-holder pipped. Caught I was, foully.
"HOW DARK?" . . . I had not misheard . . .
"ARE YOU LIGHT OR VERY DARK?"

"That doesn't matter to me." The voice of my conversation partner sounded annoyed. "What a question!"

"I'm sorry. I only wanted you to know."

I was unsettled. I had not expected such a vehement reaction, but something more along the lines of "That's no problem!" or an excuse as to why it couldn't work in this case, for they would prefer a native speaker. *I can forget this job,* I thought. Instead, the question came from the other end of the line, "So can you work for us?"

All was not lost, I realized with relief. "Of course," I said.

We discussed all the necessary arrangements and then said good-bye. At the time, I did not yet know that the man with whom I, sitting on the carpeted floor of the hallway in the student residence hall, had spoken on the phone would be my future husband and the father of my daughter.

When Ian entered my life, Karl and I had just broken up. I was dissatisfied with my studies in Bayreuth as well as those in Berlin. With my professor's waning interest in my dissertation, it was progressing only slowly, and the film school had turned out to be too "alternative" for me, making it difficult to find a platform for the more ordinary human stories I wanted to tell. I felt like a swaying ship with no sense of direction, looking for a place to anchor. I needed something solid and stable in my life. Suddenly Ian appeared, a man who seemed confident and grounded, something I had found lacking in Karl.

I plunged into the relationship with Ian, convinced that I had finally found a man who would take care of me. I visited him on several occasions in England, and he also came to Germany. It didn't matter to me that he didn't speak much and seemed to be a rather serious type. I myself talked so much that I didn't really notice that at first. He was happy to let me keep our conversations going. But as time went on, I got tired of always determining the course of the conversation. Though we spent a lot of time with Ian's family, who were wonderful people and welcomed me warmly, he did not seem to socialize much outside of that. I was itching to explore London, which was not too far away from where he lived. However, Ian, though he readily tagged along with me on social outings in Germany, was unfortunately not as enthusiastic back home. "Been there, done that, burned the T-shirt!" was his reply when I suggested a night out in the capital.

Inevitably, I, too, began to be silent more often when we were together. I wanted to see whether he was really so quiet or whether he could make an evening with friends or family interesting without my help. Ian remained taciturn—even when we were with his family. More and more often I would find myself grouped with the women, while the male family members, Ian among them, sat apart and chatted about soccer and politics. Ian's silence began to frustrate me, and I started to doubt whether he was really the right partner for me. I wanted to be with someone who participated more in what was going on around him. But Ian seemed content simply to be there and let me take the lead. It thus became clear to me that what I had mistaken for stability based on his down-to-earth, confident nature was, in fact, more a reflection of his shy, introverted temperament. I was no longer so sure about my relationship with Ian. And after a while, we went our separate ways. I returned to Germany and resigned myself to never seeing him again. The relationship had lasted just under a year.

When Barack and Michelle got married in Chicago in 1992, I was still with Ian, however. I was really looking forward to the wedding, not least of all because I had been chosen as one of the bridesmaids. Michelle sent me an elegant, black dress, with just enough time for me to lose a few more pounds before the occasion. I was astonished that black was worn at an American wedding.

In Chicago, I met Michelle's family and was warmly received by them. She had many relatives, but the immediate family consisted only of her brother, Craig, and her mother. Her father had died the previous year. From our side, Barack's mother, Ann, and his sister Maya had come, as well as Barack and Maya's grandmother, whom the grandchildren fondly called "Toot." Abongo also participated in the ceremony. Unfortunately, Ian had not been able to join me, for he had to work. Barack's old school friends from Hawaii came, too, and I had great fun asking them questions about my brother and hearing what he'd been like as a child.

The ceremony took place in late summer in magnificent weather. The sun was high in a cloudless sky and offered the perfect backdrop for a storybook wedding. And that's really what it was. I still remember how impressed I was that we were driven around in a limousine. Michelle looked heavenly in her long, white wedding gown. And the sight of Barack in a classically tailored tux, which accentuated his slender figure and his good looks, filled me with pride. *If only our father had been able to witness this day*—that sad thought went fleetingly through my head several times, like a dark cloud, which I quickly drove away.

We bridesmaids and groomsmen were nothing to sneeze at, either, as we accompanied the couple into the church and then stood near the altar. A great party ended the big day.

After the celebration, I stayed with my brother and his new wife for a few more days. Their honeymoon would only begin several days after the wedding. At the time, the two of them were living in a small apartment attached to Michelle's parents' house. I was glad to spend a few days alone with Barack and Michelle again, without relatives and friends, for I got to see my brother and his wife so rarely.

When I returned from America, I spent most of my time in Berlin. I had completed my required courses in Bayreuth and now only had to finish my dissertation before taking my final exams. In Berlin, I experienced firsthand the far-reaching effects of the fall of the Wall, including its negative ramifications, such as the racist attacks that ensued in the German towns of Hoyerswerda, Rostock, Mölln, and Solingen.

One day a letter arrived from Ben, one of my mother's younger sons. He wrote that he was barely able to feed himself in Nairobi, found no work, and could no longer fend for himself. He sounded desperate.

Ben was my mother's fourth child, one of two sons born after she had separated from my father; the other was named Samson. I had gotten to know these two brothers better when, while studying at Kenyatta University, I spent more time at Aunty Jane's house, where Ben lived and Samson was a frequent visitor.

Ben now asked me whether he could come and stay with me in Germany. After careful consideration—I wasn't sure whether Germany, especially in winter, was really the right place for him—I said yes and sent him a plane ticket.

The stay was, in fact, largely ruined for him by the winter cold. On top of that, I was afraid of the racist attacks the media frequently reported. He felt the same way and practically never left my home. I lived in a small apartment near the Spree River at the time, and he felt really isolated, because I often had to leave him alone to go to the film school or the library.

When we parted, I hoped that he was at least flying back in a somewhat better frame of mind and would now appreciate warm Kenya more. For me, his visit had also been an attempt to do my duty as a modern "chosen one," so to speak, and help my little brother. But the feeling remained that there wasn't much I could have done for him.

My mother visited me a year later in Berlin, also in winter. But this time I was the one who needed emotional support. I had just gone through a very difficult phase. Although I had some friends in Berlin by then and had joined a group of black women who met regularly, I was afflicted by a profound sense of loneliness that I couldn't talk about with my new friends. This difficulty communicating about personal problems transported me back to the time at Kenya High School, when I had also usually kept them to myself. As I had been then, now, too, I was outwardly friendly, lively, and fun. As was the case back then, people probably couldn't tell now by looking at me how much forlornness and sadness I was carrying around with me.

I sank deeper and deeper into a gloomy state, and often my participation in activities was only mechanical. When I began to fear that I might end up hospitalized for depression, I asked my mother to visit me in Berlin and stay for a while.

It was a cold and snowy winter, so we didn't go out much and often sat at home. Most of the time, I worked on my dissertation while my mother busied herself with domestic activities. I was happy to have her around. But her presence ultimately could not dispel my sense of dissatisfaction with my overall situation.

As she had in Heidelberg, my mother worried about the fact that I didn't have a boyfriend—Ian and I had broken up. I explained to her that I didn't even want a boyfriend. Then she began to get worked up about Karl, and accused him of robbing me of my time and deceiving me for six years. But I didn't accept that.

"*We* broke up," I said emphatically. "It always takes two."

The argument did not convince her.

"I had asked him when he was with you in Kenya what plans he had with you," she said. "But he couldn't give me an answer to that. Now I know why. He didn't have any at all."

I let her talk. There was no sense in arguing with her. After all, I was burdened by all that myself. Deep inside, I knew that I had not yet recovered from the breakup. We had been together for so long and had done so much together; I had imagined all sorts of things for the future, only to realize in the end that he didn't love me as much as I loved him. He had definitely loved me at the time, just not enough to marry me after being together for six years. That experience had taken the wind out of my sails and left me drifting aimlessly in a sea called Germany. My brief relationship with Ian had been an attempt for me to cast anchor on more solid ground. But it hadn't worked.

Eventually, I told my mother about Ian and our relationship. I hadn't actually wanted to do so at all, because I did not regard the episode with him as worth mentioning.

"Why did you leave him?" she asked me, when I had finished.

My answer confused her.

"Boredom?" she repeated. "But that's no reason, especially since he was apparently good to you."

What could I say to that? My mother and I lived in two different worlds. She had grown up in a traditional Luo setting, in which a woman demands nothing of her husband but to feed the family and help raise the children. The husband is not necessarily expected to be a fun life companion for the wife.

"You expect too much of a man," my mother now said emphatically.

When I thought back on my previous year, I wondered whether she might be right.

As if a higher power had answered her prayers, just a few days later I received a call from my brother Abongo in the United States. He explained to me that he was planning to import a car to Kenya, but wanted to buy it in England, because people drove on the left side of the road there, too. He wanted to know whether I had any contacts there. I immediately thought of Ian, and a bit later I spoke to him and got his permission to give my brother his telephone number.

It felt strange to talk with him again after all those months. And I was surprised to realize that I secretly missed him. He really was a "good" man, as my mother had assumed; I actually had nothing to reproach him for. He wasn't responsible for my restlessness.

But he faded into the background again—until February 14, 1995, when I received a large, stiff envelope in the mail. It was obviously a card. There was no return address on the envelope. My mother, who was still staying with me, could hardly wait to find out its contents.

"Go ahead, open it!" she encouraged me impatiently. "Who's the secret admirer you've told me nothing about?"

I think her greatest fear was that I, in my stubbornness, with which she was all too familiar, would refuse to marry once and for all and she would ultimately get no grandchild from me. For her, a woman had to be with a man, had to be married. Anything else seemed unnatural to her.

I wanted to take my time opening the card, but that did not suit my mother at all.

"Come on, Auma! Let's see who it's from."

I surrendered, opened the envelope, and took out what was

indeed a Valentine's Day card. To my surprise, Ian had sent it to me. *You will always be my valentine,* he had written on it in his neat handwriting, a few words that spoke volumes. I was confused. What was I supposed to do with that?

My mother had read along with me, of course.

"Wonderful, wonderful!" she cried, clapping her hands joyfully. "The good man loves you!"

Shaking my head, I looked at her. Was she crazy?

"How do you know? It's only a card."

"No, he's still thinking about you! Just look at the size of the card."

I had to admit that it was huge, almost tastelessly huge. Ian wanted to tell me something in no uncertain terms.

"Give him another chance, Auma. You have nothing to lose."

When I heard my mother talking like that, I suddenly thought: *She's actually right. What do I have to lose?* I was alone and had the sensation that I was drifting. I was not sure what I felt for Ian, but it was clearly not anything negative. So why not give it another shot with him? Something about me really seemed to appeal to him. If the size of the card corresponded to his love, I couldn't really go wrong.

I reached for the telephone. For a start, I could at least thank him for the beautiful big Valentine's Day card, and then we would see.

ENGLAND and KENYA

23.

I SEEMED DESTINED to shuttle back and forth. Ian and I had gotten back together, and so I resumed my trips between Germany and England. But because our relationship had now strengthened, I had decided to move in with him.

"You can make films here, too," Ian assured me confidently. "I'll help you with it."

The way he said this, it sounded like the simplest thing in the world. Might I have found in him exactly the person I needed, who would help me realize my dream of telling stories in images? I could no longer really imagine an academic career, neither in Germany nor in Kenya.

"I've even put some money aside," he said. "We can put that into your film."

What more did I want? *My mother had been right after all,* I thought. Here was someone who not only loved me but also had an interest in my career. *And what about the boredom?* I nonetheless heard her ask in my mind. Surely, only my restless nature was to blame for that. As soon as I settled down in England, that would be over. At that time, it was precisely Ian's calm temperament that I needed.

But moving to England was not as smooth a transition as I had imagined it would be. By then, Kenyans were no longer exempt from the requirement of a British visa, as they had been in the past when being part of the Commonwealth was enough. Now I had to fill out numerous forms and wait for hours at the British consulate in Düsseldorf to undergo a grueling interview about my plans in England. A visa was by no means guaranteed.

To expedite the bureaucratic procedure to some extent, I applied immediately for a fiancée visa, for Ian had asked me to marry him on one of my visits to England. I had said yes.

On that occasion, we were sitting in a small French restaurant in a village near London. Ian had picked me up from the airport the day before, and despite the rainy weather I was glad to be back in England—with him.

"Close your eyes," he said, after we had ordered and the waiter had left.

"Why?" I asked with curiosity. To fulfill a request without asking about the reason was simply not in my nature.

"Just do it!" Ian said in mock exasperation. At the same time, there was a smile in his voice. "Just this once," he added softly.

Reluctantly and curiously, I obeyed. Then I felt him gently taking my hand and putting a small box in it. I suspected what this act meant, but I kept my eyes closed. I wanted to give myself time to digest the significance of this moment.

"Don't you want to open your eyes?" I heard Ian asking. I opened them and looked at him, still holding the box in my hand. He was looking at me so lovingly that I kissed him on the mouth.

"Is that a yes?"

I still hadn't said anything. "I have to think about it," I finally answered with a wink. "A yes would mean that I was defecting to the enemy."

Ian gave me such a confused look that I had to laugh out loud. "You must have forgotten history," I added. "England. Kenya. The colonial era!"

Finally, he understood. He burst out laughing and raised his arm with a balled fist. Lowering it again, he shouted: "YES!"

"That's exactly what I mean," I said, laughing.

"Yes! Yes! Yes!" Ian continued, and made the same triumphant gesture with each *yes.* Completely unromantic, but fitting. When I met him, I had claimed smugly that I could never imagine living in England, let alone marrying an Englishman, because England had done so much damage to my fellow Kenyans through colonialism.

The waiter, who was approaching with our drinks, stopped uncertainly a few paces away. "Is everything all right, sir and madam?" he asked worriedly.

"Everything's great!" Ian replied happily and looked over at me with raised eyebrows. "Right?"

I nodded, grinning. "Everything's perfect."

"Will there be champagne now or not?"

"Yes!"

"Yes! Yes! Yes!" Ian exclaimed a second time, before turning to the waiter. "You heard it, sir. Champagne! We're getting married!" With these words, he leaned over to me, took the box from my hand, opened it, pulled out a ring, and put it carefully on my finger.

"And you thought you could escape the British," he whispered in my ear, kissing me on the neck.

Ian and I got married in August 1996. It was a wonderful, very happy day. Not only was the weather gorgeous, but also my closest family members and many friends came from Kenya, Germany, and the United States. Even Toot, Barack's maternal grandmother, made the long journey from Hawaii to England. We only missed Ann, Barack's mother, who had died the previous year of cancer.

I had not managed to finish my graduation film at the DFFB before the wedding. The editing still needed to be done, for which I had to travel to Berlin several times. I was able to stay with Elke, who after sixteen years in America had moved to Potsdam, near Berlin, with Robert, who was now her husband, and their two children, Jan and Lena.

During one of those stays, I felt tired all the time and wanted to do nothing but sleep. When I lost my appetite, too, and told Elke that certain smells nauseated me, she said with a knowing expression, "I think you're pregnant!"

Taken aback, I stared at her. "You really think so?"

I must have sounded pretty naïve. And I *was,* in fact, naïve.

"We can find out quickly. Take a pregnancy test."

Ian and I had spoken about children only once, and that was when I had worked for him and we were not yet a couple. He had explained at the time, full of conviction, that he didn't want any more children, because he already had a daughter from a previous marriage. In response, I had asked him, "And what if you have a girlfriend who absolutely wants to get pregnant?"

"Then she's out of luck," he answered with a laugh.

Just as convinced of my words as he was of his—only very seriously—I had replied, "If I were that woman, I wouldn't go out with you! I definitely want to have children one day."

After that, we had never talked about the topic again. And

now, a few years later, we were married. And I might be pregnant. How would Ian react if it were true?

"You're pregnant! You're pregnant! Hooray!"

Elke hopped from one leg to the other. I had come out of the bathroom with the colored test strip, after I had let out a telltale cry. Suddenly, everything seemed like a dream to me. I tried to imagine that a little person was growing inside me, but the thought was completely strange to me. Nor could I connect my nausea with the emerging life inside me, no matter how hard I tried.

"It's really true! You're pregnant! I'm happy for you, Auma!"

Elke hugged me tight; her excitement was palpable. When she was pregnant with Jan and Lena, she could imagine nothing more wonderful. When I had visited her in Carbondale for the first time, she had walked around the room with a pillow under her overalls for fun and played mother-to-be.

And now I was pregnant, and she was again seized with euphoria. Her high spirits were downright contagious.

"We're having a baby," I said to her, smiling, but my voice wavered a little. "And you'll be an aunt. I'm happy about that."

The rest of the afternoon, we sat together and imagined my future.

"It will be a girl!" I said confidently.

"You can't know that." Elke laughed.

"Yes, it will be a girl."

"And why are you so sure?"

"I just know. I want a girl, and I know that this child will be a girl."

Elke gave up trying to convince me that the opposite was possible, but in my head the discussion went on. I really wanted a girl. I could not imagine having a boy. A girl simply suited my temperament much better.

I could hardly wait to tell Ian the joyful news. During our phone calls, I barely managed to keep it to myself. I had decided to surprise him with it on my return home, and my plan succeeded. I bought a card, on the front of which was a picture of tiny baby hands, and gave it to him when I was back in England and we were sitting together at dinner. Ian carefully opened the card and discovered on one side the ultrasound image of a baby and on the other a few corny words like "Hello, Daddy!"

With a broad smile, he looked at me. And before he could say anything, I declared, "It will be a girl."

"Of course!" he answered with a laugh. "Real men have girls."

I was overjoyed. And that night, as I fell asleep with my husband's arms around me, I knew that our little girl was in good hands and would be received with great love into our world.

My graduation film was finally finished and could be submitted for approval. It was December 1996. I was in Berlin again for a few weeks, and each evening when we spoke on the phone, Ian asked impatiently when I would be returning to England. "After the film's first screening," I said each time.

My film was titled *All That Glitters Is Not Gold* and was about an African woman living in rural Germany as the wife of a wealthy but rather cold German husband. She is extremely lonely. One day, she loses her seven-year-old daughter under unusual circumstances.

When I showed my film to faculty and students, it was very

quiet in the hall and it was impossible to tell how it went down with the audience.

After the lights came back on, it took a while before the silence was broken. Finally, a student raised her hand and said, "The whole thing is unrealistic! In real life something like that would never happen."

With that she set something in motion that resembled a tsunami. Suddenly, I was subjected to a multitude of questions and criticisms. I tried to respond to the many attacks, some of which did not make sense to me. I felt as if I could not really defend myself at all. My film seemed to have offended people, but what exactly it was that was offensive no one could explain clearly to me. Even when I later asked Elke and some other friends, whom I had invited to the screening, what on earth I had done wrong, they were not able to give me a clear answer. I could only suspect that from the point of view of the Germans, the film made the African woman too much a victim and so triggered among the viewers an unpleasant sense of complicity.

Feeling rather bruised, I left the hall. Shortly before leaving the building, I went to the bathroom. There I discovered that I was bleeding. *My baby!* I thought in horror. I was in my third month, a critical time for miscarriages. In a panic, I rushed out of the bathroom to look for Elke. Fortunately, she had not gone home, but was absorbed in a conversation with some other people. I took her aside and told her what had just happened to me.

"We're going to the hospital immediately!" she said resolutely. "Don't get worked up and don't move more than necessary." With these words, she took me by the elbow and led me toward the exit. "Sit down here on the stairs. I'll get my car."

In the hospital, I was informed that I might, in fact, have a miscarriage. But I was reassured, told to just lie still on my back and everything would be all right.

I expected a few days of prescribed bed rest, but the doctor who examined me the next day said I would have to remain lying down until the birth. Almost seven months!

From day to day, I grew more distressed, especially as I could not pry a clear explanation for my condition out of him. A few days before Christmas, Ian, who had heard the despair in my voice, made a decision. "I'm coming to get you," he said. I did not feel comfortable with the idea—what would the doctors say about it?—but I simply could no longer bear to stay in the hospital and agreed to his plan.

"We can't be held responsible if you take your wife with you," the doctor treating me told Ian, when he showed up the next day in the hospital. "Anything can happen."

"I understand," he replied, and asked for the necessary documents. "We'll deal with this in England."

The doctor in the British hospital, where I went immediately on arrival, sent me back home after the examination.

"If you have any pain, take these pills here. Otherwise, you can do everything without any problems."

"But in Germany I was told . . ."

"Everything is fine with you. There's no reason to lie in bed all day."

Was this a classic case of "different countries, different norms," or was I the victim of an error in judgment? In Germany, the doctors had insisted on total bed rest; in England, however, I was advised to keep a stiff upper lip and carry on with things as usual. And that's what I did!

On the morning of May 3, 1997, I gave birth to a perfectly healthy daughter—I had been right. I took her in my arms and at the sight of her little face felt a love such as I had never previously experienced. I was insanely happy—and at the same time panic-stricken. She was so little and seemed so fragile. I was afraid of pressing her too tightly, not holding her securely enough, being incapable of looking after her. I was beset by all the fears that most women probably have at the birth of their first child. Suddenly, I was responsible for the survival of this little being who was completely dependent on me. There's no doubt that happiness and fear are closely related.

Ian sat at my bedside. He had missed the actual birth. When the contractions had begun the previous evening and he drove me to the hospital, it had been assumed that the delivery would take substantially longer than the two hours my daughter needed the next morning to come into the world. For that reason, Ian had been told on the telephone that he did not have to hurry. So by the time he had woven his way through the rush-hour traffic, his daughter was already there.

"It can't be true!" he exclaimed as he rushed into the room. I lay exhausted on the bed. Aunty Jane, who was visiting us at the time, entered the room behind him.

"Look, over there." With my head I gestured to the bassinet in which our little girl was sleeping peacefully in a white romper. "There's our daughter." I was overjoyed. It sounded so good. Our daughter. My daughter. I had a daughter.

"Can I pick her up?" Ian asked hesitantly.

"Of course!" said Aunty Jane, beating me to it. She, too, was smiling from ear to ear. "And hurry, or else I'll take her from you. I want to hold my granddaughter in my arms." In place of her older sister, my mother, Aunty Jane was at that moment the grandmother.

Then came the obligatory photos: the baby with the father, then with the exhausted but elated mother, finally another picture with Aunty Jane, and, of course, a shot of the leading lady lying in her bassinet. We had named her Akinyi, which means "morning child" in Luo. I looked through the wide window of the room. The sun shone brightly. It was a magnificent, almost cloudless day. Here in the room, my husband and my aunt admired our child, and outside a wonderful early summer day was dawning.

In my first days as a mother, my everyday life revolved exclusively around our daughter. I had eyes almost only for her. For the fear that had seized me in the hospital and the doubts about whether I would manage to take care of her were still alive. It became really difficult when Aunty Jane left and I was alone with the little one during the day. Ian had to work, and in the neighborhood—we had just moved to Bracknell, a town in Berkshire—I still didn't know anyone. My one attempt to get closer to my neighbors had failed miserably.

Shortly after we had moved into our house, I invited our immediate neighbors—to the right and left and across from us—for tea one afternoon. And they all came. We sat in our small living room, drank tea, and made small talk, as I imagined it was done in England. And when they said their friendly goodbyes, I thought the afternoon had been a success, especially as they said things like "You should definitely stop by our place, too." Then I waited, but in vain. Not a single return invitation came from our neighbors.

"I find that really impolite," I said, disappointed. We were sitting in the kitchen, Ian was making dinner, and I was nursing the baby. "In Kenya, you always return an invitation after visiting someone. Anything else is impolite."

Ian just shrugged.

"Don't you think so?" I was a bit irritated by his silence.

"It's somewhat different here," he began, as he peeled the last of the potatoes. As he said this, he turned to me, because he had heard the sadness in my voice. It was not the first time we had spoken about the—in my eyes—somewhat strange social behavior of British people. But now that I was alone all day with the child, I suffered increasingly from their distance. I longed for friends and companionship.

"Here people don't deal with each other as openly and freely," Ian explained.

"Then why did they come to our house at all?" I asked, annoyed. "I thought they had a genuine interest in getting to know us."

"Unfortunately, it was probably only curiosity," Ian replied, as he put the potatoes on the stove. There would be fish and a salad as well. "But it might also be that they don't invite us because they don't want to disturb us. We Brits are somewhat strange in that regard."

It surprised me that our neighbors' behavior seemed not to bother him.

After a while, my loneliness became mixed with resentment toward Ian. I didn't understand why he had not taken time off after the birth of our daughter. Almost immediately after I returned home from the hospital, he had gone back to work. It occurred to me that the loner who was now my husband had told me once at the very beginning of our acquaintance that he could easily imagine living on a secluded farm somewhere in Scotland. There, he wouldn't need more than a sheepdog.

"Why don't you join a mother and toddler group in our area? There you'll definitely meet other mothers." With these words, Ian put the fish in the oven.

"What is a mother and toddler group?" My question sounded only moderately interested. I actually wanted to do something with him, not with mothers I didn't know.

"It's a group of mothers with babies or newborns. They meet regularly and do various things together. There, you'd have the chance to get to know people."

But everything was not as simple as Ian imagined—at least not for me. Although I tried out several mother and toddler groups, I did not really feel comfortable at any of them. The fact that I had little desire to talk only about diapers and burping techniques didn't make it any easier. Because many British women—unlike in Germany—have their children rather early, I frequently met very young mothers in the groups. I myself was already thirty-seven. On top of that, almost all of them were housewives, had entirely different interests than I did, were—with the exception of one mother—white, and came from the conservative British middle class.

I felt out of place and missed my friends in Germany, missed the vibrant life in Berlin. Even Bayreuth seemed to me lively and exciting from afar.

"Can't you take a few weeks off?" I asked Ian. "Then we could invite the neighbors over again."

"I can't do that."

"Why not? You've just become a father."

"I have to earn money, Auma!" Ian replied adamantly.

His words had reduced me to silence. I could not compete with the need to make money. Since my move to England, I had not had a chance to contribute to our income, which was due primarily to the pregnancy and my ensuing situation as a young mother. Ian did all the shopping. I had my pride, and it was hard for me to ask him for money. I had never before had to rely financially on someone. First, I had my scholarships; later, my well-paid trade fair jobs as an interpreter and my fees as a freelance journalist. Now Ian was the sole earner, and I was completely dependent on him.

When Akinyi was five months old, we took her with us on a trip to visit my brother in Chicago. I wanted Barack to meet his niece—and vice versa. It was October. A cold autumn wind swept through the streets, though the sun was still high in an almost cloudless sky. I was surprised at the cold. My brother said it came from Lake Michigan, directly from Canada.

"In Canada, it's already much colder than here," he added.

"I'm glad you don't live in Canada," I replied with a laugh.

Over a year had passed since I had last seen my brother. In the meantime, he was living with his wife, Michelle, in their own apartment, and the two of them seemed to have a happy marriage. They were delighted to see their little niece, especially Michelle, who didn't have any children yet. Maya, too, came to visit and greeted Akinyi with a gift that was supposed to keep all evil spirits away from her.

We stayed only a week in the United States. Mich, as everyone called Michelle, and Barack had to work during the day—he as a civil rights lawyer, she as vice president for community and external affairs at the University of Chicago. In the evening, we cooked together and sat at the table for a long time after the meal and talked. At one point, Michelle's brother, Craig, who lived in Chicago, too, came for a visit with his wife and two young children.

The time with Barack was short, but it did me good. It felt great to be back in the family circle after the loneliness in Bracknell, and I enjoyed the attention bestowed on me, the young mother. I experienced those days almost as a sort of compensation for the fact that I had not been treated like a *manyur* up to that point. That is what the Luo call a woman who has just given birth to a child. In our tradition, a *manyur* is not supposed to do any work or is permitted to do only very light tasks in the first six weeks after her delivery. Her main job consists of nursing the infant. She is spoiled by her mother and the rest of the women of the family; she gets only the best food to eat and as much rest and relaxation as she needs before she fully assumes the role of mother and guardian of her child.

Akinyi was eleven months old when Ian and I took her with us to Kenya to introduce her to my family there. Ian, who had worked hard all year, wanted to go to the coast to relax. A visit to Nairobi did not much appeal to him, because he did not particularly like the city. But I wanted to go to the city in which I had grown up and in which all of my friends and most of my relatives lived. So we decided that I would fly there alone with the little one and then he would follow. Afterward, we planned to take the train together to Mombasa, where we had rented a vacation apartment. My mother would accompany us. That way she would not only get to spend time with her first granddaughter, but also lighten my load a bit.

I was disappointed that Ian did not want to spend more than

a few days in Nairobi. I myself never lasted long on the hot coast—nor was I keen on possibly being treated there like a woman who had managed to snap up a *muzungu,* a white man. Although I was not aware of it at the time, I now think that this was the beginning of the end of our marriage. I had simply not managed to convey to my husband how much the people who loved me and wanted to be with me meant to me and what I so intensely missed in England: friendships.

The British and their culture remained foreign to me. I often spoke on the telephone with my friends, who all thought that I lived near London and did not understand why I was so lonely.

"But there's so much to do in that city, even more than in Berlin," Elke said during one of our phone calls.

I explained to her that we lived quite a ways outside of the city and Ian preferred anyhow to keep his distance from it.

"Then invite people over. You have a garden, and I assume that British people like to barbecue, right?"

"I'd like to, but Ian works all the time. And when he's at home, he wants to rest."

"But he can't be in the office every weekend!"

"Almost every."

Most of the conversations with my other friends, who were unfortunately all too far away to offer me more than words of comfort through the telephone, went similarly. And soon the high telephone bills would become another contentious issue between Ian and me.

Our shared social life was limited mostly to going to a pub together once a week to eat curry. Curry is a popular dish and an integral part of British people's Friday night out. On those evenings, you usually meet with friends, eat together, and drink beer. For Ian, too, those occasions were an established institution.

As I had experienced at other social gatherings, here, too, the women sat separately from the men, who mainly stood at the bar and talked about politics, but above all about sports. Then, after a few (or too many) glasses of beer, it was time for the—to my mind—often-tasteless jokes. The women conversed about housework and children. I had never witnessed such a separation of the sexes in Germany. Nonetheless, I did make a few nice acquaintances, though the contact remained limited mostly to the meetings at the pub.

In the meantime, our daughter had begun to walk, and I had learned the art of being a mother and no longer felt overwhelmed and daunted by my new responsibilities. And because I loved Ian, I wanted our marriage to work. To overcome my difficulties adjusting and my loneliness, I decided to delve into the world of work in order to have a meaningful occupation and meet people.

Bracknell was not the right place to teach German or get a job in film. That would have been London, but I could go there only rarely, because I needed to be close to home for Akinyi. On top of that, I had not been involved in film circles for a while and first would have had to develop a network of relationships. So I had to look for other prospects.

"I'm sorry, but you are overqualified," I was told again and again, until I finally got a job as a personal assistant to a purchasing manager at Boehringer Ingelheim, a German pharmaceutical company. The company had a British branch in Bracknell.

To this day, I am grateful to Gayle Reis for offering me the opportunity to do administrative work for her and thereby get out of the house. On the whole, the job was undemanding and monotonous. But Gayle, an older, maternal woman, was a wonderful boss and never hemmed me in. We also got along very well. I could on occasion even talk to her about my loneliness. She must have suspected that Ian and I were slowly drifting apart.

I did not stay long at Boehringer Ingelheim because my contract expired after eight months. I left the company with a heavy heart. At that time, Akinyi was going to preschool, which I paid for from my salary. It was very expensive, which was due to the fact that in England those institutions are privately run. Now I understood why so many British mothers stayed home. They probably didn't see why they should give up all their earnings for preschool.

I applied at the University of Reading, which is about half an hour away from Bracknell. There, I was hired as a part-time lecturer. A few hours a week I now taught German literature and grammar to undergraduates. But the job was not very fulfilling.

Meanwhile, the relationship between Ian and me was worsening. We barely had anything in common anymore; our conversations revolved only around our daughter, her well-being, her activities.

"Just do something," Ian often said when I complained that I found no satisfying occupation in our town.

However, I didn't want to do just anything. He had once wanted to help me make films in England, but there was no longer any mention of that. And I was too proud to remind him of his promise. In a way, I was not only angry with Ian, but also with myself. I was, in a sense, trapped. *Why has this happened to me?* I thought reproachfully. *I should have known better.*

Eventually, I resigned myself to my role as mother and housewife. Often, after I had brought the little one to preschool, I lay down in bed again and did not get up until it was time to pick her up. In retrospect, I can say that in those days I was functioning more than I was living.

"Auma, is that you?" The ringing of the telephone had roused me from the half-sleep into which I had sunk that morning as I so often did.

"Yes, who is it?" I asked drowsily.

"Tsitsi."

"Tsitsi?" Suddenly I was awake and sat up in bed. "Tsitsi? How's it going? What's up?"

"I searched for your number for a long time," she replied.

Tsitsi was from Zimbabwe and had, like me, studied at the film academy. I was happy to hear a friendly voice from the past. We talked about what had happened since we had last seen each other. After a few sentences, she knew that something was wrong with me.

"What's going on, Auma? You sound so different," Tsitsi asked worriedly.

"I'm doing fine." I tried to sound cheerful. "Really!"

"I don't believe you. I can hear that you're faking."

Her words cracked a dam. Her familiar voice, which awakened memories of all that I had once been, and the thought of what had become of me, brought tears to my eyes. Silently, I let them flow.

"Auma, what's going on? Talk to me."

"There's not much to say. I'm here, have the sweetest daughter in the world, and have a husband who loves me and works hard. What more can you ask for?" With almost every word my voice broke.

"What more can you ask for?" Tsitsi repeated in her dry way. I began to cry again.

"Much more. Much, much more," I said softly.

For a few seconds, she just let me cry. Then she said, "I have something for you. That's why I'm calling."

Tsitsi explained to me that in her native Zimbabwe an event called the African Screenwriters Workshop was being planned. The organizers were looking for young, talented filmmakers who wanted to write screenplays. Of course, prospective participants would not be accepted automatically, but had to apply for one of the few places.

"You definitely have to give it a shot. I know how well you write stories," she said enthusiastically, after she had finished explaining.

"I don't even remember how. It's been so long. I don't know if I can still do it." Fear welled up in me; I had grown so insecure that I had no more confidence in myself.

"Auma, you have so much talent. What happened to the energetic woman I met in Berlin?" Tsitsi said many more things about me. She brought back to my mind a person who had become a stranger to me.

Finally, I asked her what I had to do for this project. Her relief was palpable even through the phone. She would not have hung up without a yes; in retrospect, I was certain of that.

"Well, you don't have much time and here's what you have to do. . . ."

She gave me all the necessary information and let me know that I had to send the organizers a screenplay as soon as possible.

"And Auma!" she said at the end of the call. "You don't need to be afraid. Really. You just have to write. And you can do that. I'm sure that you'll get in."

Tsitsi's phone call was my salvation. After I had hung up, I suddenly felt less alone and lost. I realized that I was excited about the possibility of being admitted to the screenwriting workshop.

I called Ian and told him what I had been offered.

"And who's going to pay for it?" he asked.

"The organizers cover everything. The whole thing lasts ten days."

Ian hesitated briefly, and then he said, "Maybe you'll actually get in."

It was not only a chance for me that presented itself here, but perhaps also for our marriage.

The trip to Zimbabwe was like a resurrection; I recognized that I was heading toward a better place and a better stage in my life. The workshop was exactly what I needed. I had applied with a screenplay that revolved around my parents' youth. It depicted how they had grown up under British colonialism and how, at the time when Kenya attained independence, both of them had abandoned themselves to their love of ballroom dancing. The participants from all different African countries as well as the instructors were enthusiastic about my story.

In this friendly atmosphere, I could open up and let my old self come out. It was like coming back to life. Surrounded by people who believed in me even though they hardly knew me, I recovered my energy, my ambition, and my enthusiasm for life.

24.

When I had boarded the plane to Harare, Zimbabwe's capital, at Gatwick Airport on a mild spring evening in 1999, I did not yet suspect that the impending trip not only would save me from slipping into deep despair but that I would also meet the love of my life on the way back.

On my return flight to London, Marvin was on the plane. He had boarded late and only caught my eye when he moved up two rows, having apparently sat in the wrong seat. Because the plane was pretty empty, I, too, had previously changed my seat. I had barely seen the stranger's face, only his profile, which was also concealed by a small leather cap.

Because I had gotten into the habit of reading during takeoff, I was soon absorbed in a book—or at least I thought I was, for my eyes repeatedly moved away from the pages and wandered over to the stranger who had in the meantime taken off his cap so that I could see his clean-shaven head.

Back then I did not yet fly as much as I do now, and I liked to strike up conversations with other passengers. Never before, however, had a fellow passenger attracted my attention as much as this man. In vain, I tried to focus on my book. I noticed how nervous I was. I simply could not sit still, so I got up and went to the bathroom. There I stood in the ridiculously small space and looked into the mirror. "What's the matter with you?" I admonished my reflection. "You don't even know the man!" I slapped my cheeks, washed my face with cold water, and tried to come to my senses. But nothing helped.

When I had returned to my seat, I was again powerfully drawn to him, with a downright palpable magnetic energy, which was stronger than I was. Again I fled to the bathroom and talked to myself. "You haven't even seen his face!" I reproached myself. I simply could not figure myself out. "Are you interested in the back of a stranger's bald head?" Shaking my head, I left the bathroom and returned again to my seat. But the desire to get to know this man did not abate.

He was sitting by the window, alone in a row of three seats. After my initial change of seats, I, too, had claimed a row of three seats for myself, so that I would be able to spend the night on the plane lying down.

Suddenly, it occurred to me that the man was sitting in the exact same row I myself had abandoned to look for a better one. If I had remained in the seat designated on my boarding pass, I would now be sitting next to him!

That must be fate, I thought, although I am not at all superstitious—and then the solution came to me. I would simply go back to my old seat! Now I had a good reason to sit down next to him. My heart raced, and I felt my palms become damp. *You can't do this!* said an inner voice. But like a remote-controlled being, I hung from an invisible wire; I resembled a will-less marionette. For the third time I proceeded to the cramped, now-familiar bathroom. From the sympathetic looks of some fellow passengers, I could tell that they suspected some sort of gastrointestinal problem behind my repeated urge to visit this place. They were not entirely wrong. For, out of sheer nervousness, I now felt ill.

"Now go over there and ask for your seat back. He can't say no," I said, emboldening myself in front of the mirror. "It's your seat, after all, right?" I looked myself sternly in the eyes. *Oh God, I can't let him notice how flustered I am.*

Someone tried to open the bathroom door. That meant that at least one passenger was waiting outside. This time I had stayed a little too long in the tiny room. In my nervous excitement, I would have preferred never to come out again. But I had no choice; I had to free up the room. Slowly, I walked back to my seat. No more restless trips to the bathroom, I decided. I would simply yield to the magnetic power of attraction. I promptly took from the seat pocket in front of me the small bottle of wine that had been served with the meal and that I had saved to calm my nerves and walked down the corridor toward the front.

"Um . . . I . . . This here is my seat." I pointed to the aisle seat. "I . . . uh, changed my seat, but . . . ," I stammered, "I'm bored back there . . . all alone. Can I have it back?" I quickly added the last words before my courage threatened to abandon me.

The man at first gave me a puzzled look. Then he smiled.

"Of course." He had a deep voice and an American accent.

I sat down and put the small wine bottle in the seat pocket in front of me. The seat between us remained empty. I did not dare to look at the man.

It was he who finally turned to me with a friendly, polite smile. A handsome, strong face, I thought. His expression revealed that he was open to small talk. I had, after all, given boredom as the reason for my seat change.

"You're flying to England?"

If I hadn't been so nervous, I would have answered cheekily, "No, to China!" But all I managed was to ask politely where he was heading.

He told me that he was on the way home. He lived in Auckland, California, about half an hour away from San Francisco. Because our conversation became more intense from minute to minute, I could finally get a good look at his face. I liked it. His shaved head formed an interesting contrast to his gentle and masculine features, the narrow eyes and the full mouth under a neatly trimmed mustache. His prominent forehead, strong cheekbones, and large nose stood out against the gentleness that emanated from his eyes and mouth. He radiated an inner peace, which made him even more attractive.

He was a businessman in the United States, as I now learned, and traded in arts and crafts from southern Africa. I told him enthusiastically about my week in Harare, about my family, about Ian and my daughter. I talked almost nonstop.

In the course of our conversation, I found out with mixed feelings that he had already been married twice and now lived with his girlfriend. *No surprise,* I thought. He was well built; the rolled-up sleeves of his denim shirt revealed muscular arms. His dark skin was a few shades lighter than mine and had a slightly reddish tint. I had a practically irresistible desire to run my hand over the fine, downy hair on his dark skin—and was startled by what was such an unfamiliar thought for me.

After a while, my neck began to hurt from turning my head and shoulders to the right the whole time in order to chat better. At first I tried to ignore the pain, but ultimately I brought myself to ask Marvin—we had introduced ourselves in the meantime—whether he would have anything against my moving one seat closer to be able to talk to him more comfortably. It was somewhat embarrassing for me to say this, but he just smiled and said completely without irony, "Be my guest!" And in the next instant I was as close to him as I had desired the whole time.

In the course of the next few hours, I eventually noticed that he liked me, too. There was something very cozy and intimate about the way we sat next to each other and talked. At one point, I thought I glimpsed an amused smile on the face of the passing stewardess. She had seen me change my seat. But that seemed unimportant. I was finally seated next to this attractive stranger and nothing else mattered.

A couple sitting in the middle row of the plane who, judging by their outward appearance, might have been from Somalia, kept looking over at us disapprovingly. For, in the meantime, I had asked Marvin's permission to lay my head on his shoulder. The nervous tension and the desire to be really close to him had actually intensified to the point that I could no longer restrain myself and again gave my neck pain as the reason for my request. Once again he answered without batting an eye, "Be my guest!"

"Please don't get the wrong idea . . ."

"Of course not!" he reassured me, and immediately I leaned on him and lay my head on his shoulder. I felt his body shake slightly. At that moment I knew that he was laughing.

"Fine, go ahead and laugh," I said, laughing myself. "Okay," I confessed, "my neck is not to blame—I just wanted to lean on you."

He looked at me with amusement. "That's what I thought. I just wanted to be sure." And then he drew me to him and gently pressed my head to his shoulder.

In this position we continued to talk, repeatedly joking about what the stewardesses and the people sitting near us must have been thinking. Ultimately, we stopped speaking in order to sleep a little. I enjoyed the intimacy between us, knowing well that our togetherness would only be short-lived. But in the few hours aboard this airplane inevitably approaching London, all that existed was the small world in which the two of us sat close together on our narrow seats.

"Looks like we'll be there soon," Marvin said softly. It had gotten light out, and the sun was coming out behind a layer of clouds. My head was still lying on his shoulder. His voice was barely audible, as if he wasn't sure whether I was awake yet.

"Yes, looks like it," I whispered. I had been staring out the window for quite a while and thinking with some sadness about the fact that I would soon be leaving Marvin and would never see him again. The feeling that we belonged together had crept up on me—but it was apparently simply not to be. It was the wrong time.

As if he could read my mind, Marvin suddenly said, "Bad timing, huh?"

"Sure is," I answered. "Sure is."

We had agreed not to exchange contact information so as to avoid painful complications in our lives. I was married, albeit unhappily, and he had a girlfriend.

"You know that I'll never forget you," I said, after a pause, with a hoarse voice.

"I won't forget you, either," Marvin replied.

"And that I usually don't do things like this," I added.

"Like what?"

I sat up and pushed him lightly away from me.

"This here, of course," I said with a laugh, and gestured to the two of us.

"Oh, I never would have guessed that. It seemed very skillful."

I nudged him again and punched him playfully in the shoulder.

"I really mean it. I have no idea what came over me."

"This guy here!" he said, laughing and pointing to himself. And I, who didn't at all want to, couldn't help laughing, too.

"You're impossible!"

"Ladies and gentlemen, we are now approaching London Gatwick Airport. Please get back to your seats, fasten your seatbelts, and bring your seats to the upright position."

"That was it, I guess." Marvin looked at me.

I took his hand and held it tight. He returned the pressure, as he averted his eyes from me. And so we remained in our seats, our gazes lost in the clouds, until the landing in Gatwick.

"Take care," Marvin said for the third time.

"You, too."

Our ways parted; he had to leave the airport and take a bus from Gatwick to Heathrow.

"You really have to go now," I said, "or else you'll miss the connecting flight."

Marvin let go of my hand and moved toward the transit exit. He took a step and then suddenly turned around at the exact moment I was about to call him back. Almost simultaneously both of us began to talk. We couldn't just separate like that, without a chance of seeing each other again. And when he gave me his business card, which he had apparently had ready in his jacket pocket, I opened my hand, which contained my own card. Both of us knew: We should not get in contact with each other. But Marvin looked at me so intently that it almost took my breath away.

"Good-bye for now," he said, then he blew me a kiss—and

now really went to the exit. I just stood there, emotionally drained, and watched him disappear behind a door.

Ian picked me up at the airport. In the car, I asked about Akinyi and my mother, who had come to England in my absence to look after our daughter.

"She's doing well," he answered.

"Could I have your cell phone? I want to talk to Akinyi. And I want to tell my mother not to take her to preschool today."

"Why not?" Ian asked sharply.

"I haven't seen Akinyi for ten days. I've missed her, and she has probably missed me, too. I want to spend some time with her."

"That's selfish. She likes to go to preschool, and you'll get to see her soon enough."

Taken aback, I looked at Ian.

"She'd rather go to preschool than see her mother again? I don't think so!"

"You're really selfish, Auma," my husband merely repeated.

"Akinyi is just two years old. I don't think it will do her any harm to miss one day of preschool and see her mother instead," I replied irritably.

Ian just shrugged and looked at the road. In the crawling London traffic, we made only slow progress. But the heavy atmosphere between the two of us was even more impenetrable than the mass of cars around us. I wondered how the man who sat next to me at the wheel, the father of my child, had become such a stranger to me. An immense sadness came over me.

Ultimately, I ignored his disapproving demeanor and spoke on his cell phone with my mother. Ian and I then continued to sit next to each other in silence. I was anxious and couldn't wait to see my daughter again. At the same time, my thoughts kept wandering back to the airport, where Marvin and I had just parted.

I didn't dare to look at Ian, out of fear that he could read in my eyes what had happened the previous night on the airplane. So I turned my head away from his rigid profile and looked out the window.

At that exact moment, the Heathrow Gatwick Express, which shuttled passengers from one airport to the other, passed our car, a high four-wheel drive, the windows of which were almost level with the bus. Absentmindedly, I looked at the vehicle, which was two lanes over from us. I caught my breath—and I fervently hoped that Ian hadn't noticed it. For there, in the bus, sat Marvin, only a few yards away! His head was bowed; he was probably absorbed in a book or a magazine. His black leather cap and the blue denim shirt left no room for doubt. Startled, I looked away, out of fear of my own reaction.

Luckily, the lines of cars in the various lanes shifted so that the express bus remained behind us. After a second of relief, however, I wished with all my might that it would pull up again and bring Marvin back alongside me. And it actually did catch up. But Marvin still didn't raise his head. Then began an arduous process of the two vehicles nearing each other and drifting apart again, which must have lasted about half an hour, until Ian declared that he was now going to take another route, not the usual one, to escape the heavy traffic. Although I was inwardly in complete turmoil, I prayed for Marvin to look up just once, to give me one last chance to look at his face. But it was not to be.

Overwhelmed by the intensity of my emotions, I heaved a deep sigh as we finally turned off the highway.

"What's wrong?" Ian asked.

"Oh, I'm just tired."

After a while, I came to terms with the idea that I would never see Marvin again. At first, life in Bracknell took its familiar course. Ian and I returned to everyday life and tried to patch up the cracks in our marriage. But neither of us was happier as a result, and we knew that our separation was only a question of time. We even broached the topic of divorce. Ian blamed me for our rifts; he had the impression that he himself had tried everything. He regarded me as ungrateful and too demanding. All my explanations that I had wanted something different from him fell on deaf ears. I felt like one of his children—even worse, like a piece of his furniture, without my own identity. I didn't want to go on living like that.

The second African screenwriting workshop took place six months after the first. This time, I wanted to take Akinyi with me. On the way to Zimbabwe, I planned to stop in Nairobi and leave her with my mother, so that after the seminar I could then spend three months in Kenya with the two of them. In the meantime, Ian and I had actually filed for divorce, and I felt exhausted from the domestic tensions. I was looking forward to an eagerly awaited break in my native country.

In the first days before the workshop, Akinyi and I stayed with my friend Keziah in Nairobi, who had offered to share the care of my daughter with my mother during my two-week absence.

I was playing with her in the garden when Keziah's domestic help called me to the telephone.

"A call for you from abroad!"

I ran into the house and took the receiver on the assumption that it was Ian.

"Hello," said a soft, deep voice. "Do you still remember me?"

"I'm not sure," I said hesitantly. I couldn't believe my ears. And then I blurted out, "How did you find me?" The butterflies in my stomach were suddenly back.

"Believe it or not, your husband gave me this number."

"What? How? What did you say to him?" I stammered.

"I asked for you, and he gave me this number," Marvin said dryly. But I could tell that he could not quite believe his luck that he really had me at the other end of the line. "I think he thought I was a brother of yours who lives in the United States, a certain Mark, can that be?"

"Mark!" I burst out laughing, almost hysterical in the face of the irony of fate. "Yes, I have a brother in America named Mark. As far as I know, he lives in California like you."

"A lucky coincidence," said Marvin.

I told him how close we had been to each other on the drive through London after our encounter, he on the express bus, I in the car with Ian. Then he told me that he had sent me a home-made card disguised as a prize voucher, which I must, however, have thrown directly in the trash, not recognizing what it was. He had remembered my second workshop in Zimbabwe, which had already been planned back then. That's why he was calling, he said, because he, too, would be there again at the same time.

I could hardly believe it. Eventually, we arranged a meeting in Zimbabwe; there, he would give me more details about his further travel plans.

As much as I was looking forward to seeing him again, the thought of it also made me uneasy. I didn't know him at all. What would it be like to spend time with him, how would it end?

"Aren't you nervous?" I asked him.

"No, just excited at the idea of seeing you again," he said with a seductive undertone in his voice.

I laughed. I was happy, and tried to disregard my fears. We said good-bye, and I remained seated next to the telephone for a while longer. No, I really hadn't planned my Africa trip this way.

When he entered the restaurant, I had been waiting for him nearly an entire day. At the arranged time, he had not shown up, and so I had stayed an hour and had finally gone back to my hotel, where I found a message from him: He had missed the train and had to wait for a bus; unfortunately, that could take hours.

The previous day I had arrived in Harare. I had a free weekend ahead of me, since the workshop would not begin until Monday. Because several other participants had also arrived early, the organizers had invited us to a barbecue. I had thought up an excuse in order to be free for my rendezvous. And now I had to be patient.

"Sorry for the delay," said Marvin, when he finally sat down with me. He was wearing a straw hat and a Hawaiian shirt and looked very American.

"No problem. I had no other plans anyway."

We smiled at each other across the table and enjoyed looking at each other in peace, without the semidarkness and the tension of the first encounter. Finally he broke the silence.

"Who would have thought it?"

"Who would have thought it?" I repeated.

He took my hand. "Who would have thought that we would see each other again so soon?"

"That we would see each other again at all," I corrected him, smiling.

"True. Who would have thought that we would even meet?"

I shrugged.

"It must have been meant to be."

Thus Marvin came back into my life. Yes, it was meant to be.

Over the next two days of his stay in Harare, we saw each other almost without interruption. Because he knew the city well, he showed me where he bought his arts and crafts, as well as other beautiful places. He took me out to eat and spoiled me. We talked nonstop. He told me about himself, about his two daughters, and that he—though I initially refused to believe it—was already a grandfather.

In the excitement of seeing each other again, we forgot to give each other more detailed information on the further course of our travels. So I assumed wrongly that he would be in Kenya while I was in South Africa, where I had been invited to a film festival after the workshop. Later, I found out that he was there at the same time as I was; he came to Kenya on the last leg of his business trip.

Thus, after my return from South Africa, I was surprised once again by a phone call in Keziah's house. Marvin had been staying in Nairobi for a week and was convinced that I was still in South Africa. He had merely wanted to try to reach me. I was terribly disappointed that we had missed each other, especially as his plane was leaving that same evening. A meeting at the airport seemed to be our last chance, but due to timing issues we couldn't manage that, either. What a tragedy! But could I complain? The fact that our paths had crossed again at all was astonishing enough. I had gotten more than I had ever imagined.

25.

THE DIVORCE PROCEEDINGS went quite smoothly. As I left the courtroom, I heaved a sigh of relief: A new stage was now beginning in my life. But at the same time, an intense fear of a fresh start made itself felt. For four years I had been by Ian's side in England. Together we had moved into our two-story single-family house in Bracknell, where I had spent the whole time, with only brief interruptions, as a housewife and mother of a small child. Everything beyond that Ian had taken care of. I didn't even know how to pay the electricity and water bills. Somehow, I had forgotten that I had handled all my affairs on my own for years before moving to Great Britain. The many responsibilities that now seemed to be in store for me frightened me.

Ian kept the single-family house, while Akinyi and I moved into a small two-bedroom row house, which I had a hard time getting used to. I functioned like a robot, took care of my daughter, tried to do the necessary paperwork properly, and kept my eye out for a job. In the evening, I sat alone in front of the television.

I was in contact with Marvin mainly by e-mail, though only sporadically. What I had at the time imagined as true love was in reality something one-sided, coming from me. I gathered from our occasional exchanges that Marvin, even though he felt really drawn to me, was in a phase of his life in which he did not want to get involved in any relationship. Soon after our encounter, he broke up with his girlfriend and was happy to be alone. *What luck!* I thought, frustrated. Now, of all times. It reminded me of my time in Germany, when everyone was on a self-discovery trip. I had not understood this phenomenon back then, either. Either you liked someone and wanted to be together with that person—or not. For me, it was that simple. The suspicion that Marvin didn't love me tormented me, and yet I could not let go. I longed for him and, against my rational judgment, eagerly took all his phone calls and promptly answered all his e-mails, even if I sometimes had to wait weeks for a response from him.

Little by little, I found my feet in my new existence in Bracknell; I got a job in a marketing firm and thus managed to pay the expenses for the house, the food, and Akinyi's preschool. Even though the job was not very interesting, I met people, and gradually the loneliness that had accompanied me for so long in England left me. A reassuring routine took its place. The small house became cozy, and I came to appreciate my new life.

For financial reasons, I took a job in elder care on alternate weekends, which Akinyi spent with her father. In that way, I unexpectedly gained insight into the life of older people in England. I was shocked by how many of them were alone. Often, they were ill and required a great deal of attention. For days, they saw no one, only the uniformed care staff who, like me, briefly dropped by and quickly dealt with the bare necessities. The fact that we were always in a hurry was due to the strictly limited time available to us for each of these women and men, an hour maximum, usually scarcely more than half an hour. Thus, on my house visits, I quickly prepared a microwave meal, helped the old people out of bed or got them ready for it, assisted them with washing or bathing, and chatted for a few minutes with them—always with a side glance at the clock, because I sometimes had up to twelve visits to make in a day.

Many of the stories I heard from those old people made me melancholy. As an African, I found it inconceivable that so many parents had been abandoned by their children. Often, at the end of a long day with those sad people, I came home completely exhausted. In comparison to them, I was doing really well. I still had my family and a home in Kenya that was close to my heart. But these people no longer found pleasure in anything. Many were only waiting for death. And some of their relatives who no longer showed their faces were probably doing the same.

"They'll all come back," an old man once told me with resignation. "As soon as I'm dead. They want my house."

After brief spells with various marketing firms, I worked for a company in telemarketing, where I was responsible for drumming up German customers for products from the computer technology sector. That at least gave me the opportunity to speak German. I brought in many new buyers, and after not even a year—when I had, parallel to my job, completed the required further training at Bracknell College—I was offered a position as project manager.

With the new position, my salary improved, too, and I felt as if I finally had a "real" job with a "serious" title. No one in the company knew that I held a doctorate. When I applied, I had deliberately withheld this information for fear of being rejected as overqualified.

The work was now considerably more demanding and also more interesting. I assumed greater responsibility, was more committed as a result, and enjoyed the contact with customers. But as time went on, it bothered me that in the world of marketing only the product and the profit had priority, while people seemed to be more a means to an end. I wanted to work for people and not for a product, especially one that was overpriced and rather superfluous, because there were more than enough of them on the market. For me, everything didn't always have to be faster, better, and more compact. But that was precisely what was expected in the computer industry.

So I looked for something more suitable, for work with people, preferably with young people. Soon I managed, through an ad, to get a second job at the Youth Service in Bracknell. Two evenings a week, I now worked on a bus that had been converted into a mobile youth center. A distant relative who lived with me at the time took care of my daughter while I worked.

We would drive the bus to a designated location where the vehicle would be parked and open for the young people to board. We dealt mostly with members of the marginalized Sinti and Roma peoples.

Working with young people gave me great pleasure. We not only offered them the chance to spend time with friends in a safe environment, but we also used the opportunity to teach them about safe sex, drug abuse, and other challenging topics. The three hours in the youth bus flew by, and I sensed that I had found something that was really for me.

26.

ONE DAY, while I was working as a project manager, the phone rang. It was my brother Ben, who asked me to call him back. This immediately made me uneasy, because in recent years I had always been the one who contacted the family. During my next break, I called him back.

"Mum is sick and in the hospital," said my younger brother. "The doctors don't know what she has. You have to do something."

Although Ben's news frightened me, I had to smile to myself. As had happened so often in recent years, this time, too, I was expected to fix things. That would probably never change.

"What's wrong with her?" I asked. "What are the doctors saying?"

"Oh, all sorts of things. They seem unsure."

"Haven't you asked for more details?"

"Yes, but they're groping in the dark."

Since Ben had given me a telephone number of the hospital where my mother was staying, I asked him to get a doctor. He sounded relieved that I was taking the matter in hand.

For a while now, my mother had been unwell. Whenever I

spoke to her, she complained of fatigue, and at our last encounter, after my workshop in Zimbabwe the previous year, she had looked thinner to me. I felt guilty, because I had not flown to Kenya during my last vacation, but had gone to Greece with Akinyi instead. The divorce, the move, and the various jobs had exhausted me, and I had needed to get away from everything.

After fifteen minutes, I again dialed the telephone number that Ben had given me. He immediately put me on with the doctor.

"My sister is on the phone," I heard him say, and then an unfamiliar, somewhat exhausted-sounding and slightly testy voice reached my ear.

"Hello, I'm Auma," I introduced myself. "I hear you are treating my mother, Kezia."

"Yes, she has been with us in the hospital for a few days."

"Can you tell me what's wrong with her?" I held my breath. I didn't really want to know. I wanted to avoid the anxiety and the unavoidable responsibility for what might now lie ahead of me.

"We can't say exactly, but it looks as if something might be wrong with her kidneys."

"Her kidneys? What do you mean?"

The doctor described my mother's symptoms, spoke about the medical diagnosis, and told me how critical her condition was. Though he didn't want to frighten me, he finally said it would be best if I came immediately.

When I had Ben on the phone again, I explained to him that we absolutely needed a second opinion. That evening, I would give him the address of another doctor to whom he should bring our mother. I also told him that I would come home soon. Yet I had no idea how I would pay for the trip. And then something else occurred to me.

"Does Abongo know about this?"

"I've tried to reach him, but so far it hasn't worked."

"Okay, I'll try, too. Now I have to go. Talk to you this evening."

My thoughts raced as I returned to my workstation. I was terribly afraid that time could run out for my mother. I could already see myself as an orphan—even at my age, I needed my mother, and Akinyi should not lose her grandmother, whom she was only just getting to know. I had taught her Luo so that she would be able to communicate with all her Kenyan relatives without any difficulty.

However the second medical examination turned out, I knew that I would fly to my mother. That was the only way to be sure that everything necessary was being done for her.

I ultimately took out a bank loan, not only to pay for the plane tickets for Akinyi and me, but also to cover my mother's hospital bills. Ben had no money, and he also had no idea where to get any. He still had no job. Disappointed, I wondered where my mother's many brothers and sisters were now.

"Look at this!" Harris exclaimed. We had all crowded around his computer. He was the only one who dared to surf the Internet during working hours—probably because, of all of us, he had been project manager the longest and was practically part of the establishment.

"Who would invent such a macabre game?" asked one of our coworkers. On the screen, a BBC News site was open, on which a video showed a plane that had just hurtled into a skyscraper. The building seemed to be one of the Twin Towers in the New York financial district.

"It's not a game," Harris said, suddenly very serious, and read the accompanying text aloud. At the same time, we observed in horror as a second airplane hurtled into the other tower.

"Oh, my God! This can't really be happening!" someone cried. The rest of us stared silently at the screen and could not believe what was unfolding before our eyes. It must have been some digital animation; a sick joke that a bored computer freak had put on the Net to shock the world. But why were all those people jumping out of the top floors of the two towers? And what did all the commotion down on the street mean? Helplessly, we followed the horrifying event, which, as we later learned, incredulous eyes all over the world were watching over and over again. My stomach turned at the sight. The air in the room suddenly felt cold, and shivers ran down my arms and back as I looked at the screen clouding up with smoke and dust. And those screams of the people fleeing in panic! Just the day before I had bought our tickets for the impending trip to Kenya in two days.

In the airport, I was immediately struck by the low level of activity. Two days after the horror of September 11, 2001, no one wanted to fly. The plane to Nairobi was quite empty, too. But I was too worried about my mother to let that deter me. That was the price of living abroad. If I was needed at home, a long-distance flight was part of the deal.

I wasn't sure whether Abongo would come, too, but I really hoped so. Before September 11, I had sent him a telegram, in which I had informed him of my upcoming arrival in Nairobi. But I hadn't heard from him since. His presence was important, however. In the meantime, I knew that my mother had a kidney ailment, and we children had to decide together how her treatment should be handled. I had already paid the hospital, and hoped that my brother would reimburse me for some of the expenses.

"This is your responsibility. You take care of it."

I couldn't believe my ears. We were in Nairobi, in the Kileleshwa neighborhood, where I had put my mother up with my friend Diana. From there, she could undergo further medical examinations as an outpatient in the hospital. Akinyi and I were also staying in Diana's large, two-story house. Abongo, who had finally arrived and had just come to visit our mother, was now standing in front of me and explaining that, because I had initiated our mother's treatment without his prior consent, he would not share in the medical expenses.

"What was I supposed to do?" I asked, dumbfounded. "You couldn't be reached. Was the illness supposed to wait for you to get in touch?"

"This is your affair. As I said, you independently made decisions about our mother's treatment, so now you can see this through on your own."

I stared at this brother, who had never done anything for me in his whole life. I felt nothing but profound sorrow. He was still competing with me, as always, but now at the expense of our mother's health. I turned away from him, went upstairs without a word, and returned to the room in which our sick mother lay.

Abongo was already on his way out again. Why he had undergone the long flight at all was a mystery to me. He had visited his mother but done nothing for her. Later, I found out that he had actually only come to check on his children. At the time, they were living on my mother's compound in Alego and were temporarily being looked after by her.

"Mama! Mama!"

I pulled myself together and looked down at my four-year-old daughter, who was tugging on my skirt.

"Mama, Uncle Abongo forgot my gift for Little Auma," she cried, holding a rag doll in her hand. We had bought the doll at the airport in London for my niece, Abongo's daughter. I took the toy from her. Aunt Agnes, who was sitting with my mother and had been taking care of her since her release from the hospital, said bitterly, "He's Muslim now and probably won't accept something like that."

I gave her a confused look.

"I've heard that according to his religion, it is forbidden to worship an image of Allah. A doll is regarded as a copy of a human being and therefore of Allah, too. Do you understand?"

"No," I replied dryly. "Since when is he so religious anyway?"

My mother answered with a weak voice. "Since he came back temporarily from America. He not only rediscovered his African roots, but also found Islam. In his view, dolls are an attempt to copy the image of Allah. And that's a sin for him."

"What nonsense," I said, annoyed. "He's crazy!"

"Akinyi can give it a try," said Aunt Agnes. "Maybe he'll accept it from her."

I gave Akinyi the doll and waited as she went downstairs. My brother was already standing at the open door.

"Here, Uncle Abongo, you forgot the doll for Auma."

My brother took it. But judging by the way he held it, by the legs and with the head dangling, my niece would probably never set eyes on it.

"He took it, he took it," Akinyi rejoiced, when she was back upstairs with us. I smiled and took her in my arms.

"Well-done, Muu," I said, using my pet name for her.

With a heavy heart, I flew back to England. My mother had been able to stay with my friend Diana for only a short while. Her condition had worsened again, so that she had to return to the hospital. Although the stay there was very expensive and I had no idea how I would pay for it, there was no alternative. She had suddenly had difficulty breathing and needed an oxygen mask.

I learned that relatives visited her at the hospital every day to check on her. This meant that at least she was never alone. In the summer of 2003, when she was doing considerably better, I invited her to Bracknell along with my brother Ben. Akinyi and I had not seen her for over a year and were looking forward to her visit. Because other family members arrived with her, too, my small house was suddenly filled with people, laughter, and chitchat. Every morning I had to weave my way through the living room, where some guests were sleeping, before I could leave the house and go to work. Akinyi, who had just started school, enjoyed coming home after classes to a house full of people who gave her a lot of attention. She liked to dance and now always had a large audience in the evening and on the weekend.

Before I was really aware of it, the time had come for my mother to fly back to Kenya. However, for several days she had been complaining that she didn't feel well. We suspected a case of the flu and gave her medication. On the day before her departure, however, she felt particularly bad.

"We're going to the doctor!" I said resolutely, although my mother was against it.

"It will be all right, I just have to rest," she protested.

I remained firm and called my family doctor.

"I'm sorry," he said with a serious voice, "but your mother cannot fly under any circumstances."

"What?"

My mother lay completely exhausted on the examination table. She had taken off her blouse and the doctor was listening to her chest. I sat on a chair next to his desk.

"I cannot responsibly condone her flying. Something's wrong with her kidneys. She has to go to the hospital immediately," he went on.

Suddenly, my secret fears were confirmed. Over the past few days, my mother had barely gotten out of bed, hadn't eaten much, had suffered from pain and facial swelling, and incessantly had to go to the bathroom. Now it was unavoidable. She had to go to the hospital.

"Everything's going to be all right," I said to her, clasping her hand. She smiled faintly and closed her eyes. She believed me. She, too, had at some point gotten used to me taking care of everything.

Wexham Park Hospital, the largest in Berkshire County, had the necessary equipment to examine my mother more closely. But after a few days, it turned out that that was not enough. It lacked an important machine needed for her treatment.

"We have to transfer your mother immediately to a hospital in London," said a young doctor. He stood in front of me and looked tired. His blond hair looked disheveled, as if he were constantly ruffling it with his hand. He was doing so now, too. "We have to connect her to a dialysis machine, and we don't have one here."

"A dialysis machine?" I asked, alarmed. "Isn't that used to clean the blood?"

"Exactly." He again tousled his hair with his hand. That irritated me, because it gave me the impression that he was not entirely confident. I wanted him to tell me clearly where things stood with my mother.

"Without this intervention she won't survive," he went on. "Her blood has to be cleansed."

I had to sit down. Over the past few days I had once again had to face up to the fact that my mother was seriously ill. Every day, after picking up Akinyi from school, I had driven to the hospital to speak with the doctors and make sure that my mother was receiving the proper treatment. I shuttled back and forth between work, child, and hospital, always in the certainty that she would soon recover. Now I was confronted with the fact that her life was in danger unless she was brought to a specialist hospital in London. But Wexham Park Hospital was already far away from Bracknell. In rush-hour traffic, it took me almost an hour to get there, and I would hardly be able to drive to London every day.

"Shall we arrange for the transfer? We need your signature for it." I just nodded. In my head, my mother was already in London.

"She is being put in the intensive care unit."

"Why?"

"It's not certain whether she will survive," he said matter-of-factly. As he said that, he no longer ran his hand through his hair.

I accompanied my mother to London, where I was housed in an apartment on the hospital grounds reserved for family members of critically ill patients. Fortunately, school break was just beginning for Akinyi. I had brought her to her father, so that I could devote myself entirely to my mother.

It was a terrible time. Every day I sat at her bedside and watched nurses and doctors stick needles in her skin and administer various medications to her. In the background the dialysis machine worked around the clock.

"Can I please speak with you?" Once again a young doctor stood in front of me—this time, however, one whose short, pitch-black, neatly combed-back, and pomaded hair suggested extensive grooming. "It's about your mother."

I might have guessed as much—the words were on the tip of my tongue, but I swallowed the comment. I had seen the young doctor in the unit a few times. He seemed to be always in a hurry and was clearly fully aware of his position of power as a doctor in the midst of the many nurses.

"When would you like to speak with me?" I asked politely instead.

"Now, if you have time."

My mother was asleep.

"I have time."

"Good, then come with me."

He turned around and left the unit. I followed him with a sense of apprehension.

The room to which he led me was actually reserved for family members who spent the whole day with their sick relatives. It was comfortably furnished and had a pleasant color scheme. Later, I learned that people were only brought there when a doctor had bad news.

Now I stood in the small room by the window, where I had fled from the words of the young doctor.

"Are you really trying to tell me that you intend to shut off the dialysis machine, even though you know that my mother might die?" I asked, after the doctor had finished speaking.

He was unfazed by my tone of voice. He had shown not the faintest trace of sympathy as he had explained his plan.

"And on top of that, you want to tell my mother?"

"Yes, I think we should tell her. If her condition has not stabilized from the medication by the end of the week, we have to shut off the machine."

"Just like that?" I asked incredulously.

"Of course not just like that," he replied, frowning. "We're really sorry, of course. But it costs a lot of money to run the machine, and your mother unfortunately has no insurance. Who is paying for her treatment? The hospital cannot afford these expenses."

"Aha, it's because of the money. That's why you want to shut off the machine?"

Without batting an eye, he replied, "That's the way it is, unfortunately."

Slowly, I approached the doctor. I sat down opposite him, looked him directly in the eyes, and said resolutely, "Listen to me closely. You will tell my mother nothing. Not a thing! Nor will you shut off the machine! First of all: When and how my mother learns that she is going to die the family still gets to decide. Secondly: As for the costs, I will find out what is doable and what is not. And thirdly: You gave me this news without any preparation, without any advice on how I could cope with it. You know that my mother has other relatives, too. You've seen that she has visitors. And still you did not think it necessary to ask me whether

I might need the support of other family members during this conversation? For that reason alone, I do not accept your diagnosis or your decision. And I will tell that to your superior, too."

I had spoken without interruption, almost in one breath, with anger and distress in my voice. The doctor was about to reply, but before he could say anything, I stood up and left the room.

Ben had come with my mother to England, and now he had extended his stay so that the two of us could take care of her and could make sure that she received the best possible treatment. We were also supported by relatives and friends, and I was astonished when I found out how many of them lived in London. Despite the anxiety-provoking situation, I was glad that it had given us the opportunity to meet. After several years of isolation in Bracknell, I really enjoyed their company. My mother's illness brought us all closer together. We comforted each other and talked about our lives in England. During that time, I definitely could not complain of loneliness.

Over all those weeks and months, I had remained in contact with Marvin. Once I had even been able to meet him in Windsor, when he had an extended layover in England on one of his flights. As much as I wanted to be together with him, my pride did not allow me to make moves in that direction, and so we maintained a distance that was agonizing for me. So I was all the more surprised when one day—my mother was still in the London hospital—he offered to come to England to be by my side.

"I don't have much to do at the moment, and I'm sure you could use some support. If you want, I'll come."

Of course I wanted that! Not a day passed that I didn't think of him, despite everything that preoccupied and weighed on me. Not a day passed without the painful hope that he longed to be close to me as much as I longed to be close to him.

I explained to him how badly my mother was doing. "The doctors are afraid that she won't survive."

"I'm already on my way," he replied. "Stay strong."

I was grateful for his encouragement. That was just what I needed now—besides a shoulder to lean on, of course. After that phone call, I finally saw light at the end of the tunnel.

Soon after our conversation, Marvin arrived in England. We sat together daily at my mother's bedside—she apparently took the stranger to be some friend, and I let her believe that. Marvin and I often took long walks on the bank of the Thames. The tension of the past months drained away from me as we strolled along the water, and for a brief time I had the soothing feeling of not having to bear the worry for my mother alone. Marvin helped me make decisions, and when the pressure became overwhelming, I wept on his shoulder. He managed to make me laugh. And one evening, he even took me out to a salsa club, for he knew how much I loved to dance.

But as wonderful as it was to have Marvin with me, his visit left a bitter aftertaste. Even though he obviously liked me—otherwise he would not have come all that way to see me—he did not seem to find it hard to head back to the States.

As if by a miracle, just a few days after my conversation with the doctor, my mother could be taken off her dialysis machine. She had turned the corner, and it was now possible to transfer her back to Wexham Park Hospital, to a normal ward.

"Your mother is a true fighter," a nurse remarked admiringly.

"Thank God." That was all I could say in response.

When my mother was finally released from the hospital, she was still far from recovered. She suffered not only from the effects of the intense medication, but also from a lack of companionship. The friends and family members from London lived too far away, and around Bracknell there was no one she knew well. She was completely dependent on Akinyi and me for company.

Her loneliness exacerbated my own. I now no longer left the house much, because I was taking care of her most of the time. She was afflicted by intense leg pain, and there was already talk of hip replacements. All this often put her in a morose mood, and I had to muster a lot of patience in dealing with her.

Because I could understand her despondency and the oppressive loneliness only too well, I looked desperately for a way to help her. Finally, I found a group of older women who met once a week for tea and did various activities together. Though my mother had her difficulties with English, I was certain that she would overcome them with time. Gradually things started looking up.

At that time, I often wondered which of us was the child and which the mother. After all the worry and the exhausting period spent taking care of my mother, I eventually could not help feeling some indignation. The relationship between my mother and me was complicated, even though we never spoke about it. Ever since I had gotten to know her at the age of thirteen, I carried around with me the feeling that I owed her something. Perhaps that was because I had actually forgotten her over the long years of separation and had not loved her from afar. In some way, I felt as if I had to make up for that and as if I were responsible for her. Although it should have actually been the other way around—it had been she, after all, who had given me up, deprived me of her motherly love.

These thoughts troubled me. I wished that I at least had a shared history with her, shared experiences of joy and sorrow—everything that belonged to a family life. And something that could serve as a justification for the hard work and the sacrifices I now had to bear for her sake. But then I thought of my own daughter and knew instantly why I was doing all this. It was for her. Even if it might be too late for me, Akinyi still had a chance to develop a good relationship with my mother. My daughter could nurture an intact connection with her grandmother without the burden of any family tragedies, I thought. When I managed to see things that way, it was suddenly no longer so hard for me to be there for my mother.

During her hospital stay, I had explained to the authorities why my mother could not leave the country after the expiration of her visa. Now the worrisome question arose as to what would become of her if she were deported. In Kenya, we had not had the best experiences with family care. All our relatives were too preoccupied with their own problems. And it seemed just as questionable whether my mother would get the proper further medical treatment there.

"Why don't you ask whether she can stay with you permanently?" a friend suggested to me, when I had told her about my misgivings.

"Impossible. They're so strict with us Africans."

"Just try it. Inquire with a lawyer."

"I would need money for that," I replied with resignation.

"Certainly—ordinarily. But your case is unusual. Your mother is sick. I'll look into what can be done."

So I took on, with my friend's encouragement, the long, arduous process—involving red tape, driving from one place to another, endless telephone calls and appointments—of obtaining permanent residence for my mother in England. One day, to our joy, a letter finally arrived informing us of the decision of the Home Office that Grace Kezia Aoko Obama was permitted to stay in Great Britain. An official document followed, complete with the royal seal of her majesty Elizabeth II.

27.

IN THE MEANTIME, I had taken a new position with the Bracknell Youth Service in a program called Connexions. I was able to leave my job as project manager and could now work full-time for the Youth Service. I was tasked with helping children and youth from difficult family circumstances get an education or find training or employment opportunities.

I had been doing this for almost two years when I was entrusted with the Bridget Case. Bridget had just turned seventeen and was homeless. Because she was underage and without fixed abode, she was entitled to state support, for which she had applied with the authorities in Bracknell, where she had last resided.

When we inquired about the application at the office, we were told that a different agency was now responsible for it. But there, no one knew anything, and we were sent to a third agency, which itself referred us elsewhere, until we ended up back at the first office, where now someone was able to produce the sought-after application after all. The whole back and forth involved hours of phone calls, which the girl would never have been able to handle successfully on her own. Without my help she would have given up and gone on sleeping "under a bridge."

Bureaucratic obstacle courses of this sort went with the territory of this work. But as a staff member under the Social Services Department, I could at least insist on responses and the expediting of processes, even if often not much came of it. To expect young people who lived on the fringes of society to find their way in all this on their own was, however, too much to ask. Most of them had no idea that they had rights. They did not even expect to be treated better when they ended up caught in the wheels of bureaucracy, in which they constantly had the feeling that the right hand didn't know what the left hand was doing.

Although I knew many colleagues who really strove to make a difference, I was frustrated by the often rather scant sympathy the authorities showed the youth in need. As a result, I had to struggle hard to allay the young people's mistrust toward adults, including myself. In light of my cultural background, I was often astonished by the enormous gulf that divided the youth and adults where I worked. I was convinced that the adults needed to be much more responsive to the young people. In most cases, unfortunately, the exact opposite was the case: The youth had to adapt. They were expected to fit in and assume their predetermined place in the social structure. In Kenya, too, there were certainly strict rules to which you had to adhere, but family had such a strong influence on the lives of the children and youth that such a wide gap between the generations was not likely in the first place.

In light of these experiences, I began to reflect on how I could contribute to fundamentally changing the situation for these young people. It was clear to me that as a Connexions staff member I could take them by the hand for only a brief time and could not really improve much about their lives. So I applied one day for a position that had been created some time ago in the

Youth Service of the neighboring town of Wokingham. The work there essentially consisted of giving children and youth the opportunity to participate more intensely in decisions affecting them. Following orders from on high, the initiative sought to provide them with a platform from which they could express themselves and be taken seriously. This work seemed to be tailor-made for me and my vision.

I prepared thoroughly for the interview and was overjoyed when I got the job.

But my plans and those of my colleagues were often thwarted by lack of funds. The second most important task besides the attempt to give children and youth a voice and greater self-esteem was the struggle for financial resources. For without the necessary money I, too, came under suspicion of making only empty promises.

Increasingly, I compared the British children with whom I worked at that time to Kenyan children. It pained me to see that they had so many more possibilities in comparison to their African counterparts and yet made so little of them. At the same time, I knew that these reflections were pointless (and would hardly have motivated the youth more). In many ways, the British boys and girls faced challenges that, under the prevailing circumstances, were just as difficult as those confronted by young people in my native country.

One such challenge was the scarcity of meeting places for young people that were not also centers where they were required to participate in specific character-building activities, leaving little room for them to just "hang out." I never really understood why young people did not meet at each other's homes, until a colleague explained to me that the parents were often against it out of fear that their children and their friends would make a mess.

"But wouldn't that be better in the end than your daughter or son roaming around in some dark park and you as a parent not knowing what your child is up to?" I asked.

"I think these fathers and mothers have given up," the colleague replied. "They don't want their children coming home late at night, but the children no longer obey them. They just do what they want."

"Still, the parents could definitely do more," I insisted.

"No. The British have ceded their responsibility in many respects to the state. For that reason they accept the status quo."

So how was I supposed to improve anything for young people, if the parents themselves weren't pulling together? I wondered. More than ever, I was aware of how little I could change the existing conditions. I thought of Akinyi, who was eight already, and at that moment, only a few miles away, lay safely ensconced in her bed. What would become of her once she was a teenager? Would I be able to keep tabs on her behavior outside the home? For some time, the thought had been repeatedly crossing my mind that it would be better to leave England before I was confronted with such a situation. I simply could not imagine my daughter in a poorly lit park, hanging around with other, possibly unstable young people, even if it might be only under peer pressure.

Finally, I made a decision: It would only be a matter of time before I left. At the same time, I was more and more convinced that I could achieve more working in my own country.

28.

BARACK HAD BECOME A LAWYER and, as he had once told me he would do, had gone into politics instead of working in a law firm. Over the years, he had never lost sight of his goal of trying to influence policy to improve people's lives.

When I one day received an e-mail from him in which he informed me that he was running for election as a senator and wanted to know what I thought of that, there was not much I could say. I wrote back that I did not really understand the significance of this; the American system of government was too foreign to me. But if it was an important step toward achieving his vision, I would definitely support him.

After a few months, he got in touch again to invite me to his official inauguration as a senator. Wow, I thought proudly, he actually got elected. In the meantime, I had done my homework and learned—also because it was all over the newspapers—that my brother's new post was not exactly a minor accomplishment. Barack was one of five black people who had succeeded up to that point in getting elected to the United States Senate. And it had been years since the last black person had assumed such an office.

"You have to come, Auma. I'd really like to have you there," my brother told me on the phone.

"I can't afford it. Two tickets cost—"

He cut me off. "I'll pay!"

"No, that's out of the question. *You* shouldn't be doing something for *me.* To celebrate this event, *I* should be doing something for *you.*"

"Listen." Barack sounded impatient. "I'm also inviting other relatives from Kenya, and I'm paying for them, too. It's really important to me that you participate in this inauguration, as well as Akinyi and your mother. That's why you have to come."

After some back and forth, I agreed.

"So we'll see each other in Washington, right?"

"Absolutely! You're very persistent. That's why I love you!"

Not until I was in Washington did I truly grasp what it meant for Barack to be elected senator. Although we stayed in the same hotel, he was barely present, because there were so many demands on his time. A celebratory thrill was in the air, and everywhere great enthusiasm could be felt for what he had achieved. When a black woman from the hotel security service learned that I was Barack's sister, she spoke to me excitedly.

"We're all so proud of him!" she said, beaming. "Congratulations! Congratulations!"

And so it went the whole time. People were constantly shaking my hand and complimenting us. I was taken aback and overwhelmed, and I almost felt as if I myself, solely by virtue of my relation to my brother, had accomplished something special.

The days in the capital of the United States were filled with invitations to various events and ceremonies, where I got to witness again and again how popular Barack was. People cheered him enthusiastically as soon as he entered a room, listened to him attentively when he spoke, and applauded him wildly and repeatedly.

Without a doubt, I was extremely proud of my brother and his success. At the same time, I was astounded at the effect he had on others. Marveling, and also smiling to myself a little, I observed the man who was my little brother. I remembered our conversation on the porch of my apartment in Nairobi, when he had told me about his Harvard plans and his desire to change people's lives. And now here he was, able to completely transform the mood in a room through his presence alone. The faces of the people who had come to celebrate with him and listen to him reflected the great expectations, hopes, and possibilities that he embodied. Even Barack's colleagues seemed hypnotized by him. My little brother was now a big man, I thought. If only the old man were still alive to see all this!

Apart from my brother's inauguration as senator, a major highlight of our trip to Washington was meeting my nieces Malia and Sasha for the first time. My last visit to the States had been before the two of them were born.

Malia was six, a year younger than Akinyi. Sasha was almost four. As I hugged them, I caught myself looking for signs of family resemblance. Malia, I could see at a glance, looked a lot like her father's maternal side of the family. Little Sasha was more difficult to place. "Could those be the Obama high cheekbones?" I asked myself. "The forehead perhaps . . . ?" It was hard to tell. She also looked a lot like her mother.

Although I was still a stranger to them, the girls graciously let me hug them. They tolerated my many "aunty" questions before turning their attention to a more interesting new member of the family, their cousin Akinyi. The three of them slipped easily into a sense of familiarity and for the rest of the visit were inseparable.

Despite Barack's hectic schedule, we were able to congregate one evening for an intimate dinner with family and friends. Coincidentally, it was also my forty-fifth birthday. Maya promptly saw to it that a birthday cake would be served. As we all sat at our tables, laughing and chatting, and later, when we gathered to take photos to capture the moment forever, I felt a great sense of family and belonging. It crossed my mind that this might have been what my father had wanted to achieve when he longed for Barack and his mother to come join us in Kenya.

"Hey, Sister!" That was how Barack always greeted me on the telephone, and this time was no different.

"Hello! What have I done to deserve this phone call?" I replied jokingly. "Is everything all right with you?"

Automatically, I suspected the possibility of bad news as the reason for the unexpected call. We had not spoken for a long time. Since his inauguration as senator, both of us had always been busy and had not had much time to talk on the phone.

"Everything's great." He really did sound in good spirits. "We're doing fabulously. And you? And Akinyi?"

It was not his way to beat around the bush and make small talk. So he got straight to the point with his next sentence. He was planning a trip to Kenya and wanted to have me there with him. In August, he would pay the country an official visit. At the same time, he wanted to visit our grandmother with me.

I could not give him an immediate answer. For one thing, it

was really short notice. For another, there was the familiar challenge of the expenses.

"I'll call you back once I've calculated everything," I finally said.

But he offered to pay for the flights; I myself would then only need to arrange our accommodations.

"Not again." I had to laugh. "You can't pay for our plane tickets all the time."

Barack laughed, too. "That seems to be the price I have to pay for a long-distance relationship with my sister and the fact that I want her to take part in my life."

But this time I was able to come up with the money for the trip myself and give him a positive answer shortly after his phone call. Akinyi and I would accompany him, Michelle, Malia, and Sasha to Kenya.

We arrived in Nairobi before Barack and his family and checked into a hotel that was only a few paces away from theirs. That way the children could be together most of the time, while I accompanied my brother and Michelle on several official visits. Despite all the spectacle and the various ceremonies, I found it wonderful to be in Africa with the two of them again. The August weather was mild, with considerably cooler temperatures on some days.

What particularly astonished me on this trip was how Barack was received everywhere in Kenya. From the day of his arrival, the whole country was seized with Obama mania. Crowds of people flocked to hear him speak. When he gave a speech at the University of Nairobi, the hall was packed. Many people were standing, and some were even sitting on the floor. When he planted a tree in Uhuru Park in the business center of the capital, countless people came to watch him. When we drove in a motorcade through the streets, they craned their necks out the windows of buses and cars. The police escort ensured the smooth flow of traffic, which in essence meant clearing and blocking off the road for us. And I, who had always been disapproving of politicians or dignitaries who caused traffic jams with their motorcades, was myself suddenly sitting in one of those official cars holding up traffic. It was a crazy situation for me.

"Do you remember your last visit?" I asked my brother jokingly as we hurtled down the Uhuru Highway.

"I do indeed. What to say?" he replied, and shrugged with a smile.

Back then we had sat in my old Beetle—or rather, on the roadside, while two strangers had tried to repair the burning car.

"What to say?" I echoed, mimicking his gesture with a laugh. I was so proud of him. He really had become a statesman.

The arrival of Barack and Michelle in Kisumu was a major event. The small city on the shore of Lake Victoria was abuzz with excitement about Obama, and everything else came practically to a standstill. Thousands wanted to see my brother. T-shirts and caps with his name printed on them and other souvenirs were being sold. The crowd chanted: "Obama! Obama!" To hear my family name from all those mouths was confusing and uplifting at the same time. In anticipation of his arrival, people had lined up along the road from the airport into the city. This was my first brief impression of the rock star aura surrounding Barack, which I would later witness again and again in his encounters with crowds of people. In Kisumu, of course, there was the added element that the people were incredibly proud that such an important person had his family roots in their region. The fact that Barack was Luo increased their self-esteem immensely. Every single one of them standing there on the roadside or gathering on the grounds of the hospital we visited experienced Barack's success as their own.

Masses of people also awaited us in Alego. The area around the local school he visited was a sea of onlookers. We virtually had to fight our way through to the tent in which my brother was to speak to the people. And making our way back to the car and to my grandmother's homestead a few minutes away from the school was just as arduous. There was pushing and shoving. Everyone wanted to grasp Barack's hand and exchange a few words with him. As a welcome gift, he was given a white goat that got lost in the crowd. No one seemed to know what had happened to it when I inquired about it later. We could only hope that it had found a good home and had not immediately ended up in the cooking pot of a hungry family.

Nor did the insanity stop when we finally made it to my grandmother's compound. The four acres of land on which Granny Sarah's house stood were teeming with people. Many relatives had come from far away to see and greet Barack. Things were similarly chaotic at my mother's homestead, the adjacent property, where she had lived with Abongo's family before she joined me in England. We had planned that my brother—in accordance with tradition—would visit each of the homesteads. He wanted to bring gifts to Abongo's wives and then join our grandmother for a meal. Only with difficulty did we manage to stick to this plan amid the crowds jostling for Barack's attention. Unfortunately, only a small amount of time remained for the meal with Granny Sarah.

"And he will come again?" she asked me, as we were again

walking to the waiting cars after the brief visit with her, which had lasted not even an hour.

"Absolutely," I answered.

"What is Granny saying?" asked Barack, who stood next to me. I translated, and my brother nodded vigorously.

"Tell her that I will definitely come again. I had to leave my *chapatis* on the table, and for that reason alone, I'll have to visit her again, to eat up that outstanding flatbread!"

Our grandmother gave Barack her broad, warm smile, followed by a deep laugh and finally her usual "give me five." This routine was reserved for Barack alone—it had started between them when they first met many years earlier. I couldn't help marveling once again at how the two of them were able to convey their feelings to each other through nothing but laughter, embraces, and gestures. Our children, too, watched this deeply emotional communication, and it pained me that the time they had been able to spend with their great-grandmother had been so limited. Barack's daughters had only caught a glimpse of the wonderful energy of this old woman they were meeting for the first time.

Back in England, I again had to deal with work-related challenges. And things did not get easier. Often I felt frustrated because I could not bring about lasting change in the lives of the young people I worked with. What difference was I making? I asked myself again and again. What could I really achieve?

Increasingly, my thoughts wandered to Kenya and my possibilities there. I had lived for over twenty years on another continent, and now I was putting all my energy into the youth there, seeking to attain something for them. When I compared the fate of European children with that of African children, I noted that in England, at least most of the boys and girls had a social safety net to fall back on. In Kenya, there was nowhere near anything comparable. A large number of children and young people in that country struggled under the most difficult circumstances to get by in a society that was often unable to provide for their basic needs. The more I thought about it, the more strongly I felt compelled to return to my native country.

My mother was meanwhile living in her own small apartment in Bracknell. Besides her permanent residence, I had managed to obtain for her a small partial disability pension with which she could pay her living expenses. That way my mother had more freedom and could shape her existence on her own, independent from me, while still nearby. I was happy that her situation had stabilized. Once a week Akinyi stayed overnight with her, in order to spend time with her grandmother and continue to improve her command of Luo.

Although I now had more time for myself again, it was still not enough to lead a satisfying social life. And the situation with Marvin—though I was still in love with him—had not changed, either. He had come to Bracknell once, without things developing further between us. I was increasingly unhappy about this nonrelationship and finally decided to put an end to the whole thing. I asked a friend to help me. Monika, my Swedish neighbor from across the street, with whom I was close, had met Marvin when he visited me in Bracknell. At the time she had been quite critical of our relationship.

"What sort of love is that?" she asked. "The man keeps you waiting for years—"

"But that's the thing," I interrupted her morosely. "He hasn't actually been keeping me waiting. He hasn't promised me anything at all!"

"Then why does he call you all the time? He knows that you're in love with him," she went on. "If I were you, I would immediately show him the door."

"I tried. But it doesn't work. He doesn't listen to me when I tell him not to call me anymore. That's why I need your help. You tell him."

"Why me?" Monika asked, shocked. "I barely know him."

"For that very reason! Maybe he'll take you seriously. Please, you have to do it! Or else I'll die!"

"Don't be so melodramatic, Auma. I'll do it. But only because I disapprove of his behavior. Almost seven years have gone by since the two of you first met. It really is enough!"

"That's what I'm saying!" I replied with relief, and hugged my friend. I gave her Marvin's number and sent her home immediately with it. I didn't want her to stay longer and perhaps change her mind.

I never found out what Marvin and Monika talked about on the telephone. I only know that in the aftermath I heard nothing from him.

Plans for my return to Kenya became more and more concrete.

The most important groundwork was the search for a well-paid job. Although Kenya is a developing country, a fairly comfortable life there costs a lot of money. I wanted to return to my native country only if I could ensure a certain standard of living for my daughter and me.

So I acquainted myself with the world of NGOs—nongovernmental organizations—for, it seemed to me, that was where I would most likely find an opportunity to apply my previous experience working with children and youth. My friends helped me with the search, and during a trip to the United States to visit my brother and his family, I planned to meet with various organizations in New York that I had contacted beforehand.

On that occasion, Akinyi and I experienced the American Thanksgiving celebration for the first time—and marveled at the abundant feast. Many of Michelle's family members were present, as well as Maya and her family. She had since gotten married and had a little daughter, Suhaila. The time together was mainly spent chatting and eating. Akinyi and her cousins enjoyed each other's company. I was pleased that every time the girls saw each other they got along so well, despite the fact that they were usually separated by thousands of miles.

In New York, my first appointment was with a representative of CARE, the American humanitarian organization founded in 1945. I was to meet her at Kennedy Airport, where she had an extended layover.

I booked Akinyi's and my return flight to England via JFK to coincide with the timing of the CARE executive's New York stop. We planned to meet in the airport terminal.

My brother ordered a limousine to take us from his house in Chicago to O'Hare International Airport. On arrival we were escorted to the VIP lounge. Akinyi was really impressed with the special treatment. And while she explored the lavish buffet, I made myself comfortable in a large armchair by the window with a view of the runway. The sky was gray, and it looked like rain.

"You still have time, and the lounge is only a minute away from the gate," I was told when I inquired about our plane's exact time of departure. Content, I again leaned back in my armchair. After quite a while without any boarding call, I wanted to hear again when we would be boarding.

"The plane has departed, ma'am," was the answer.

"Excuse me? It has already taken off?" I asked, aghast. "But we weren't even called!"

"I'm sorry, ma'am. We don't do that in the VIP lounge. We don't want to disturb our guests."

I could not believe it. We had just missed our flight! And of all flights, it had to be this one! What was the point of sitting in these elegant surroundings, if in the end you missed your flight?

"So what am I going to do now?" I asked. "Within the next three hours I absolutely have to be in New York!" Disbelief and panic resonated in my voice. The CARE executive would soon be waiting for me at Kennedy Airport, and I was stuck here in Chicago.

The staffer looked intently at her screen.

"Ma'am, the plane is already on the runway. Unfortunately, there's nothing I can do."

"There *must* be something you can do! I have to get to New York. Urgently!"

"The earliest possibility is in an hour, a plane landing at LaGuardia," she said, after she had looked at our tickets and pressed a few keys.

"But I have to go to Kennedy Airport. I have a meeting there." I was desperate.

"Unfortunately, there's no other option, ma'am. The next plane to JFK doesn't depart until the afternoon."

So we had no choice but to fly to LaGuardia. Beforehand, I called the CARE executive's assistant to inform her of my changed time of arrival in New York.

"Don't worry," the woman on the phone reassured me. "My boss has a long layover. There will still be enough time for your meeting."

I could have hugged the stranger on the other end of the line.

During the flight I drilled into Akinyi how she was to behave during the meeting with the CARE representative. Actually, the plan had been for her to spend that time with a friend who lived in New York. But now, due to our delayed arrival, that arrangement would probably fall through.

"It's possible that you'll be with me during my meeting," I explained to Akinyi in Luo. She looked up from her Nintendo.

"That's all right," she said calmly.

"But you are not allowed to interrupt me no matter what when I'm talking to the woman," I insisted.

I was worried that Akinyi, who as an only child was used to getting a lot of attention and often barged into conversations, might do so during the upcoming meeting. Her earnest little face looked up at me.

"I know that, Mum." Smiling, she added, "Everything will be okay."

With her nine years, my daughter exuded an enviable composure. She's so entirely different from me, I thought. While I can easily get worked up or unsettled by little things, she is rarely rattled. Even as a small child, she tended to react calmly—and often wisely—to stressful situations. "It's no big deal, Mum," she would say to me on many occasions, thus helping me respond to things with somewhat more calm.

"I have my Nintendo," Akinyi added. She waved the small

pink object, which was a lifesaver for me at that moment. I drew her into my arms and hugged her tightly.

"Mum! Stop it!"

Despite the unplanned detour, my meeting at Kennedy Airport went really well. I found out about a promising opportunity: CARE was about to launch a new program. The planned Sport for Social Change Initiative would introduce a new approach to working with children and youth in developing countries. The goal was to use sports as a way to involve girls and boys in the areas of health, education, leadership, employment, and recreational activities. The chance to contribute to a program that was not only about making a better life possible for disadvantaged children, but also about requiring their active participation—for this was key—was exactly what I was looking for. The fact that it would be coordinated from Kenya for all of East Africa made the position even more interesting.

I stayed another week on the East Coast in order to attend several more meetings. Of the organizations with which I had appointments, only UNICEF dealt directly with children and youth, but there was no suitable position for me there or with the other NGOs. So when CARE offered me the position as coordinator of the East African Sport for Social Change Initiative (SSCI), I didn't hesitate a second.

I was sitting at home with my friend Vicky, who had often looked after Akinyi back when she was still a baby. I was telling her over a glass of wine about my experiences in New York when the telephone rang. Instinctively, I knew who was calling. No one else called me so late in the evening. Disregarding all rational judgment, I picked up. And just listened.

"It's Marvin," said the voice on the other end of the line. I had guessed correctly.

"I thought it was all over," I muttered, prepared to hang up again immediately.

"No. Wait!"

"Why? I really don't have anything more to say to you."

"Then why did you write me that letter?"

Marvin was talking about a six-page letter I had written after Monika had called him. It was meant as a good-bye; in it, I explained to him what the years with him had been like for me. I wanted him to know that I did not hold it against him that he could not love me. And I wanted him to know that I in no way regretted having loved him so intensely and absolutely. Only in that way was I able to let him go.

"For three months, I carried your letter around with me," he said. "The first time I read it, I was just mad at you. Your tone had made me angry. But then I read it again—and understood it." He was silent for a moment. I didn't say anything, either. I couldn't say anything.

"I understood what you were trying to say," he went on. "This time I was able to read between the lines."

"Took you long enough," I replied sarcastically. "Let's just drop it, Marvin." I could feel the tears welling up.

"Give me a chance to explain, Auma. We have to talk. I want to be with you."

"I don't believe that anymore."

"I really want to be with you, Auma!"

I was silent. But I couldn't hang up, either.

"You need time to think, I understand that. I'll call you again in a week, okay?"

I hung up without saying another word.

"Shit!" I blurted out. Ordinarily, I never used this word. Akinyi would have been shocked if she heard me. And I caught myself looking up as if expecting to see her standing on the stairs. I turned to my friend, who had followed the conversation intently.

"What now, Vicky? Does the torment start all over again?"

Vicky knew all about the Marvin drama, and with the wisdom of her seventy-six years had often offered me advice and support.

"Do you still love him?" she asked.

"Yes, unfortunately." The two words practically burst out of me.

"Then you have nothing to lose."

"But he hurt me so much with his indecisiveness."

"And you still love him anyway."

I gave Vicky a confused look. It couldn't be that simple.

"If you let him go now," she said, "you might regret it for the rest of your life. But if you give him a chance, you'll either get what you want or you'll at least know what you don't want. One way or the other, you win."

I simply could not understand her logic.

"I guess I still have to think about it."

"You have a week's time, don't you?"

In July 2007, Akinyi and I moved to Kenya. Marvin would follow later. After a brief back and forth in the wake of that phone call, he had come to visit me in England and had convinced me of his love. I was overjoyed—and grateful to Vicky that she had persuaded me to give him another chance. Now we were planning to live together in Nairobi.

That meant big changes for all of us, especially for Akinyi, whose visits to my native country had always lasted only a few weeks. To have to switch to a new school, and in an entirely different country, was causing her anxiety.

But I was happy that we would be closer to my family and that my daughter would finally have a chance to speak Luo more often and learn more about her Kenyan heritage.

Almost immediately on arrival, with scarcely a breather, I started my job at CARE. My coordination work brought me into contact with about thirty-five East African local aid organizations, which altogether dealt with several thousand children and young people. My task was to help them develop their capacities by sponsoring trainings and workshops.

"Why sports?" the person sitting opposite me asked. I was in Washington for a large CARE conference. My role was to provide supporters of the organization with valid arguments they could then use to persuade their representatives on the Hill to champion CARE's cause of fighting global poverty.

"Because sports work especially well with children and youth," I replied. "Through sports it is easier to reach young people."

"But isn't that a luxury for the poorest of the poor?"

"Only if you don't offer the young people more than just the sports," I answered. "Though these children, too, deserve the chance to play simply for the sake of playing, don't you think?"

I knew, of course, that for the people we dealt with in our program, sports were indeed often a luxury, which they typically could not afford. The struggle for mere survival left little room for indulging in sports "just for fun."

"What do the young people get out of it if they're playing on an empty stomach?" asked another member of the group of supporters.

"That's precisely the point," I replied. "We have to offer more. Because, as you say, they cannot participate in sports on an empty stomach."

Then I explained that most of the organizations we work with also promote HIV and AIDS awareness and provide information on other illnesses. In addition, they involve their beneficiaries in income-generating activities.

To help those present better understand what our work was about, I gave an example. "Moving the Goalposts is an organization located in Kilifi, a town on the Kenyan coast in an area with a predominantly Islamic population. What makes it special is that here girls play soccer. Girls, who are normally not permitted to leave the house unaccompanied by a male family member, gain a new awareness of their bodies through the ball game. They learn to value and protect them. Their self-esteem is strengthened. They discover that they can succeed and achieve just as much as boys. In their rural, Islamic environment, they convey a downright revolutionary message: Women, too, can accomplish great things! Women, too, play soccer!"

We continued to discuss this interesting concept, and in the end it was clear to all that when girls succeed in sports, this ultimately achieves far more than a lecture on equal rights does on its own.

"It is not by chance that the motto of Moving the Goalposts is 'Yes we can!' " I said. "And that's been the case for a long time, not only since my brother made it his campaign slogan in the United States. And because they *can,* the soccer-playing girls also learn to say no without fear or hesitation."

When, in the midst of my work, I think of my own youth, I am, of course, entirely aware that most girls in Kenya do not have the protective environment I had while struggling through my difficult teenage years. The majority of them face substantially greater challenges. Many work in the fields or as street peddlers to help provide for their families and themselves, in some cases trying to go to school at the same time. Again and again I am impressed by how many girls, despite all the adversities and with a mature, realistic view of their prospects, somehow get by and make use of their limited choices.

And in everything I do, it's important to me that the children and young people with whom I work, as well as those with whom I worked before my return to Kenya, do not become victims of clichés—whether they are British children who are all too often seen by adults only as troublemakers or East African children who frequently have to serve as puzzle pieces in a prevalent perception of Africa that is all about poverty, wild animals, beautiful beaches, and a few top athletes. Through what I do, I try to show them that there is also another, positive image, which they themselves can help create.

29.

"AREN'T YOU . . . !?"

I did not let the woman standing excitedly at our table finish her sentence. She had been looking over at us the whole time. She was seated near us in the company of a man who, ever since she had noticed us, unsuccessfully sought her attention. Now she had stopped at our table on the way out, as had the man.

"I just look like her," I explained with a knowing smile and as if it never ceased to amaze me. The woman continued to look at me intently, though now somewhat uncertainly. However, she seemed to be one of those people who, once they are convinced of something, are hard to talk out of it.

"But . . . but . . . you are Auma Obama! I'm sure of it! All evening I've been saying that to my husband. Haven't I?" She turned to her escort in the expectation of a confirmation. But he just stood silently next to her and nodded with embarrassment.

"Come on, let's go," the man finally said with a hushed voice. "We're just bothering the people." Now he seemed even more self-conscious, and looked as if he would have preferred to be far away. "Please come," he murmured again, pulling the woman slightly by the arm. But she didn't budge.

"No, really, I'm always being mistaken for her." I gave it another try with feigned sympathy.

I sensed Akinyi next to me suppressing her laughter. Under the table, I gave her a slight nudge.

Marvin's face revealed nothing. I could rely on him; that I knew.

When I saw Akinyi's face screwing up and anticipated her loss of self-control, I threatened with a sharp glance to ground her or do something similarly unpleasant.

"A mosquito!" my daughter cried. "A mosquito stung me!" She bent down, pretending to scratch her leg under the table, as I turned back to the woman, who was still standing there and staring at me. I was glad that we were sitting in the garden of the restaurant and our table was only dimly lit by candlelight.

Akinyi, Marvin, and I were sitting in this restaurant to celebrate my birthday. It was supposed to be a nice, quiet evening: just the three of us, no big deal, but still something special.

Usually I ignore that day, but this year was different. Weeks earlier, I had made it clear that this time I wanted to celebrate my birthday. "I would really like you to take me out!" I had declared loudly, adding dramatically, "I need it!" Marvin and Akinyi had been astonished. I wasn't entirely sure of the reason myself, but this time the day should not be like any other. That's why we were now sitting outside of the Nairobi city center in an Italian restaurant on Argwings Kodhek Road.

It was January 2009. Perhaps I had been overcome by the desire to celebrate all that had happened in the past two years. Big changes had occurred in my life within an extremely short period of time. Among them was not only my brother's electoral victory in the States, but above all our move to Kenya. And only now did I feel as if I could catch my breath a bit. Or so I thought, at least, until the curious woman had approached me. She was still standing at our table, while her husband had long since walked to the exit.

"I'm not her," I repeated, now sharply. I was no longer in a polite mood. The woman did not seem to notice that her stubborn persistence was starting to get on my nerves.

I only rarely revealed my identity as Barack Obama's sister. Only in that way could I move around in Nairobi without arousing a lot of attention. I didn't want to forgo this luxury now, either—even if the woman only reluctantly followed her husband and still looked back at us several times, shaking her head.

No sooner was the married couple out of sight than Akinyi burst out laughing. "Mum! You can't do things like that."

"Did you want the woman to stay with us all evening?" I replied.

"All she wanted was confirmation. Then she probably would have moved on," my daughter said, defending the stranger.

"No," said Marvin. "She would have sat down and questioned your mother at length about your uncle. I've already witnessed that on several occasions. People take many liberties. They think that because they are so enamored with your uncle, they somehow have a claim on him and therefore on his family, too."

Gratefully, I nodded in agreement with Marvin.

"Yes, if I didn't react that way, I would be nothing but a prisoner of myself. Then I would no longer be able to turn away people like that woman, or else people would say that Obama's sister is rude." I sighed. "Basically, I understand how people feel. They're excited and want to share with me their enthusiasm for Barack. Or they are simply curious, because they have spotted a family member of such a prominent person—and in the process, they completely forget that I, too, have a private life."

My daughter listened to both of us and merely shrugged.

"I don't understand. I would have told her." Akinyi loved the spotlight. Her goal was to one day become a big star, for which she would, of course, need her audience. Marvin and I looked at each other—and began to laugh.

"We don't understand, either," the two of us said at the same time. And once again I caught myself wishing I possessed the innocence of an eleven-year-old.

In early 2007, the life-changing announcement had reached me: My brother Barack informed me by telephone that he intended to run for the presidency of the United States. Previously, on one of my last visits to America, we had speculated about whether he would have a chance at a victory if he ran.

But this latest plan of my brother's was truly on an entirely different scale than the winning of a senate seat. The fact that this step would affect my life, too, was made clear to me by the photographer who one day hid behind bushes in the front garden of my house while his accomplice—they can hardly be described as serious journalists—rang my doorbell and immediately pressed himself against the wall next to the door so that the photographer could quickly jump out and take a picture of me. Paparazzi! Outside my own front door!

What particularly alarmed me in retrospect was the fact that my daughter had answered the door that afternoon. We were still living in England at the time and were expecting Malcolm, a mechanic who was to pick up some money for a repair job he had done for me. When the bell rang, Akinyi opened the door, but saw no one standing outside. Presumably, the photographer did not dare to take a picture of the child who had stepped in front of his lens—or he simply wasn't interested in her, because he had been after me.

"Who's at the door, Muu?" I called from the kitchen, when after a while I still heard no voices.

"No one," answered Akinyi. She sounded surprised.

"But the doorbell rang."

"Yes, but no one is there."

I went into the living room and saw my daughter standing at the wide-open front door. When I came up to her and looked around outside, I suddenly glimpsed to my left the figure of the man trying to hide next to the door. At that same moment, something moved behind the bushes next to the garage. Instinctively and as fast as lightning, I closed the front door, just as a tall, thin man came out from behind the bushes. Inside I leaned, frozen in shock, against the door. Who were those men? And what did they want from us? Akinyi stood next to me and fortunately seemed more curious than scared. I, however, was trembling all over. I simply could not get past the image of my daughter opening the door to two completely strange men.

Then the bell rang again. I started. Did they really dare to make a second attempt? Cautiously, I looked through the peephole. At the sight of Malcolm's friendly face, I heaved a sigh of relief. I carefully opened the door, in such a way that I could not be seen from outside.

"Am I glad it's you," I said to Malcolm.

"Oh, you've never greeted me so effusively before." He laughed. "What have I done to deserve it? I guess I should bring you a bill more often."

With a serious expression, I told him what had just happened.

We were sitting in the dim living room, for I had asked him to close the curtains.

"What on earth did they want?"

"As harmless as it might sound to you, they undoubtedly wanted a photo of me. The man behind the bushes had a camera in his hand. They didn't even intend to ask me, but instead planned to take the picture then and there!"

"Probably it's more fun to take someone by surprise with the camera."

"I don't find it funny at all, Malcolm. What should I do now? Tomorrow I have to go to work. What if they are still waiting for their chance behind the bushes then?"

What could he have said to that? He had only come by to pick up his money. Still, I didn't let him leave until I had calmed down a bit.

Only hesitantly did I leave the house the next day with Akinyi. Were the paparazzi still nearby? Would they follow my every step from then on? It was a scary thought.

Indeed, scarcely two days had passed before a paparazzo again ambushed me, this time near my workplace. I had just finished work and was leaving the building in which my office was located. Lost in thought, I walked to my car. Suddenly I noticed someone half hidden behind a wall, watching me. When he saw that I had spotted him, he quickly retreated. But the camera in his hand had not escaped my notice. Hastily, I ran back into the building. I felt naked and vulnerable. How was I supposed to get home now?

"You'll have to give him something so that he leaves you alone," said the director of our communications department. I had sought her advice, and she had gone down to talk to the man. Now she had returned with this proposal.

"I can't do that. As soon as I give him something, the next one will come and want something, too. Then it will never stop. That's why I can't agree to that."

I certainly did not want to hand myself over to the British tabloid press. I was annoyed by the gall of the journalist, who had replied to the communications director's request to leave me alone that he would get a photo of me one way or the other.

"Then it would be best if you wrote a general statement as a press release. We will then pass it on to the media on your behalf," the director suggested.

"Yes, that's a good idea," I replied, relieved. "But what do we do *now*?"

"Good point," said Andrea, who also worked in the communications department and had joined us. "The photographer knows that you're here in the building. So he won't leave that easily. We have to think of a way to smuggle you out unnoticed."

And that was just what the two women did. They planned that I would leave the building through a side exit. From there, I would cover the first stretch of my way home on foot, taking a roundabout route. In the meantime, Andrea would get my car from the parking lot and drive after me. Along the way, I would take the car, and Andrea would walk back to the office. Following our plan, I felt as if I were in a James Bond movie.

Because I now had to reckon with paparazzi at any time, I sought support in dealing with the press from a friend who was himself in the public eye. Fortunately, with his help the unpleasant surprises soon stopped.

My brother Barack was now undeniably making history, and although I had over the past several years watched him from the sidelines, so to speak, and participated in his progress only in small ways, I hoped for his success—no matter what effect this might have on my life.

In any case, due to the shared family name alone, I was catapulted into a world in which the media would continue to show an interest in me and in my life. They wanted to get closer to this prominent person—possibly the next president of the United States—even if only indirectly.

Suddenly, old friends, family members, and acquaintances with whom I had long ago lost touch resumed contact with me and wanted to make up for lost time. I was invited to all sorts of meetings and events. I declined most of the invitations and shunned the newly aroused interest in me. Only with difficulty could I accept the changed attitude toward me.

In defiance of the "onslaught" on me from all sides, I made a point of behaving as "normally" as possible toward everyone. In a way, that was an attempt to force the people around me to act no differently toward me than before. That led, however, to many people finding me somewhat peculiar, incapable of grasping the enormity and significance of the situation. A question that I heard again and again, even before the presidential election, was: "Don't you get it?" Most of the time, this was asked in a casual way, but sometimes it was tinged with a serious, somewhat unsettling undertone, which made clear to me that, as far as my conversation partners were concerned, I was not behaving in keeping with the situation. Usually I responded equally jokingly: "*What* am I supposed to get?" Most of the time, they would then laugh, roll their eyes, and reply with a slap on the forehead: "Your brother might become president of the United States of America!"

Ordinarily, I then declared that my brother had always been my brother above all else and that wouldn't change no matter what great things he went on to achieve. Ultimately, that was the most important thing to me. That fact would never change. And because that was true, I told myself, I didn't need to change either.

Now, I was not so naïve, however, to think that everything could remain the way it was. I knew I would not be able to hide forever and that it was only a matter of time before I had to deal with being in the public eye. I was, after all, Barack Obama's sister, whom the media liked to refer to as his "half-sister." I find that term odd to this day, because in our polygamous Luo culture we never speak of "half" or "full" siblings, but only of brothers and sisters—unlike in the Western, "pseudo-monogamous" culture, where people are classified as full and half siblings, creating a hierarchy that does not actually exist in Luo culture.

In the year that followed Barack's decision to run, up to the day of the presidential election, I limited my communication with the media to conveying a somewhat better sense of what he meant to his family in Kenya. I explained, for example, that he had always been regarded as a son of the family, despite the distance and the fact that he first visited Africa only as an adult. It was understandable that people wanted to learn more about the Kenyan part of his background, in order to understand him better. So my grandmother and I, as well as other close family members, made ourselves available to the press to help tell Barack's "Kenyan story."

After Barack won the election, I was virtually bombarded with interview requests, which I mostly turned down. The Kenyan story was now "out," it was known, and I did not feel as if I had anything essential to add to it.

30.

"WHAT DO YOU THINK of Iowa?" the young journalist, who was visibly nervous, asked me.

Without thinking, I answered, "Very white!" I noticed how Iris, standing by my side, cringed. The journalist was diligently taking notes. I was in Iowa to take part in my brother's primary campaign.

"She doesn't mean it like that," Iris said quickly. "But more . . ." She groped for words to rephrase my answer. For a second, I was confused, and then I understood.

"Oh, I meant the weather! All the snow everywhere . . ." I smiled at everyone. "It looks really pretty. But it is a lot of snow, isn't it?"

Iris heaved a sigh of relief. I felt like laughing. She hadn't really thought that I meant the people, had she? It was true that I hadn't seen many black people in Iowa, but it never would have crossed my mind to address the proportion of blacks and whites before a journalist. I would have liked to have added a joke, but the intense expression on the young woman's face and Iris's nervous looks shut me up. The matter was too serious; a headline like "Obama's Sister Finds Iowa Very White," even if the statement had been made in the deepest winter, might have been immediately exploited by my brother's opponents.

When Barack decided to run for president, there was a hunger for a new beginning on the American political landscape. The Bush administration had embroiled the country in two wars and mired it in economic and foreign-policy problems. People wanted change, a fresh wind, and a new confidence in governance. They wanted someone who had not yet been compromised by the established Washington political scene. And my brother seemed to be that someone. I had always admired him for his tireless engagement on behalf of the disadvantaged. At our first encounter in Chicago, I had seen that clearly, in light of our conversations and his community work in the city's poor neighborhoods. Everything he said and did expressed the desire to improve the lives of his fellow human beings. He did not let anything divert him from his vision of a better world for everyone. When he stumbled on an obstacle or stood before a closed door, he tried to find another way to nonetheless overcome the hurdle or get through the barrier. He didn't study at Harvard in order to earn money later, but rather to attain the necessary tools to advocate successfully for the disadvantaged. Following that logic, my brother finally had to take on the challenge of doing the improbable and going through the door that led to the presidency.

Previously, I had not been particularly well acquainted with the political structures of the United States, and that had not really changed when my brother became a senator. Therefore, I now decided to give myself a crash course in American politics. Everything I would learn might also help me cope with the changes in my life. This included actively participating in the election campaign. I wanted to contribute to my brother's effort to achieve his goal.

I flew to the States in January 2008, and spent several weeks there as a campaigner in the primaries. I had taken Akinyi with me—Marvin would join us later—and she got to witness her uncle's victory in Iowa. I met many of my brother's supporters, not only in Iowa, but also in New Hampshire and South Carolina.

Taking part in the campaign was a special experience for me. For the first time, I encountered the diversity of America and got to learn what was important to Americans from all walks of life. The people's stories fascinated me. I met a Republican who, choked up with emotion, told me he had registered as a Democrat just so that he could vote for my brother. Then there was the family from Los Angeles who, along with the grandparents, had taken leave of their sunny California home in order to manage an Obama office in wintry Iowa. I admired their enthusiasm for the movement that my brother had launched. They had never been in Iowa before, and now they were knocking on strangers' doors in unknown towns in freezing temperatures. The two students I met at the Obama campaign office in Des Moines, the biggest city in Iowa, must have left their homes with the same enthusiasm. One of them was from Germany, the other from South Africa! Both of them had taken a one-year leave of absence in order to take part in the campaign.

"Why are you doing this? You can't even vote," I asked in amazement.

"That doesn't matter," replied the young German. "This election is too important for me to just stand by and watch what happens. The world urgently needs an Obama, and I want to make sure we get him."

The South African nodded in agreement. "It's not just about

the Americans. It's about all of us," he remarked. "We can't leave anything to chance."

I couldn't think of anything else to say. I was deeply impressed. These young people had put the American election in an entirely new perspective for me. The campaign was only just beginning, and already the whole world was participating in it. I felt as if I were part of a larger family, as if I were moving in a protected sphere in which we were all fighting for one and the same cause. None of us wanted to lose the primaries—that was obvious. We all knew and had faith that we would give our all so that Barack's "change" could become reality.

On January 20, 2009, my brother Barack became the forty-fourth president of the United States. Since his victory, a sentence had been going through my head again and again: "He did it!" And the best thing about it was that, when he walked through the door of the presidency, he left it wide open behind him.

His inauguration was indeed an event of a new, unprecedented magnitude. I was tremendously delighted for him and excitedly awaited the trip to the ceremonies and celebrations—not least of all because I would share the experience of the inauguration with our two families, the Kenyan one and the American one. It gave me the feeling that our deceased father would be there, too, in a way, and would witness his son being sworn in to the most powerful office in the world.

The fact that temperatures in Washington were freezing did not really bother any of us; we were much too excited for that. As family members, we were, of course, granted certain privileges. Thus we did not have to rely on public transportation, but had cars and drivers at our disposal. In the midst of over two million people, many road closures, and detours, that was a blessing. Our grandmother Sarah, now in the United States for the third time, accepted everything with impressive composure—not only the intense cold, but also the contact with the famous and powerful of America.

The five days of our visit in Washington, D.C., were filled with memorable encounters and events. It began with a concert at the Lincoln Memorial and ended with a service in the Washington National Cathedral. At the Lincoln Memorial, to celebrate the occasion, stars from Hollywood and the music world made their appearance—Stevie Wonder, Beyoncé, Mary J. Blige, Bono, Tom Hanks, Jamie Foxx, Denzel Washington, Usher, Queen Latifah, Samuel L. Jackson, and many others. Even Tiger Woods stepped up to the microphone and said a few words.

There was also a kids' concert—for Akinyi, *the* highlight. There, I revealed myself in her eyes as "soooo old-fashioned," for I knew practically none of the performers. Smiling, I became aware of my age, especially in light of the volume of the music. Marvin and I repeatedly had to cover our ears, so that my daughter and the scores of children and teenagers in the arena—among them, of course, my nieces Malia and Sasha—did not deafen us with their screams.

The *real* highlight of the trip was, of course, the inauguration. We had all worked hard toward this event, and now it was here. When I woke up that morning, I promised myself that absolutely nothing would spoil this day for me. Not even the icy weather! And the day began well. The sun was shining, and the sky was bright blue. When we arrived at the capitol, thousands of people had already gathered. Behind the podium, where we family members got to sit, most of the guests were already taking their seats. I recognized Ted Kennedy, John Kerry, and other members of Congress. Behind us, somewhat farther up, sat Arnold Schwarzenegger, Earvin "Magic" Johnson, and others. Then the former presidents appeared with their wives: the Carters, the Clintons, the Bushes. Finally, I looked over to the podium, where my brother would in a few minutes take his oath of office. With Barack's inauguration, the swearing-in of a man who had, so to speak, appeared out of nowhere, the office of the American president became attainable even for the average American. With his "average family" behind the podium—including his sister Maya and her husband, Konrad, sitting next to me—the change, Barack's most important message, had basically already begun. We belonged there just as he did, for Barack was one of us. With that thought, I could relax and enjoy the day. All was as it should be.

When the celebrations were finally over, I flew with Akinyi and Marvin back to Kenya, content in the awareness that I had not lost a brother but had gained a president. A president who, due to the political and economic climate in the United States, would have to face many challenges in the subsequent months and beyond.

The excitement surrounding my brother's election has in the meantime abated. The actual work is underway, and it is truly not an easy task. And unfortunately, some have forgotten Barack's repeated reminder during the election: "It won't be easy. I'll need your help."

From afar, I watch his progress and inwardly support my brother's political efforts. "Keep up the work, little brother," I whisper to him whenever his image appears on television or his voice rings out on the radio. "You are making a difference."

Tuesday, May 11, 2010.

I wait eagerly for Hillary Clinton's keynote speech in honor of CARE's 2010 National Conference and Celebration.

Afterward, we finally get a chance for a brief conversation. I'm glad to see Hillary again, in particular because I sense in those few minutes that she not only takes an interest in me, but also in my work.

In light of everything that has happened to me in the past years, I am aware that as an Obama I now have a real chance to make a difference. For me, a door has been opened, and I, too, want to open doors for others.

Epilogue

Several years have passed since my brother became the forty-fourth president of the United States. And in that time, a lot has happened. I have watched Barack achieve wonders in a job that is undeniably one of the most difficult in the world. Against all odds and with varied support he has managed, among other things, to pass a new national health care bill, add two women to the U.S. Supreme Court, and, most significantly, get his country through the worst economic crisis since the Great Depression. He has persevered tirelessly in his effort to improve the lives of his fellow countrymen and women, a task that he takes very seriously. To say that I am immensely proud of my brother would be an understatement.

Across the Atlantic, the rest of the Obama family, including myself, has seen itself projected into the limelight. The world continues to be curious about Obama's roots. And our grandmother, Mama Sarah, has a steady stream of visitors from all corners of the world, who come in pilgrimage to our ancestral home in Alego, Siaya, not far from the shores of Lake Victoria, where she resides. They all want to see the birthplace of Barack

Obama Sr., and despite all attempts to correct this misconception by explaining that although he is buried in Alego, he was actually born in Karachuonyo, on the other side of Lake Victoria, the visitors keep coming.

Over the past three years, I have watched in fascination as our homestead went from being a typically sleepy rural setting to a gated secure compound with running water and electricity. The pride in having a son of Kenya gain such high office spurred on well-wishers and family members, who had previously not taken particular interest in the Obama homestead (locally known as the Onyango Hussein homestead, after my grandfather), to push for an "upgrade" of the place. As Kenyans saw it, this was, after all, technically speaking, the home of one of America's current First Grandmothers.

As is in her nature, Mama Sarah has taken in stride all the changes in her life since Barack announced his candidacy in 2007, and in particular the interest in her personally. She remains unflustered. Her composure is reassuring because I know that should all the attention disappear, she would be just as happy to revert to her old way of life. At the age of eighty-nine, she is content with her lot.

As for me, the exposure I receive continues to allow me to touch the lives of countless children and young people. I have met wonderful people in high and low places, all of whom have enriched my life immensely. Every day, I am reminded of how blessed I am. Again and again the respect and love afforded my brother rub off on me. I have stopped trying to explain that I do not warrant this, that I have to earn it by my own merit. It is all to no avail. Everywhere I am welcomed with open arms and red carpet treatment. This is an added motivation for me to commit more fully to making a positive impact on the lives of the disadvantaged children and young people with whom I work.

As for the content of my book, quite a lot has happened since it was first published. Kenya has truly once again become home to me and has provided me the space and calm that have allowed me to establish a presence within the nonprofit arena. Beyond my work with CARE, I have forged links to exceptional grassroots organizations doing extraordinary Sport for Development work in East Africa, Bangladesh, Egypt, Brazil, South Africa, the United States, Germany, and the United Kingdom.

On a personal level, I have learned that finding the love of your life does not necessarily guarantee that it will be your last love. It takes work and commitment to keep the flame burning. And as for family and my close friends, they continue to be there for the long haul, which is what really counts the most.

I continue to be grateful for all good that comes my way, and I look forward to whatever else may be in store for me. I plan and map out my future, fully aware, however, that whatever I do, I must factor in the inevitable; no matter what, life happens.

Acknowledgments

My deepest gratitude goes to Maria Hoffmann-Dartevelle, friend and fellow linguist, who through her literary and linguistic advice and collaboration helped me put together the original German version of this book. She was tireless in her commitment to helping me get my story right in her native language of German. *Danke,* Maria!

A special thank you also goes to Elke Geisler, Thomas Schindelbeck, Barbara Sabbarth, and Trixi Mugishagwe, who all were instrumental in the production of the German book. The stories that have here been retold in English would have not been possible without them. Thank you for reading, rereading, and again reading my manuscript. A thank you, too, to Phoebe Asiyo and Paul Agali Otula, Oloo Aringo, and others not mentioned here for their patience in explaining and giving me insight into the life of my late father, Barack Obama. You are too many to all be named, but know that I dearly appreciate having been given your time and attention.

And to my agent, Anoukh Foerg, a special thank you, for always being there for me, above and beyond duty, even when the question at hand did not necessary directly have anything to do with the book. You truly understand that there is more to being an agent than ensuring contracts are signed. *Danke!*

Similarly, I want to thank Daniela Rapp, my editor, Ross Benjamin, my translator, the staff at St. Martin's Press, and not least Jane Starr, who took the time to accompany me to meetings with publishers in the United States. Thank you all for taking a chance on me and committing to helping me bring this book to fruition. As I stated at my first meeting at the St. Martin's Press offices in New York, I felt already then that I was in good hands. That feeling at no time abated, and I am grateful to you all and in particular to you, Daniela and Ross, for patiently working with me on the manuscript and remaining calm and focused while I tried to juggle work, travel, family, and writing. Know that I truly appreciate this and thank you both sincerely.

Also for being there I thank my family, without whom this book would never have happened. In particular, my grandmother Mama Sarah and my aunties Zeituni and Marsat deserve special mention for never tiring in answering all my many questions about the family, even when, in the case of my grandmother, this questioning started long before I had reached the age of ten. The information they supplied me over the years made writing this book a lot easier for me.

And to my brother Barack, without whom any such interest in a book by Auma probably never would have materialized, I owe a special thank you. I am so proud to call you my brother, Barack!

And last but not least, I want to thank my daughter, Akinyi, and Marvin, the man who, in the most unusual of ways, stole my heart. Both of them stood by me while I put all else aside to write this book. Their patience and love made it possible to do so. Thank you.

Index